John Campbell Shairp, John Veitch

**Sketches in History and Poetry**

John Campbell Shairp, John Veitch

**Sketches in History and Poetry**

ISBN/EAN: 9783337013455

Printed in Europe, USA, Canada, Australia, Japan

Cover: Foto ©ninafisch / pixelio.de

More available books at **www.hansebooks.com**

# SKETCHES

IN

# HISTORY AND POETRY

BY THE LATE

## JOHN CAMPBELL SHAIRP, LL.D.

PROFESSOR OF POETRY, OXFORD
PRINCIPAL OF THE UNITED COLLEGE, ST. ANDREWS

EDITED BY

## JOHN VEITCH,

PROFESSOR OF LOGIC AND RHETORIC IN THE
UNIVERSITY OF GLASGOW

EDINBURGH: DAVID DOUGLAS
1887

# PREFACE.

OF the ten papers, which have been named Sketches, contained in this volume, some were given to the public in periodicals by the author himself. Others are now printed for the first time. The date of the earliest is 1860; of the latest 1884, the year before the author's death. Four of them were given as Lectures in the chair of Poetry, Oxford, viz., VI., VII., IX., X. All the subjects, save one, are taken from Scottish History or Poetry, fields in which the writer showed a lifelong and special interest. One or two of the papers may be singled out as but slight in treatment of the subject; yet all of them contain passages which are highly characteristic of the author, and some are worthy of him at his best—as, for example, "The Songs of Scotland before Burns." They thus seem to me to be well deserving of collection and publication in one volume. As these papers were written at different times, and as the subjects are mainly allied, there occurred in the originals passages, slightly varied, referring to the same topic. The repetition of these has been avoided in the present publication, as far as this was consistent with the proper effect of each Sketch when read by itself. Some changes have been silently made in names and dates, the quotations revised, and a few notes have been added by me, which appear in square brackets. The volume may be regarded mainly as containing the last gleanings, in favourite fields of one, the excellence of whose literary work will be increasingly recognised as the years flow on.

J. VEITCH.

*October* 11, 1887.

# CONTENTS

|     |     | PAGE |
| --- | --- | --- |
| I. | St. Columba, | 1 |
| II. | Queen Margaret of Scotland, | 45 |
| III. | Bishop Lamberton and the Good Lord James, | 86 |
| IV. | King Robert Bruce in St. Andrews Cathedral, | 111 |
| V. | The Earliest Scottish University, | 133 |
| VI. | The Early Poetry of Scotland, | 202 |
| VII. | James I. of Scotland and the King's Quair, | 240 |
| VIII. | The Songs of Scotland before Burns, | 282 |
| IX. | The Ettrick Shepherd, | 317 |
| X. | Henry Vaughan, Silurist, | 350 |

# I.—ST. COLUMBA.[1]

Hy, Y, Ioua, Iona, Icolumcille, Icolumkill, Isle of Colum of the Cell, to the outward eye one of the least noticeable of the Hebrides, has to the inward eye a beauty and a sanctity which belong to no other Scottish ground. From our childhood the very name has been invested with an old ideal reverence, which, unless scared away by vulgarising steamboat visits and tourist crowds, lives on still when we are grown men. We think of it as a beacon burning all alone, but bright and blessed, in the deep midnight of Celtic heathenism; or rather as a solitary peak, already struck golden by the coming day, while deep darkness lay yet unbroken on all the mainland and islands of Alban. And the impression is not decreased, but deepened by the contrast we feel when, thinking of its old sanctity, we gaze on its now forlorn abandonment. Elsewhere, the spot on which some first missionary settled has grown, in time, into cathedral town, commercial mart, even into metropolitan city. But Iona—though the light first kindled there is not yet

[1] [Contributed to *Good Words*, 1860.]

disowned, yea, rather has been growing and spreading till now—Iona has become as utter a desolation, as if it had been some heathen oracle long gone dumb, or the shrine of some out-worn religion.

To those to whom it has long been a cherished imagination, one cannot but feel apprehensive lest all that can be advanced of fact and illustration should only mar its ideal consecration. But to others, who may have gone there without thought, and returned without interest—laughing, perhaps, at all things they heard there as fictions of Highland story-tellers, at best disregarding them as intangible myths—something I hope may be adduced to convince them that Iona has a real history, compared with which its oldest existing ruin is but modern, and that Columba stands out in tolerably clear outline, by several centuries the earliest human figure we can descry against the dim dawn of Scottish history.

For of him we possess, what we have not of any other Scot for five centuries afterwards, two lives, which may be called contemporary, written by two monks of his brotherhood, who had every means of knowing the truth. One of these is a short Latin life by Cummene, supposed to have been written about sixty years after the saint's death; the other, composed about eighty-five years from his death, is the longer and well-known life by Adamnan, which has been lately edited (1856) by Mr. Reeves, an Irish antiquary, with a rare fulness of erudition and accuracy of Hebridean topography. Perhaps there was no man in Europe of Columba's time of whom we have so authentic a record—certainly no native of Scotland till after the year 1000.[1]

Yet, strange to say, in both these lives Columba is seen invested with such an atmosphere of legend and miracle, that often, only with strained eye, in partial, broken glimpses, we can descry his human features. One moment we get a blink of his countenance as if by chance; the next it is lost in the mass of miracles, visions, and prophecies with which they have surrounded him. For it must be owned that the real, natural facts of his life peep out of these biographies as if accidentally. In the words of the most recent commentator on Cummene and Adamnan, "they manifest the simplicity and credulity of a rude age, but it is impossible to charge them with any intention to deceive. From them we learn the mode of life adopted in Iona. But it is not only what they have written—that was not an age of writing—it is from what they have done that we

---

[1] [Cummené was abbot of Hy from 657 to 669. The life of Columba, attributed to him, was printed by Colgan from an Antwerp MS. Substantially the same work was also published from a MS. at Compiègne. The third book of Adamnan embodies nearly the whole of this life. The remaining part is also used by Adamnan at an earlier stage in his narrative. Adamnan was abbot from 679 to 704. See *Historians of Scotland, Life of St. Columba*, pp. 287-8.]

learn the effects of the preaching of St. Columba and his disciples."

If Scotland, in the fifth century, gave to Ireland her Apostle St. Patrick, Ireland, in the sixth, repaid the debt with interest when she sent us Columba. With interest, I say. For, even according to the view which makes St. Patrick a Scotsman, Scotland gave him nothing but a birthplace—Kilpatrick (then Bonhaven) on the Clyde. His conversion occurred in Ireland, his culture he received in Gaul. But Ireland sent us Columba, a fully equipped Christian missionary, and he imparted to Scotland the zeal, the truth, the discipline, the learning which he had first imbibed in the monasteries of his native country.

His birthplace, called Gartan, lies among the wildest of the Donegal mountains, an elevated plat of ground on the hillside, looking up and down a long valley, with chain of small hill lochs. The sanctity which the place won from Columba's birth lives on there to-day. Hard by, an old burying-ground, a roofless chapel, two stone crosses rudely carved, much disfigured, beneath which the people still come to pray; a holy well, in which they still wash for supposed latent virtues; chief of all, a large flagstone, still shown as the spot on which Columba's mother bore her child. The stone is still believed to have the power of curing home-sickness; whither, therefore, emigrants, on the eve of their exile, much resort.

Colm, Colum, Colum-cille, that is, Colum of the Church (not the churches, as the latest and best Celtic scholars tell us), came, on both sides, from a race of kings—such kings or patriarchal chiefs as then existed in Ireland. He was born on the 7th December 521. His father, Fedhlimidh, was grandson of Conall of Ulster, and thus one of the northern Hy Neill, or reigning family of the Irish Scots, and closely allied to the House of Lorn, which, at the beginning of the sixth century, had passed into Argyll. These Scots were the last race who had come into Ireland—a conquering race, which lorded it over the two older races of the Hiberni and the Cruithne. Colum, therefore, belonged to the reigning family of Ireland. His mother, Eithné (Æthnea), was of Leinster extraction, descended, say the antiquaries, from Cathair Mor, the first king of Leinster, afterwards king of Ireland,—a man much renowned in the second century, but long since forgotten.

They tell that, one night, Eithné had a strange prophetic dream shortly before Colum was born. As she lay asleep she saw an angel come to her, bearing a beautiful robe, broidered all over with all shapes and hues of flowers. She laid her hand upon it, but soon the angel claimed it back, and, bearing it aloft, spread it out and let it float on the air. Whereat she, grieving, cried to the angel, "Why dost thou take from me so soon this delightsome robe?" But the angel replied, "This robe is too highly prized for you longer to detain it." Then, as she followed it with her eyes, she beheld it expand itself wider and still wider till it had covered all the plains, and the woods, and the mountains as far as she could see; and a voice fell from heaven, saying, "Woman, be no more sad. For the child which thou shalt bear shall be numbered among the holy prophets, and has been fore-ordained of God to be the guide of innumerable souls to the heavenly country." Great, therefore, were the hopes that waited on this child. And when he did appear, he came into the world, favoured not less by his outward circumstances than by his inward endowment.

This high lineage did much for Columba. It could have done nothing for him had he not been otherwise endowed with rare gifts; but it furnished to his inborn genius and early piety a ready-made scope and range of influence which, unaided, they might never have achieved. It is a fact which none can be blind to, that, even in our own day, where there is energy of character, birth and fortune give a man many years' start in life before less favoured compeers, and enable him to bring out whatever there is in him at a much earlier age, and in a wider sphere. How much more powerfully must these have told in those early ages when blood was so much more accounted of, and among a race so beholden to ancient lineage as the Celts! Happy in his natural endowments, fine genius and strong piety showing itself from a child; happy in his parentage, not only kingly, but a valiant, energetic race of kings; happy, too, in the time of his birth, the most prosperous and energetic epoch Ireland has ever known!

We are apt to think of Ireland as having always been a byword among the nations for backwardness and misery. It was not so in those early ages. From the fifth to the ninth centuries Ireland was among the foremost and most civilised of European nations—known as the island of saints, the missionary school of Europe, the storehouse of the best learning then existing. "It needed but a native Alfred, or even a Malcolm Canmore, to have given to her separate tribes the same unity which St. Patrick gave to her church organisation. But, alas for her! her Alfred was never born." But Patrick and his followers gave her the best help she has ever received from men. They made for themselves, by their own hand-labour, civilised dwellings amid the thickest forests and dreariest morasses, and covered the island with monasteries, in which, when all else was savage with clan feuds and bloodshed, the Scriptures were studied, ancient books collected and read, and missionaries trained for their own country and the rest of Europe.

Hear the great German Church historian, who

was under no temptation to exaggerate Ireland's early renown :—

"The Irish monasteries were distinguished for strict Christian discipline, for industry, zeal for the Scriptures, and general knowledge, as much as they could collect of it. The Irish monks fetched knowledge from Britain and France, preserved this knowledge and digested it in their retirements, and were destined to bring back the seeds of science, along with Christianity, to countries whence they had once received these seeds, but where they were now choked by spreading barbarism." The deeds and sufferings of Columbanus, Gallus, and a multitude of other Irish missionaries, who, in the seventh century, went preaching and founding mission schools in Gaul, Burgundy, Switzerland, and far into the heart of Germany, witness to Ireland's overflowing zeal. Strange—is it not?—to think now of that her early and excellent renown preceding her long, unhappy centuries, like the early blink of morning sunshine ushering in a dark, stormy day!

On such a time of monastic activity and missionary zeal fell the childhood of Columba. In such an atmosphere, whatever there was of more than usual purity, repugnance to vice, and ardent, imaginative temperament, was drawn, as by irresistible attraction, to the calm of the ascetic convent. Columba does not seem so much to have made deliberate choice of this course of life as to have adopted it intuitively from his very cradle. The thoughtful child we see with his mind preoccupied from the very first. There, among the Donegal mountains, in the hamlet of Doire-Eithné, he passed his boyhood, tended by a priest-tutor— a simple man, who gazed on his young pupil with wonder, even awe, as he saw him asleep with face illuminated as with a ball of fire, which he took for the outpouring of heavenly grace. Boyhood past, he left his mountains, and went to the famous monasteries of the south, just as our youth now go to the university. First to the monastery of Movilla, in County Down, then to the school of one Gemman, then on to the monastery of Clonard, in which last he had for companions students who were afterwards fathers of the Irish Church, Comgall, Ciaran, Cainnech, and others. In these monasteries he had access to the best learning of the time in the Scriptures and all other subjects. His genius was visible to his teachers, but still more his strong piety. Good Bishop Finnian, who ordained him deacon, looking on him reverently, said, he saw an angel walking by his side; meaning, perhaps, no more than that he felt sure he was being trained and guided by God for some high purpose.

Returned to his own north at the age of twenty-five, we find him at once setting vigorously to work, obtaining from his kinsman the King of Erin a grant of land and founding on it a monastery—

Daire Calgaich, afterwards Derry—on a pleasant eminence, covered with oaks, the first nucleus, out of which has grown, in due time, what has long been the town of Londonderry. Leaving this monastery under charge of a chief monk, he passes southward, and in the centre of Ireland founds Durrow—another large monastery, "equal," says Bede, "to the Iona one." Two large monasteries, besides churches here and there, were the result of his early activity between his thirtieth and fortieth year. A man of rare force, marvellous energy, if we think what founding monasteries in those days meant. Not to pay so much money down, and while you are enjoying your ease elsewhere, get the work done by proxy of contractors, overseers, and the rest; but to strip to it yourself, hew down the oaks, and make others hew them; lift them, and get others to help in bearing them from the woods; to build wattle huts for dwelling in, and a wattle church to worship in; clear and cultivate the neighbouring wood or moor for sustenance; then to lay down a stern rule of life, and make rude and untaught men obey it; to train these same rude men to be teachers and missionaries to their still ruder brethren—this is something of what he had to do who undertook to found one of those Irish monasteries. Work enough, one would think, for a life, to set one such well a-going. Columba built and organised two before he was forty, besides divers other small churches or cells. He might well be called Colum-cille, Colum of the Church, he who delighted to live and labour for the Church.

But at the age of forty-two a great crisis came to him—one of those turning-points which change abruptly a man's whole course, and shape for him a new destiny. He resolved to leave his own land and kindred, and sail away to preach Christ to the heathen tribes beyond the sea. What was the motive that impelled him to this new purpose? Adamnan says that it was the pure missionary zeal prompting him to leave all for Christ; that, like his countryman Columbanus, he felt burning within him that fire which impelled him to "go forth from his country and his kindred, and his father's house, into a land which God would show him." It may have been so, as Adamnan, and most of his biographers since have regarded it; or it may be, that the ardour of Christian zeal so blended with the natural love of adventure as to form one great overmastering passion.

There is, however, another account of the whole matter; less pleasing, perhaps, but so strongly asserted from of old, that I am in truth bound to give it. It makes Columba's departure from Ireland not so much a voluntary act as a penance to which he was forced. The story runs thus:— Diarmid, king of Connaught, sought the life of Curnan, a kinsman and disciple of Columba's. Curnan fled to Columba for protection, but the king heeded not the saint's sanctuary, seized Curnan, and summarily made an end of him. Whereon, so wroth was Columba, that he roused his whole clan, the Northern Hy Neill, and set them against Diarmid and his Connaught men, whom they overthrew, with a great slaughter of three thousand men, in the battle of Cooldrevny. The saint was praying for his kinsmen all the day the battle lasted; and they believed it was the strength of his prayers that turned the scale of victory. Straightway, according to one account, a Synod of the Church, in the interest of King Diarmid, met and excommunicated our impetuous saint; and his friends Brenden, Abbot of Birr, and Finnian, Bishop of Clonfert, advised him to go into voluntary exile. Others say that the penance was entirely self-imposed; and that in remorse for the slaughter he had caused, he resolved to reclaim from among the heathens as many souls as had perished in the ill-omened battle.[1]

But whatever the cause may have been, it was in the year 563, and in the forty-second year of his life,

[1] [This incident is variously related. Curnan was son of Aedh, who was son of Eochaidh Tirmcharna, king of Connaught. It was at the feast of Tara, held under the auspices of Diarmid, king of Ireland, that the slaughter took place, and according to the laws of the feast such a deed was a capital crime. The name of the place of the battle is in its old form Culdremhne, and is near Drumcliff in Sligo. As Curnan was son of the king of Connaught, we naturally find it stated that the Ulster men found allies in the Connaught men against Diarmid.—See *Historians of Scotland, Life of Columba*, pp. xii, xiv.]

that Columba, with his twelve companions, pushed off from the north Irish shore, and set their frail prows to the wide Atlantic. Twelve men only went with him, attracted by his character, and cheered by his strong enthusiasm. I figure him to myself, as he went forth, that island-soldier (*insulanus miles*) of Christ; tall of stature, of vigorous athletic frame; bearing, through all toils, and fasts, and vigils, the beauty of countenance, ruddy and hilarious, that made all who saw him glad, and, as Adamnan has it, with "angelic aspect" which tempered their joy with reverence. Under him, and trusting to his guidance, they put off, those twelve men—their names are all preserved—in their small curraghs or coracles, frail crafts of wicker-work covered with hides—the like of which are still to be seen in the Severn and on the Donegal coast—a slender equipment for the open Atlantic, on the swing of whose long-heaving wave no modern fishing-boat could live an hour. Right north they rowed till they came to the small Isle of Hy, lying like a tiny boat moored to the bluff western cliffs of Mull. There they found, says old Highland tradition, a Druid settlement, and bearded the old faith in its stronghold; but stricter antiquaries, on what authority I know not, assert that the only tenants they found there were the sea-gull and the heron. Soon Columba sought and obtained a grant of the island from the king. What king is not quite clear.

It may be that Conall, Scottish King of Argyll, Columba's kinsman (whom he would visit either on his way to Iona, or soon afterwards), promised not to disturb him, and that Brude, king of the Northern Picts, to whom the island belonged by right, when converted, confirmed him in possession. "And now," as Bede says of his disciples, "they neither sought nor loved anything of this world, but delighted in distributing immediately among the poor whatever was given them by the kings and rich men of the earth."

But while his end was high and unworldly, Columba was wise in his choice of means as the most prudent of this world's children. It was no part of his plan to preach the gospel among the barbarous people and leave it there to take root or die out as might happen. He knew well that in all likelihood this would be lost labour; that no isolated efforts, however great, would avail to stem the flood of barbarism and make a pure faith triumphant over old superstition unless these efforts were grounded and concentrated by firm ecclesiastical foundations. His first step, therefore, was to secure a grant of the island. His next to erect fit dwellings to cover himself and his brotherhood from rain and storm; and his third to lay down for them a strict rule of life, and train them into conformity with it. The simple conventual establishment, as it was then completed, consisted of a number of small wattle-built huts, surrounding a green court; a hut or *hospitium*, for each monk to study in by day, to sleep by night. The abbot's hut, on an eminence a little apart, in which he read by day or wrote—his servant Diormit attending him, sometimes reading to him. Near at hand rose the little church or oratory—this, too, of wattles —with its three times of prayer by day, three by night. A simple church it must have been, of wattles or rough timber; its altar remote from the door, with the paten and the cup; and at one side of the church the sacristy, in which hung the small bell to summon the brotherhood to prayer. Then the refectory, or dining-hall, in which all dined together; the kitchen with its large fireplace, round which in cold weather, the monks flocked from their huts to warm themselves during study hours. The library, with its inkhorns, pens, waxen tablets, manuscripts; and books, hung in leathern bags to pegs on the walls; and, hard by, the cemetery, where, their earthly work done, they were all to rest —a cemetery which is the same as the more modern Reilig Oran. Round all these ran a circular wall, meant rather to restrain than protect the inmates.

Outside this wall lay the byre, with pastureground, barn to store winnowed grain in, kiln to dry the corn. The land east side the island was used for pasture, the west under tillage, and thither we read of the monks in harvest going forth in the morning and returning at night—their backs laden with sheaves. Yet they had one horse at least—Columba's old white horse—and one wagon. All this establishment, in-door and out, was planned by Columba; none else there dreamt of planning. The whole was constructed of timber, brought from the mainland. They tell that once, when Columba had sent his monks to bring a boat-load of stakes for the house walls, the monks returned and told the abbot that the poor man from whose ground they had cut the stakes had grumbled sorely, and thought himself much aggrieved. One would not have thought that march fences were even then in use, nor that brushwood, in that time and country, could be so valuable. But Columba loves fair dealing, and will not rob poor men even for the Church. "Let us do him no wrong," says he. "Return, and bear to him six bushels of barley, and tell him to sow it in his ground." The saint added his blessing. The poor man sowed, and in a surprisingly short space it had grown to an abundant crop,—probably the first grain that ever found its way into these parts, which are rather scant of barley even now-a-days.

The first two years were probably spent in erecting the monastery, and arranging other conventual matters. It was then that Columba, taking some monks with him, set out on his great journey to the mainland to convert the Northern Picts. This branch of the Picts inhabited all the north-east of

Scotland, from Athole to Cape Wrath, as the other branch, the Southern Picts, stretched from Athole to the Forth. Both were probably of the Cymric branch of Celts, Columba and his friends being Gael. Columba made at once straight for the hill fort of Brude, the Pictish king, on Loch Ness. It is a peculiarity of these missions that strongly contrasts with those of the apostolic age, that everywhere they first address themselves to the kings. St. Paul says, that in his time not many wise men, not many mighty were called. With him it was the base things of the world; the poor men first, the rulers afterwards. But since the day when Constantine and the Roman world were won over, all that has been changed. And so Augustine seeks King Ethelbert; Kentigern deals much with the king of Strathclyde; Columba makes straight for Brude in his hill-fort by Loch Ness. It were injustice to our saint, however, to represent him as in any measure truckling to the great. Everywhere we find him treating the poorest and humblest with as much courtesy as the greatest king. Landing either at the head of Loch Sunart or on the mainland of Lorn, he and his monks would climb Drum Alban—the ridge of Alban—that high central ridge which crosses Scotland from south-west to north-east, from Loch Etive to Deeside in Aberdeenshire. They were the first Christian feet that had touched these mountains, or penetrated the wild country beyond them;

B

a rugged, difficult way, over mountains then tangled with woods, and infested with wild beasts, and men scarcely less wild.

Often enough it was at the peril of their lives. One night they sought shelter in some huts hard by, where a river enters a loch. They had moored on the other side of the stream the portable currachs, brought with them to ferry them over what lochs or rivers came in their way. At midnight, Columba rose and bade them bring over the boats to their own side of the stream. Scarcely had they done so, when they saw all the huts on the other side a-blaze, set on fire by some armed persecutors of Columba, probably the Druids, who everywhere resisted him. The hill-fort, in which Columba found King Brude, stood on Craig Phadrick, a commanding eminence, two miles from Inverness, looking northward to Ben Wyvis and the Ross-shire hills, eastward over Culloden Moor. Visible to this day, though moss-overgrown, are the outlines of the Pictish king's castle, in parts vitrified by the action of fire. At first the saint finds no favour with Brude. "They come, these men," he thinks, "from our enemies the Scots, with whom we have no dealings but sanguinary ones." And the Druids, who are in the fort with them, foster this impression. "They shall not enter here," says Brude; "close the gates against them." Columba draws near; signs the gates with the cross; strikes them with his hand, and they at once fly open. Awe-stricken, the king rises, and, with his chief men, comes forth and meets Columba with words of peace. The king's heart is henceforth as open to Columba as are his gates. From that day forward Brude treats the saint with reverence, listens devoutly to his words; and it was, in all likelihood, not long till he was, in a certain sense, converted and baptized. But there were harder hearts there than Brude's. Chief of these, Broichan, a Druid, who many ways withstood Columba.[1]

While the Christian monks are in a retired spot, engaged in evening prayer, Broichan and other Druids come upon them and try to put a stop to their devotion. Columba immediately chants aloud the 144th Psalm, and his voice, which could be heard a mile away, sounds in the evening air like thunder, and terrifies the Druids and king. Again Columba demands from Broichan restoration of a young Scottish maiden, who had been made a slave by the Picts. It is to the lasting honour of Columba and the Church to which he belonged, that they everywhere set their face stoutly against the slave-trade in captives, which was then carried on among all the tribes; and in time they were able to crush it. Broichan stoutly refuses to give up his captive. Thereon Columba declares to him

[1] [On the true character of Celtic Druidism, as compared with that of Gaul, see Skene's *Celtic Scotland*, vol. ii. p. 118.]

that unless he gives her up death will ensue, and leaves the fort. Ere long messengers come to Columba, reporting that Broichan lies sick and ready to die. Columba sends back two of his monks, bearing a stone which he has blessed, to heal Broichan if he consents to give up the maiden; to leave him to die if he refuse. The Druid at once consents; the stone is dipped in water, whereof he drinks, and is restored. The stone was laid up among the treasures of Brude, but when sought for on his death-day could nowhere be found.

It were easy to multiply these stories. Those already given are enough for samples.

Not to the king only he preached during his first journey to Pictland. We read of him preaching, by an interpreter, to a poor man among the Picts, and converting him and his entire household. A great impediment must have been his inability to speak the Pictish tongue. He needed an interpreter, just as a Highlander, at the present day, might require one when speaking to the Welsh. But these and many more difficulties gave way before Columba's energy. Once and again he revisited Pictland, and spent now several months, and now only a few days among his converts. His method seems to have been, wherever he preached, there to establish a small cell or church, and in some places a monastery and brotherhood, to complete what he had begun—thus covering the whole North

Highlands with a network of mission stations or monasteries—so many miniature Ionas. This was the machinery by which he worked; a machinery answering as effectually for his time and purpose as the parochial system does for ours.

The result of all these labours in the North Highlands is summed up in the phrase, "the conversion of the Northern Picts." What this really meant—how much, or rather how little, of spiritual change or moral renovation it at first implied— is hard to determine. But not harder in this case than in all those so-called conversions in the early ages, in which we read of a king and his people, a general and his battalions, being baptized in a mass. Their savage but simple natures, when confronted with Columba's clear, cultivated mind, and patient, Christian spirit, felt no doubt that they were in the presence of a higher being than themselves. The man was greater, better, wiser—that was the chief point; and then the truth he brought seemed, as far as they at all apprehended it, better than their old faith—appealed to the needs of all hearts, and seemed to satisfy them as decaying Druidism had never done. So, after the first opposition was over, they turned to him with reverence, and listened to his words like children. Not but that there may have been individual cases in which conversion meant something more than recognition of the missionary's personal nobleness—meant, in fact, the conviction of the convert that this was Divine truth which he had heard. But such instances were, I should think, the exception. In the case of Brude, probably, and the great mass of his people, conversion meant no more than this :— Columba, we must own, is a wiser, better man than any we have yet met with, therefore we will take his word for all the rest of it. And so, in due time, by this machinery, teaching and celebrating Christian rites, the moral impression made by Columba would be perpetuated, perhaps deepened and enlarged, into a habitual outward belief in Christianity, which, under the teaching of a higher than Columba, might, in some cases, become an inward one also. That there were instances, more or less numerous, of real inward conversion among these Picts, one cannot doubt; else a merely external Christianity, having no root in any hearts, could not long have lived on. But at the same time, it would seem probable that, on the great bulk of the people, his influence was only of that outward personal kind I have described. Who can say how much good even this may have done—the effect on all who witnessed it, of a man who manifested the kingdom of God in that dark time "by deeds of mercy and righteousness, and the rebuke of sin"?

It was this conversion of King Brude and his people that stamped Columba as the Apostle of the

Northern Picts. But not to these only were his labours of charity and mercy confined. Continual notices of Adamnan, immemorial tradition, and many a moss-grown ruin on lonely islands bear witness to his voyagings to and fro, preachings, baptizings, foundings of monasteries and cells throughout all the Hebrides. We read of continual goings to and from the island of Himba, which some take for Canna, others for Oronsay, on which Columba founded a large monastery, and set over it his uncle Ernan. Elachnave, or Holy Isle, lying north-west of Jura, had its monastery, over which Lugneus ruled; and to this day the traveller can trace its bee-hive cells of slate, covered with sods—the grass-grown burial-ground, with immemorial graves and few rude headstones. On Tiree, too, the low, sandy, corn island that supplied Iona with grain, he founded several conventual seats—one a training college for priests, over which Baithen presided; another, a penitential station, to which we read that the saint sent a great criminal who came from Ireland, confessing his sins, there to spend seven years in repentance. On Inch Kenneth, lying between Ulva and Iona, he placed a cell for his friend Kenneth—that Kenneth who, when Columba was at sea during a storm and like to perish in the Corrievrechan whirlpool, rose from his meal, crying out—"It is no time to eat when Columba is in peril," and ran to the church, with but one shoe on, to pray for his safety. We read, too, of our saint's being in Skye, and in danger of death by a wild boar, and of his preaching and baptizing there. And all the district of Trotternish round Loch Snizort still bears witness to his presence there, as well as the small, desolate islands of Troda and Fladda-Huna out in the Minch, by their all but obliterated chapels and cemeteries still bearing something of sanctity from the name they bear of Columbkill. Some think that Columba himself penetrated as far as the Orkneys, and established cells there; but however this may be, it is certain that a companion of his, St. Cormac, did; and having been saved from death there by the Orkneyan prince, returned to Iona, and entered the oratory while the monks were at prayer, to tell them of his wonderful deliverance.

Three times this same Cormac sailed into these northern seas, and was once, for fourteen days together, out of sight of land, seeking for a desert in the ocean, of which, perhaps, he had heard some rumour. We know not whether he or any other reached Iceland in Columba's lifetime, in their little coracles; but it seems almost certain that, not long after it, some of the Iona brotherhood did. For when the Norsemen first visited Iceland in the latter half of the ninth century, they found it deserted of its inhabitants, but they found substantial traces that Irish monks had been there before them. The poor monks were all gone; perished, probably of cold, but there were still their books, croziers, and bells—mute records of their self-devoted piety.

Taking the whole field of his labours—in Ireland, among the Northern Picts, the Argyll Scots, and over all the Hebrides—tradition attributes to him the foundation of one hundred monasteries and three hundred cells or churches; an exaggeration, perhaps, but a proof how deep was the impression made on men's minds by his boundless activity. It is quite clear that he and the twelve brethren who first emigrated with him were wholly inadequate for so wide a work. But the original monastery, with its twelve huts, seems gradually to have expanded itself, so as to receive many youths, attracted from Ireland and elsewhere by Columba's fame. These men were educated and trained as priests in the central monastery of Iona. In Tiree there was another training college for the same purpose; and from his monasteries in Ireland, over which he still presided, it is probable that Columba draughted large supplies of young and zealous men for missionary work. With these he peopled the numerous cells and smaller conventicles which he had planted everywhere throughout the Highlands and the Hebrides.

A few words are all that can here be given to the character of the Iona monasticism and the constitution of its monastery. The Church polity and the monastic institutions which St. Patrick, in the fifth century, implanted in Ireland differed, in many respects, from the Roman rule. It is quite possible that St. Patrick, during his travels in Gaul, may have come in contact with churchmen from the East at Marseilles, itself a Greek colony, which had continual intercourse with the Levant, and near which, at the beginning of the fifth century, Cassian established a convent, on the model that he had learnt from the ascetics of Bethlehem and the Nile. The Eastern institution, though rigidly ascetic, fostered more of the free and independent spirit of personal religion; the Roman had more of the Church spirit, and adhered more obstinately to outward statute and observance. This Eastern, as opposed to the Roman spirit, seems to have characterised all the views and institutions of St. Patrick.

The connection with the East seems to be further indicated by three usages which differenced the Irish from the Roman monks, and which, after the age of Columba, became, in England and Scotland, the chief subjects of controversy between the two bodies.

1. The Irish had different mass-books or rituals from the Roman monks.

2. They had a different tonsure, the whole front half of the head, from ear to ear, instead of the Roman tonsure, on the crown.

3. They kept Easter according to the Oriental, not the Roman time.

In the sixth century Columba and his contemporaries seem to have carried still further the free spirit of their country's monasteries, so little adhering to form and usage, that every abbot seems to have moulded his monastery according to his own views of fitness. Nothing could be further from the stringency of Benedict and the Italian monastics than this free and pliant spirit which pervaded the Irish Churchmen of Columba's day. And he was not the man to circumscribe his own freedom of action more than was absolutely required. In fact, born of a kingly race, he reigned in Iona a spiritual king, alongside of his kinsmen, the temporal kings of Ireland and Argyll, but with a more powerful rule, and over a wider realm. For this Iona was happily placed; near enough those seats of government to derive strength from the proximity, far enough removed not to clash with their pretensions. A king he was in the best sense of the word; that is, a powerful, yet enlightened ruler of men—a true shepherd of the people. It is his highest praise, that, holding such absolute power, he used it so largely for wise and beneficent ends. Half-patriarchal, half-monastic was the kingship he held. Patriarchal, in that the tie of kinship was so strongly recognised, that Iona was a home for all the founder's kin—a rallying point for all the wide-scattered family. So strongly was this marked, that the abbacy, though, of course, it could not be lineal, was continued, with only two exceptions, in Columba's kin through eleven successive abbots. How true to the Celtic character this admission of clanship even into a religious community! Perhaps it may have been from this that all the brotherhood of monks were called "the family of Iona," and that Columba so often speaks of them as his sons, his little children. But not the less, though patriarchal, was the system of Iona monastic. So monastic, that whereas St. Patrick and his immediate followers did not avoid the society or services of women, Columba and the presbyter abbots who were his contemporaries, entirely repudiated them. No woman was allowed to approach Iona while he lived, or whilst his rule was maintained. Columba regarded his monks and himself as soldiers of Christ, and his office was to train himself and them, by rule and example, for this service. To him the monks rendered absolute obedience, but he required nothing of them which he did not in larger measure exact from himself. If he laid down for them hours of prayer, at which they flocked to the oratory three times a day, three times a night; hours for reading, for writing, for labour in the fields, it was noted of himself that he allowed no time to pass when he was not engaged in either prayer, or reading, or writing, or in some useful work. If he required of his followers rigorous penance for their faults, and even made a penitent stranger, who came from Ireland, kneel down while he confessed his sins, and then sent him to spend some time in the penitential station at Tiree, he was not less rigorous on himself, sleeping only on a bare stone bed, with a stone for pillow, whence he would rise at the dead of night, and spend whole hours, besides the stated one, praying alone in the oratory. If the door was closed, he would pray outside, or retire to thickets or lonely places in the hills, there to pray, the winter night long, beneath the cold, starry sky.

He himself and his monks lived sparely; yet not sparely, compared with other ascetics. Two meals a day, but on the fast-days, which were very frequent, only one; their food barley bread from their own field, milk, fish. No meat, except on Sundays or feast-days, or when guests appeared. Hospitality, which was a virtue in all ancient monasteries, in Hy was practised in truly national abundance. Again and again, in Adamnan's book, we read that Columba tells the monks that a stranger is shouting for a boat across the ferry that divides Iona from Mull, just as the Highlanders shout for the ferry-boat across those firths at this day. Straightway they put off in a boat, land him on the island, and lead him to the abbot, if he has not already come forth to meet the guest. Bringing him into the oratory, they give thanks for his safe arrival, and then, conducting him to his hut, give him water for his feet. Often the abbot himself personally attended his guests, loosing their shoes, and washing their feet, after the old Eastern fashion. If the day be one of the weekly fasts, the fast is at once, by the abbot's order, relaxed, and a better than their ordinary meal prepared. Indeed, the monastery seems never to have been empty of guests from Ireland, from the mainland, from Northumbria, and other distant parts.

Columba, too, was a good friend to the poor, and a large almsgiver. Bede remarks that though his monks lived by the labour of their own hands, they gave away to the poor all they did not absolutely need. Often he blessed the grain and the cattle of the poor, and this they believed always increased their store. A great, but not a promiscuous almsgiver, sturdy beggars with wallets met no countenance from him.

A great physician, too, our saint was, if we may trust tradition: skilful in such therapeutics as were then in vogue. The sick flocked to the monastery of Iona from far and near; and his power to relieve them, like his power to counsel the perplexed, was so great that it was reckoned to be miraculous. Sometimes his patients came and stayed at the monastery; at other times he is said to have prescribed for patients at a distance, and to have sent his medicines as far as Ireland.

Sometimes he received proffered presents for these services, but generally took no fee, regarding this skill chiefly as a means of getting at the patient's heart. His medical knowledge is said to have lived on amongst his monks, and perhaps from them to have passed to the famous race of doctors in Islay and Mull. This at least is certain, that about the oldest Celtic manuscripts found in the Hebrides are on medical subjects—some of them said to be as old as the twelfth century.

I cannot pass from these notices without adverting for a moment to the much-vexed question of Columba's clerical order.

It is well known that he was a presbyter, not a bishop—a peculiarity common to him with all the great Irish abbots of his age. Add to this the well-known declaration of Bede, that in his own day, the earlier part of the eighth century, to the presbyter abbot of Iona "all the province, even the bishops, contrary to the usual method, were subject, according to the example of their first teacher Columba."

It is wonderful how loud the ecclesiastical cackle has arisen round this short sentence; Presbyterians crowing most lustily to find, as they thought, Columba one of themselves; Episcopalians struggling hard to explain away its damaging testimony. It is a vain, not to say absurd, attempt to prove that Columba finds his modern counterpart in the moderator of a Scottish presbytery, or even of a general assembly. Presbyterians must give it up, unless they can reconcile presbytery with monkery, parity with priestly kingship, such as Columba held. On the other hand, it is equally clear that if we are to go by Adamnan's book, the bishop by no means held the place in Columba's arrangements which he holds in modern and most ancient episcopacies. For it is quite clear that within the whole range of Columba's domain the bishop, or even a dozen bishops, would be but very subordinate figures whenever he appeared. Probably in this, as in other things, Columba did not adhere very closely to Church rules where he saw they could be set aside with advantage. But as one fact is worth many probabilities, I am bound to say that there is in Adamnan no evidence that Columba ever took on himself the office of ordaining priests—the peculiar office and test of a bishop. On the other hand, there is one recorded instance where a presbyter was to be ordained in Tiree, in which they summoned a bishop (*accito episcopo*) for the purpose.

One cannot expect to settle in these few remarks so old and obstinate a dispute. But thus much may be said, that Episcopalians and Presbyterians will have to bring forward some clearer evidence than any they have yet done before they prove that Columba was quite conformable to either type. Certainly the Iona Episcopacy of that day would ill assort with any modern Episcopacy, either Anglican or Roman. And as for Presbytery, it may be safely asserted that the first taste Iona had of that form of Church polity was when the redoubtable Presbytery of Argyll in one day hurled its three hundred and sixty crosses into the sea — wicked monuments of idolatry that they were. But this is not the place to enter fully into the question of Columba's Church polity. One remark only. The truth seems to be that since Ireland had derived her earliest Christianity from Gaul, at a time before the Roman system had got matured or begun to claim for itself universal dominion, the naturally free Celtic spirit maintained this independence; Columba carried it out to the full, and owned no fealty to Rome; and when, in after-ages, his descendants confronted the fully Romanised clergy of Saxon England, there were found to be between them differences irreconcilable. But though this proves Columba to have been no son of Rome, it does not prove that he or any of his generation were free, as they could not have been free, from that taint of sacerdotalism which entered into the Church the very next age after the apostles; which pervaded it more and more each new generation; which Rome did not create, but found already existing, and which she only gathered up and organised more completely into one gigantic system.

It was thus that Columba settled himself and his twelve monks in Hy, converted the Northern Picts, spread his religion over the Northern Highlands and all the Hebrides, and organised and ruled his monastery. It now only remains that I should notice his dealings with his kinsmen—the Dalriad kings of Argyll. It is every way probable that the Abbot of Hy superintended all the churches among these Irish Scots of Argyll; and there seem to be traces of a cell of his planting at Kilduin by Loch Awe, over which a monk (Cailten) was placed. Often in his wanderings he must have visited these kings in their earliest regal seat, Dun Monadh, near Loch Crinan.

But his most authentic and important dealing with them was, when their king, Conall, died, and doubt arose who was to succeed. Columba did not in anywise push himself forward as an arbiter, but to him his kinsmen seem instinctively to have turned. He had no force to command their respect, had used no intrigue or petty craft to win influence. It was the instinctive recognition of one worthier, wiser, more righteous than themselves which made them look to him for counsel, a recognition stronger often and more unerring among simple, half-barbarous men, than among the educated and highly civilised.

Columba at the time was staying in the island Himba. There, in a dream by night, he seemed to see an angel draw near to him, holding out a book of glass, containing Heaven's decrees about the succession of earthly kings. The saint took the book and read therein. But when the angel bade him arise and ordain Aidan king of the Argyll Scots, Columba refused to go, for he loved Aidan's brother Eogenan better. Thereupon the angel raised his hand and smote him on the side with a lash, whereof the mark remained blue even to the day of his death. Three nights successively this was repeated, till at last Columba arose and returned to Hy. There he found Aidan newly come to the island, and at once proceeded to make him king, as he had been commanded. He read over him words of inauguration, ordained and blessed him, and spake to him of his descendants to the fourth generation. Thenceforward Columba became attached to Aidan, and called him his "soul's friend;" and Aidan returned his affection. From their connection they gained reciprocal advantages—Aidan religious sanction to his disputed title, the Abbot of Hy, for all time to come, ecclesiastical supremacy over all Argyll.

This Aidan was an able king, the first of his line who showed real ability. He refused any longer to hold Argyll in fee from the king of Erin. Thence fell out a great strife between the men of Alban and the men of Erin, to settle which a convention was summoned of all the Irish princes to Drumceatt. Thither Columba and King Aidan set out together in a small boat, and being overtaken by a storm in mid-ocean, they hardly made Loch Foyle. At Drumceatt, Columba stood forward as peace-maker between the two kings; and so powerful was his influence in that assembly, that he prevailed with them formally to recognise the Argyll Scots as an independent people, and Aidan as an independent king. At the same convention, when it was proposed to extirpate the whole Bardic order of Ireland, by their arrogance become unbearable, Columba, though as opposers of Christianity they were naturally his enemies, magnanimously pleaded their cause with the assembly, and prevailed so that they spared the Bards on condition of a limitation in their number, and their better conduct in time to come.

Then he visited his two Irish monasteries of Derry and Durrow, over which he still held supremacy. Wherever he went the monks from cell and convent went forth to meet him, the people did him reverence.

Perhaps the chief thing that strikes us in all this is the exhaustless energy of the man, the great and numberless enterprises he laid hand to, and the power with which he clenched them all. Yet all these, various as they were, bearing on the one great end to which he gave his life, the Christianising and civilising these wild Celtic races. Evidently one of those unresting, unhasting men, who find time for all things,—time to convert Pictland and plant the Church there—time to Christianise all the Hebrides, and to order both the religious and the civil affairs of Argyll—time to shape and organise his own Iona monastery, and to manage and provide for innumerable missionary outposts—time to keep up large intercourse with Ireland, and care of his own Irish monasteries—time to give sympathy and counsel to his monks one by one, to prescribe for the sick near and far off, to give alms to the poor and comfort to the perplexed; long hours, too, of laborious studying, much transcribing of the Scriptures and other books, poems and hymns of his own composing; long seasons of solitary prayer, midnight watching in the oratory, praying beneath the starry heavens—time, too, to receive guests who came from Ireland and other lands for converse or counsel, welcoming them with kindness, and entertaining them with becoming hospitality. If it were not for some instances of a like boundless activity in times nearer our own, we might have believed that these things were exaggerations of his biographers. But they are no figments. Adamnan nowhere dwells on them, but they drop out only as by the way.

Such a life would soon wear out most men. It took thirty-four years of it to wear out Columba. On the very day when his thirty years in Iona were complete, his monks saw his face suddenly grow bright with joy, and then overcloud with sadness. They asked him the reason. He told them that he had long wished and prayed that when his thirty years' service was fulfilled the yoke might be unloosed, and he summoned to the heavenly country. To-day the thirty years were ended, and the angels had descended to take him; but they had been arrested by the prayer of the churches that he might be longer spared. Now he was to tarry four years longer on earth. This it was that turned his joy into sorrow. The meaning of this may be that, having been visited with sickness and brought near to death, he had been restored for a time, when he had rather have departed. His last four years seem to have been passed in comparative repose.

At length the time came when he could no more go out and come in, but must lie down with his fathers. In the month of May, a few days before the end, the old man, unable to walk, made them bear him in the wagon to the west of the island, where his monks were busy at their field work. He told them that he had been spared through the month of April, that his going might not darken their Easter joy. They were grieved, seeing they were so soon to lose him; but he comforted them with what kind words he could. Then, as he sat in the wagon, he turned his face to the east, and blessed the island and all the inhabitants thereof.

On the last day of that week, the Saturday, he went with his faithful servant Diormet to see the granary. After they had entered, he blessed the house, and the two heaps of grain that were stored therein. Then turning to Diormet, he said, "I am thankful to see that my faithful monks will have sufficient provision for this year also, if I shall have to go away any whither." Diormet looked round and said, "Why are you always saddening us this year by talking of your going away?" Columba replied, "I have something to tell thee, Diormet, if thou wilt promise faithfully to reveal it to none till after I depart." Diormet vowed solemnly on bended knees. Then Columba said, "This day, in the Sacred Scriptures, is called Sabbath, which means rest. And a Sabbath verily it is to me, the last day of this toilsome life, after which I shall cease from all my labours and enter into rest." Hearing this, Diormet began to weep bitterly, but Columba comforted him as he could. On their way home to the monastery, the old man, wearied, sat down to rest on a stone. And the old white horse, the one horse of the island, which used to carry the milk pails from the byre to the monastery, came up to them, and, laying his head in the saint's lap, began to moan and to make the best semblance of weeping that he could. Seeing this, Diormet began to drive the horse away. But the saint forbade him, and blessed the faithful creature, and passed on.

Then they ascended a small eminence, probably Croc-nan-Carnan, which overlooks the monastery. On the top he stood, and lifting up both his hands, blessed the cœnobium himself had built, and spake of the honour it would have in future time, not only among people and kings of the Scots, but also from many foreign peoples and their kings.

After this they came down from the hill, and the saint retiring to his own hut, or hospice, set himself to finish transcribing a Psalter which he had begun. He got as far as that verse of the 34th Psalm—"They that seek the Lord shall not want any good thing." "Here," says he, "I must stop at the bottom of the page. What follows, let Baithen write." "That," says Adamnan, "well might be the last verse Columba wrote, for he will not want any good thing for ever." And the next verse suited well Baithen his worthy successor. "Come, ye children, hearken unto me. I will teach you the fear of the Lord."

When he had done writing, he attended vespers, or even-song, in the church. That over, returning to his hut, he reclined on his bed of stone, as of old, with a stone for his pillow. As he sat or lay there, with Diormet still attending, he delivered to him his last charges for all the brotherhood, entreating them to dwell together in mutual charity and peace ; and "God the Comforter will bless you ; and I, with Him abiding, will pray for you, that you may have what is needful for this life, as well as all eternal good."

The saint then kept silence till the bell sounded at twelve o'clock for the midnight vigil. Rising up quickly, he was the first to enter the church, and fell down on his knees in prayer beside the altar.

Diormet hastened after him, but on entering the church he found all dark, for the brethren had not yet arrived with their lanterns. Groping his way, he found the saint lying before the altar, raised him a little, and placed his head on his knees. During this the monks came thronging in with their lanterns, and, seeing their father dying, began to wail aloud. As they entered, the holy man opened his eyes and looked round on them with strange hilarity and joy in his countenance, as though he saw the angels come to meet him. Diormet then raised his right hand, and he, as well as he could, moved it to wave the blessing he could no longer speak. And when he had done this, he fell asleep. A while he lay there, his whole face suffused with brightness, while the church resounded with the wailing of the brotherhood. So passed Columba, in his own small church in Hy, early on Sunday morning, the 9th of June A.D. 597.

When the matin service was done, the monks bore his body from the church back to his own hut, singing psalmody all the way. Three days and three nights they waked him there, and then, his body wrapt in clean linen, they laid him with due veneration in the tomb.

And so concludes Adamnan :—" Our patron ceased from his labours, and went to join the eternal triumph—the companion of fathers, prophets, and apostles, a virgin soul made clean from stain—one more added to the white-robed multitude, who have washed their robes in the blood of the Lamb, and now follow Him whithersoever He goeth."

These facts and incidents may have given, I hope, some impression of Columba's work and character. If they have not, I could scarcely expect to do so by any more formal portraiture.

That youth of royal race, high bearing, and noble lineaments, of tall, athletic, and commanding frame, of a countenance so ruddy and hilarious, that, even when worn with long toil and fasting, "he looked like one who lived in luxury," large store of natural genius, quite herculean energy, by nature irascible and explosive, yet unselfish withal, placable, affectionate, full of tenderness for those about him, and most compassionate to the weak, he was born to win the hearts and the reverence of men, and to mould them as he would.

Such a character comes only once a century to any time or country. As far as we know, no equal to Columba was born in these islands during the whole sixth or several succeeding centuries. Perhaps no other such appeared till Alfred, England's king. In the natural course of things Columba would have been a great warrior, or a most potent king; but Heaven had predestined him for something better. A large portion of his Celtic race were still living in a wholly inhuman state—bloodshed, rapine, and clan feuds—unreclaimed from the old night of barbarism;

their chiefs, kinglets, and Druids not lessening, only aggravating the evil.

Columba saw the evil case of his people, felt it as his own, his heart yearned towards them. For on him from his early years had fallen the divine fire, which entering in, transfigured his great natural endowments into far more than their natural effectiveness. He early learned that hardest of all lessons,—to have done with self; and this made his strength to be

> "As the strength of ten,
> Because his heart was pure."

So, forgetting comfort and power and renown, he sought only to do for his race the utmost good that could be done during his threescore years and ten. He went forth in the power of faith, into that chaos bringing order, into that heathendom bringing the purest light of Christian truth then attainable, into that dark ignorance bringing knowledge, into that lazy, bloodthirsty life bringing the first seeds of peaceful industry, into that foul impurity bringing pure manners, domestic happiness; in short, out of anarchic disorder and utter savagery, moulding harmony and order and civilisation by the transforming power of Christian faith.

He chose the highest end a man could choose in that day, perhaps in any day; and for thirty long years he wrestled against the opposing forces with all his herculean energy, till he overcame them and victoriously achieved his end. His work he left to others, whom he himself had formed, to propagate it for centuries after he was gone. Well may the Celtic people remember Columba with grateful devotion—a devotion that seems folly to those who do not know his history. They are the better to this hour, because he lived. In fact, as far as we know, no benefactor at all comparable to him has ever since risen up among them. And not to the Gael only, but to all Scots, even those who care least for the Celts, he is worthy of honourable remembrance. For the work he did in the Highlands overflowed all the Lowlands with its benign effects, and spread through the kingdom of Northumbria, and far south into England. In truth, no countryman of ours was worthy to be placed beside him till William Wallace and Robert Bruce appeared.

If Scotland had ever possessed for herself a Pantheon, a Valhalla, or Temple of her good and brave, the three earliest niches would deserve to have been filled by Ninian, Kentigern, and, high above both, Columba.[1]

[1] [It may be added that the remains of Columba were buried in Iona, and rested there for more than a century. They were then taken and placed in a shrine, which was conveyed to Ireland in 878. The shrine, with its contents, is now untraceable.]

## II.—QUEEN MARGARET OF SCOTLAND.[1]

As one looks back into the dim beginnings of Scotland's history, the first great character that rises out of the darkness is that of Saint Columba, Abbot of Iona at the end of the sixth century. The next, at an interval of more than four hundred years, is Margaret, Queen of Scotland, towards the close of the eleventh. In the long dark blank between them there are names of kings and dates of battles, but hardly a vestige of what can be called personal history. Some characters there probably were, missionary priests, or chiefs of conflicting tribes, who did things worthy to have been had in remembrance, but "they had no poet and they died." Columba and Margaret might likewise have been lost to posterity, certainly the image of both would long ere now have waxed faint and vague, had it been intrusted only to tradition. But they were fortunate each in "having a poet"—that is, a biographer, who could both appreciate their virtues and record them. Columba has been handed down by Adamnan, a successor of his own in the Abbey of Iona, who

[1] [Contributed to *Good Words*, 1867.]

wrote his life about eighty-five years after his death; Margaret, by Turgot, her own confessor, who shortly after her death wrote in readable Latin some small part of what he had seen and known of his queen and friend.[1] These books are not, of course, such biographies as those written now-a-days, neither so strictly accurate, nor so sharp in outline, nor so rich in detail. They leave untold many things we would like to know, and tell some that have lost meaning for us. Still they are full of interest. They are remarkable examples of the tone of thinking and feeling in the day when they were written. They are by far the earliest genuine biographies which Scotland possesses. They may almost be said to furnish the first authentic facts of Scottish history. Instead, therefore, of grumbling with them for what they are not, we may well be thankful for what they are.

It is a noteworthy fact that neither of these two earliest benefactors of Scotland was of native origin. Celtic Ireland gave us the first, Saxon England the second; the one the great Celtic, the other the great Saxon saint of the Scottish people. The one stands at the head of the purely Celtic period of our history, the other at the head of the mixed Scoto-Saxon epoch, which she herself inaugurated. Each has in Scotland a local habitation hallowed by their

---

[1] [Turgot, Prior of Durham, was consecrated Bishop of St. Andrews in 1107; he died in 1115.]

memory. Iona is scarcely more identified with Columba than Dunfermline with Queen Margaret. The western island has not more royal memories, and can scarcely contain more royal dust than the romantically-seated eastern town. There stand the ruins of that palace of Scottish kings in which James VI. lived often with his Danish queen before he ascended the throne of England; and there is still shown the chamber-window which let in the first light of this world on the eyes of Charles, their ill-fated son. There stands, still unimpaired after eight hundred years, the sombre Norman nave which for three centuries continued to be the burial-place of our Scottish kings, with the choir, twice ruined and twice rebuilt, under which still rest the bones of Robert Bruce. But far older than the palace, older too than the abbey church, are still seen in the glen hard by, on a knoll almost hidden among dense trees, crumbling moss-grown walls, now scarce the height of a man, which are all that remains of the Dun or Fort of Malcolm Canmore. This knoll, on which the fort stood, overhanging precipitously a deeply-grooved burn, which underneath it crooks into an elbow, seems to have given from its situation the name to the town, the Dun or Fort over the Linn, or the Fort on the Crooked Linn. That tower was the chief abode of Malcolm Canmore, the contemporary of William the Conqueror. Therein he received the Saxon Princess Margaret and her family when they fled from England before the wrath of the Conqueror, and that was the home in which they lived together when she had become his queen. No other event was more momentous to Scotland than that coming of Margaret to Dunfermline. It marks the beginning of a new era. For by her own life, and through her descendants who followed in her steps, she changed the whole future destiny of the land which adopted her.

The story you hear on the spot, and history confirms it, is, that once when Malcolm "of the big head" was living in that tower, it was told him that a strange ship had just cast anchor in a bay of the Forth, about three miles off. The king straightway sent messengers down to the Forth to find out whence the ship came and whom it had on board. They brought back word that the ship was larger and better equipped than common ships, but nothing more. The king then sent other messengers more numerous and of higher rank than the first. These were kindly received by the strangers, were struck by the tallness of the men and the fair complexion and the beauty of the women, and returned to the king reporting that they were none other than the Saxon Royal line of England, Edgar Atheling and his sisters Margaret and Christina, with their mother Agatha. With them were Gospatrick and other Northumbrian nobles, who, disgusted with the Norman tyranny, had resolved to share the fate of the old Royal family. They had sailed for the Continent, intending to take refuge in Hungary, the native land of Agatha; but a great wind had arisen and driven them from their course, and they had been fain to seek shelter in the Forth. The king hearing this hastened to the shore. He was touched with compassion for the exiles, as well he might be, for he had himself been an exile, and had received much kindness from Edward the Confessor, uncle of Edgar and Margaret. He could converse with them, too, more freely than his nobles, for he had learned the Saxon tongue during his sojourn in England. The king conducted them all to his tower, and entertained them there with much kindness. Scotland became the home of the exiled princes. In due time Malcolm won Margaret for his bride. The dark Celtic king with the large head wed the high-souled Saxon princess with the flaxen hair, said to be the most beautiful woman of all her time; but it was something more than beauty of face and form that endeared her to the hearts of her new people. The local names of the neighbourhood are witnesses to the impression she made on them. Ever since her time the bay on the north side of the Forth in which her ship cast anchor has been called Margaret's Hope. A large grey stone on the north side of the road between Margaret's Hope and Dunfermline is still called St. Margaret's seat, and tradition tells how Margaret, wearied with journeying on foot from the Forth to Malcolm's tower in the glen, sat down on it to rest. The ferry from the Dunfermline to the Lothian side of the Forth after her time lost its old Celtic name, and was called from her the Queen's Ferry. No wonder she should have left such traces of herself; for no name of equal beauty or of deeper interest appears on the whole roll of Scotland's worthies. She opens the line of Scottish queens, as a direct descendant of hers, of as deep interest, but far other character, closes it—Mary Stuart.

To appreciate aright the character of Margaret and the nature of her work, they must be looked at against the contrasted background of Scotland as it was in the eleventh century. When, in 1057, Malcolm Canmore had the crown of Alban placed on his head by the Thane of Fife at Scone, the land he was called to rule was not one compact kingdom, but a number of different tribes as yet unamalgamated, and even hostile to each other. Nay, even his own Celtic people were divided between the descendants of the gracious Duncan and the faction of Macbeth. In Celtic Alban, or the land north of the Forth and Clyde, the Scottish line of kings had for nearly two centuries superseded the Pictish, but probably the two peoples were not yet fully united. The eastern and northern seaboard, as well as all the islands, were occupied by a sea-borne population from Denmark or Scandinavia. To the south of the Forth, though Lothian, with its Saxon people, had been ceded to the Scots in the middle of the tenth century, and the Welsh kingdom of Strathclyde had been absorbed early in the eleventh, yet that whole southern region lay still unfused, almost unappropriated. Add to this, during all Malcolm's time, the continual migration northward of ousted Saxons, noble and serf, flying first from the disorders that preceded the fall of the Anglo-Saxon dynasty, then from the terrible oppression of the Conqueror. Lastly, numbers of discontented Norman adventurers were seeking in the land of Malcolm larger domains than had been granted them by their Norman master. Here were elements of discord enough—Pict, Scot, Briton, Scandinavian, Saxon, Norman, Fleming—a very seething caldron of conflicting elements, a very Babel of strange tongues. The throne of Malcolm, called to rule over these, and to reduce them to some sort of unity, must have been no easy seat. He was the last of the old and purely Celtic order, and the introducer of the new or Scoto-Saxon. For though the Celtic language was still spoken from Tweed to the Moray Firth, and was still the language of the Court, though a prince of the Scottish line was still placed, with the old Celtic forms, at his coronation on the "stone of destiny" at Scone, yet ancient Alban was on the eve of being nearly de-Celticised —the end of the Celtic supremacy was at hand. The Gael in the land of their fathers were to be paramount no more.

He who, whether intentionally or not, was the author of this revolution, the Malcolm of Shakespeare's drama, the son of the gracious Duncan, was a prince of purely Celtic extraction. How he fled to England and returned in time to avenge his father's death, and to wrest his kingdom from the murderer, need not be told now, for Shakespeare has told it. But a closer examination of the old chroniclers modifies in some important respects the incidents of the great drama. Fordun and the register of St. Andrew's Priory make Elgin, not Inverness, the scene of Duncan's murder. They say that he was attacked and wounded by Macbeth at a place near Elgin called Bothgowan, the Smith's Hut, and returned thence to Elgin to die. The real name of the famous Lady Macbeth was Gruach, through whom her lord possessed some real claim to the crown. Again, Wyntoun makes Malcolm not the legitimate son and heir of Duncan, but a natural son by the daughter of a miller near Forteviot. The same chronicler makes Macbeth's rule of seventeen years not that of a bloody tyrant, but—

> "All his time was great plenty,
> Abounding both in land and sea,
> He was in justice right lawful,
> And till his lieges all awful." [1]

Many more variations from Shakespeare's version of the story might be pointed out. Wyntoun tells us

---

[1] [*The Cronykil of Scotland*, B. VI. c. xviii.]

that when Malcolm, with Macduff, had reached Birnam, he there heard of Macbeth's superstitious belief about the moving wood, and resolved to avail himself of it; that ever since that wood has been called "the flitting wood;" that Macbeth did not stay to fight at Dunsinane, but fled over the Mounth (the Grampians) and across the Dee to Lumphanan wood, in Aberdeenshire; that there he was overtaken and slain, and his head conveyed to Malcolm, who was two miles off, at Kincardine O'Neil. But though crowned king, Malcolm was not at ease. Even the Celtic people were divided—some favouring the house of Malcolm, some that of Macbeth. To this early part of Malcolm's reign probably belongs an anecdote given by more than one chronicler, which shows the king's disposition in a favourable light. Having heard on good authority that one of his nobles, in whom he most confided, had plotted against his life, he summoned his vassals to "keep tryst," with their hounds, on a certain day at an appointed place, to take with him their pastime in the woods. In the midst of the forest was a knoll, surrounded with thick trees and covered with wild flowers. On this knoll the king took his station, and having dismissed the several nobles with their hounds each to his appointed post in the wood, he stayed there himself, and bade the accused man stay with him. As soon as they were alone, the king took the traitor aside to a yet more retired spot, and, drawing his sword, said, "I know all your treachery. We are now alone, and on equal terms. You have sought my life. Draw now, and take it if you can." At this the knight was so smitten with contrition, that he knelt down and begged the king's forgiveness, and at once received it. There is another characteristic story told of the king later in his life. His daughter Matilda, afterwards queen of Henry I., was educated in the nunnery of Wilton, of which her aunt Christina, sister of Margaret, was abbess. It seems that Matilda had on some occasions been seen wearing a veil, or something that looked like one. Anselm was doubtful whether after this he could celebrate the marriage. But Matilda, when questioned, told him that she had worn a veil in public at her aunt's command, with no intention of becoming a nun, but to protect herself against the insults of the licentious Normans. She added that once, when her father Malcolm saw it on her head, he was so angry that he pulled it off and tore it to pieces.

After Malcolm had secured himself on the throne, his life was mainly occupied in wars with the Conqueror and his son the Red King. Again and again he broke with terrible fury into the ill-fated Northumbria, burning, plundering, laying waste, and driving off such crowds of captives, that they might afterwards be found, one chronicler says, in every village and every hut north of Tweed. Not less furiously did the Conqueror retaliate; and at length, to spread a wilderness between himself and the troublesome Scot, burnt all the land between the Humber and the Tees "into somewhat stern repose." It was during one of those border wars in the reign of Rufus, that Malcolm and his son Edward perished at the siege of Alnwick. All through he must have had a busy, troublous life of it, sweetened only by the calm presence of Margaret. For his country was seething with change. A twofold revolution was going on in it. The one side of it arose, as we have seen, from the clash of many diverse populations, in which the old Celtic one gradually had to succumb, and yield its supremacy to the hated Sassenach.

The other form of the revolution, the ecclesiastical one, was not less important in itself, and had far more bearing on the life of Margaret. In the civil change she bore only an indirect part, by disposing her husband to look favourably on her countrymen and their customs, and by preparing a ready welcome in the north for all of them who, like herself, were driven from England. There is, however, no record of any harshness or want of friendliness on her part towards the native Celts. We never hear that in her boundless charity she had any regard to difference of race; only that the poorer any were, the more they drew forth her compassion.

But to effect an ecclesiastical and religious revolution in Scotland, Margaret gave her whole heart. The native Church, with its Culdee clergy, she found cold and lifeless—deep sunk in worldliness, and little able to supply nutriment to a faith ardent and energetic as hers. To describe fully the condition of the Culdee Church when Margaret arrived in Scotland, or even to state clearly who the Culdees were, is no easy, perhaps a hardly possible, task; for almost all our accounts of them are from the records of that Church which was opposed to them, and bent on their suppression. These scanty and imperfect notices of them give little enough footing of evidence; but even these fragments have been, as it were, trodden into mire by the feet of innumerable disputants. One party have set themselves to find in these Culdees nothing but the purest life and doctrine, combined with the simplicity of Presbyterian discipline. Nay, some would even seem to antedate the Disruption by a thousand years, and to find them Non-Intrusionists and Free Churchmen in the ninth century. High Churchmen, on the other hand, make them out to be good Episcopalians, perfect in their order and apostolic succession, wanting only somewhat in strictness of discipline. From views such as these it is refreshing to turn to the

"Book on the Culdees," recently published by Dr. Reeves, the great Celtic antiquary. He there condenses into a short space all the evidence that is extant, giving the original documents. Every one, therefore, has now before him the grounds at least on which alone a true judgment can be formed. One thing is still wanted: that Dr. Reeves or some one else well versed in church history and ecclesiastical usage, not only in these islands, but throughout Christendom, should, as it were, sum up the evidence, and, comparing what it tells of the Culdees with what is known of contemporary churchmen in other countries, give, in the light of likeness and of contrast, the complete result.[1]

The first fact which Dr. Reeves makes plain is, that the Culdees had nothing to do with St. Columba and his Iona Church. The name is found not in Scotland only, but in Ireland also, and even in England, at York, and in Wales, at Bardsey; in fact, wherever the native Church retained any of its original elements unsubdued by Romanising influence. The name, it seems, means "Gillies," or Servants of God. To Columba or his immediate followers, the name is never applied either by Adamnan or Bede, or indeed by any writer till modern times. It belongs to a set

[1] [This has been in great measure and ably done since the date of this paper, by Mr. W. F. Skene in his *Celtic Scotland*, vol. ii. *Church and Culture*. 1877.]

of Churchmen of the tenth and eleventh, not of the seventh, century. The earliest Scottish record of the name occurs in Jocelyn's "Life of Kentigern," a work of the twelfth century. Let us dismiss, then, the groundless belief that the Culdees were Columbites or followers of Columba, as we read of Benedictines or followers of the rule of Benedict. No doubt Culdees were found in the tenth and eleventh centuries in churches and monasteries which had been founded by Columba and his immediate followers. But though they filled the places of the Columbites, they led another manner of life, and were of another spirit. The Columbite Church, indeed, acknowledged no homage to the Pope; and its Presbyter Abbot was the superior of the Bishop. But its rule was strictly monastic, celibate, and ascetic. Columba would not allow a woman even to land on his isle of Hy. He and his followers were fervent missionaries, undergoing all hardships to preach the Gospel to heathens. They loved knowledge, too, possessed all the learning of their age, were unwearied in multiplying copies of books, and in teaching others. But this light was trampled out both in Iona and in the other monasteries that sprung from her by the devastating Norsemen of the ninth century. And when the calamity was overpast, and the clergy, towards the close of the ninth and in the tenth century, gathered once again to the ruined churches and monasteries, they practised no more the old austerity. This at least, besides the natural tendency of monasticism to degenerate, may perhaps account for the state of the Culdees in the days of Margaret. For ages they had ceased to be celibates; they had little learning, and no missionary zeal; but they still lived a conventual life, yet with few rules, and these but loosely observed. Married men were as eligible to be Culdees as single; and though they could not take with them their wives and children into their conventual residences, yet, it would seem, they returned to their families as soon as their period of service was over. The result was, that the priesthood became a hereditary caste; and the wealthier priests left the Church lands to their sons, and very often these were not priests at all, but laymen. Sometimes even the abbot was not in holy orders; but the abbacy became a mere secular dignity. Several well-known Celtic names, as M'Nab, M'Pherson, bear witness to their secularisation. When those wealthy secularists had yet the lion's share of the church property, they left the prior and a few irregular monks, who still kept up a sort of conventual life, to perform the church services; for the whole Church system of the Culdees, it must be remembered, was, however lax, still monastic, not parochial. In the eleventh century there were no parishes in Scotland, and no dioceses. The Culdee priests lived in humble cottages, grouped together, probably, so as to form, as it were, colleges. And although there may have been a few convents here and there which still maintained the older and stricter system of Columba, and though there certainly were solitary hermits of severe life scattered over the country, yet the general religious instruction of the people depended in the main on the Culdees. The system itself was in its last decrepitude, and the greater part of the Church lands was absorbed by laymen. It was on this secularised portion of the old institution that the new abbeys, with their regular canons, were founded, when, in the twelfth century, the stricter system of Rome was introduced into Scotland by Margaret. These enjoyed the Church estates now recovered from their secular owners. Besides them, for a time, existed the Culdee prior, with his twelve secular priests, as in the Kirkheugh at St. Andrews; but bit by bit they dwindled, and were shorn of their rights and lands, till at last they wholly disappeared. Such at least was their history at St. Andrews, which seems to have been their chief seat in Scotland. It is not without a pathetic feeling that we trace the gradual ousting and final absorption by the new clergy of these Culdees, who were

> "Albyn's earlier priests of God,
> Ere yet an island of these seas
> By foot of Saxon monk was trod."

But whatever may be the truth about their ecclesiastical constitution, it cannot be doubted that a deep decay had by Margaret's time overtaken the Culdee brotherhoods. This, however, was but a small sample of what had been witnessed on a much larger scale throughout the monasticism of the whole western Church. Again and again since its first institution had the monasticism of all Latin Christendom sunk into worldly indifference or something worse; and again and again had it been quickened into new fervour by the zeal of some ardent spirit: now Benedict of Nursia, again a Berno, founder of the Clunians.

Throughout its whole history it was ever repeating the same ebb and flow. First, fervour, self-abnegation, poverty, asceticism; then, honour, wealth, sumptuous living, indolence, profligacy. The most that is alleged against the Culdees in the eleventh century, even by their enemies, does not nearly equal the charges made from age to age by Church historians against the monks of most other parts of Europe. In the middle of the eighth century Bede gives a picture of the corruption, both in discipline and morals, of the Saxon monks and clergy, which stands in dark contrast with what he tells of the primitive purity which then distinguished the Columbite missionaries. But in the eleventh century monasticism throughout Europe and in England had been quickened by a fresh revival; and Margaret was come of a race, and had lived under influences, which had made her keenly alive to the new fervour. She was the granddaughter of Edmund Ironside, and the niece of Edward the Confessor. Her father Edward, driven an exile to Hungary, had married Agatha, the daughter of the Emperor; Henry II. and the exiles at the court of St. Stephen had seen the work of that great evangeliser of pagan Hungary. And after Margaret came to Scotland, Turgot, a Durham monk, was her confessor, Lanfranc, the great Norman archbishop, her friend and adviser; and strange it is to find the learned prelate waging the same war against the vices of the Saxon clergy in England, as Margaret had to carry on against those of the Celtic clergy in Scotland.

The marriage of Malcolm with Margaret was celebrated at Dunfermline, probably in 1070,[1] that would be in less than two years after Margaret's first arrival in Scotland. It was the Culdee Bishop of St. Andrews, the second Fothad, who performed that ceremony, or, as Wyntoun has it, "devoutly made that sacrament." As a memorial of their marriage, Malcolm and Margaret soon afterwards founded in Dunfermline a church, which they dedicated to the Holy Trinity. The sombre nave, with its massy Norman pillars, still seen there, was probably first built by them, even if it was enlarged

---

[1] [According to Mr. Skene, in the spring of 1069.]

by their sons. This is made the more likely by its striking architectural likeness to the Cathedral of Durham, founded by Malcolm, just three months before his death. Margaret founded at Dunfermline a monastery also, which she filled with Benedictine monks brought from her friend Lanfranc's Cathedral of Canterbury. Besides these two foundations, she, out of reverence for St. Columba, rebuilt the monastery of Iona, which had long lain waste since its devastation by the Norsemen. I am not sure that any other churches or large benefactions to the Church are attributed to her. It was not by heaping up riches on the clergy that she won her saintship, nor could any of her descendants say of her as the first James of Scotland did of her son David, that she was "a sair sanct for the Croun."

And now to turn to the biography which Turgot, her chaplain, has left of his Queen and friend. One cannot but feel surprise that the most recent historian of Scotland should have failed to recognise the truthfulness and beauty of that narrative. It is thus he speaks of it: "The life gives us scarcely anything to bring before us St. Margaret in her fashion as she lived. One cannot help still more regretting that there is so little to be found realising the nature of her husband." Even when giving some of the details preserved by Turgot, he introduces them with such phrases as these: "It is likely enough that," "It is not much worth doubting the assertion that." On the other hand, the late Dr. Joseph Robertson—in whose lamented death Scottish history has lost one of its profoundest investigators, and all historical inquirers the wisest and most generous counsellor—has thus written: "There is no nobler picture in the Northern annals than that of St. Margaret—illustrious by birth and majestic in her beauty—as she appears in the artless pages of her chaplain, Turgot. The representative of Alfred and the niece of the Confessor, she showed in womanly type the wisdom and magnanimity of the one, and more than all the meek virtues of the other." But it is time now to lay before the reader some portion of its contents, leaving any one at all acquainted with mediæval biographers to judge whether the estimate of John Hill Burton or of Joseph Robertson is the truer one. I shall give as far as possible the words of the original, only condensing them.

At the outset Turgot tells her daughter Matilda, King Henry's Queen, that he writes the biography in order that she who could hardly remember her mother's countenance might have before her a true image of her character. "Far be it," he says, "from my hoary head to flatter in describing such virtues as hers. I shall state nothing but what is simply true, and I shall omit much which I know to be true, lest it be not believed." What follows is consistent, I think, with this solemn asseveration. If it seem too much of an unrelieved panegyric, still there is nothing in it but what seems natural in that age, or in any age, when writing of one who is gone, and for whom the writer had the profoundest admiration. The whole has a truthful air about it. There is not one miracle—an unusual feature in a mediæval life—nothing that is not quite within the bounds of historic credibility.

Turgot then tells us that Margaret was come from high and virtuous ancestry on both sides. From her childhood she was of a sober cast of thought, and early began to love God before all things. She employed, while still young, much of her time in divine readings, and took great delight in these. She was by nature quick to apprehend, faithful to retain, and eloquent to express what she had read. Day and night she meditated in the law of the Lord, and, like another Mary, sat listening at His feet. Such she was before she came to Scotland. Turgot hints that her marriage with Malcolm was brought about by the will of her family, more than by her own, or rather, he says, by the ordinance of God. Her heart was in heaven,—she desired the kingdom of God and not the kingdoms of this world. Compelled, however, by her station to move in the world, she was not of it. She was faithful in all that became a queen. By her good advice to her husband, the laws were executed with righteousness, religion was revived, the people's welfare promoted.

The church which as we have seen she built in Dunfermline, Turgot tells us, was, according to the custom of the time, an offering for the salvation of her own and her husband's soul, and for the welfare of her children, both in this world and in that to come. This church she enriched with many vessels of pure gold and silver for the service of the altar. In it she placed a rood with an image of the Saviour of pure silver and gold, interlaced with precious stones. Her chamber was a very workshop of church furniture. This part of the biography reads like a description of some ritualistic English lady's boudoir at the present hour. But eight centuries make some difference in the wisdom or folly of these things. There were seen copes for choristers, chasubles, stoles, altar-coverings, and all other priestly garments and church adornments. Her household was in all things well ordered. The noble ladies who attended her were employed in working at these sacred vestments. They were sober and serious in their lives, after the example of their mistress. Men were not allowed to enter where they sat at work, unless the queen brought them. All who served, both feared and loved her. Her own demeanour was calm and thoughtful: in all she said and did she seemed to breathe the air of heaven.

She was the mother of a numerous family—six

sons and two daughters. The decisive Saxonising of Scotland that took place under Margaret is strongly marked by the fact that not one of these eight children was named after any of the ancient kings or queens of Alban. She was very earnest about their upbringing. She bade their instructor restrain and chastise them as often as he saw in them any levity of conduct, and not spare the rod. So they grew up in love and kindness to each other, the younger showing deference to the elder. When they went to the solemn service of the mass, the children used to walk behind their parents in the order of their age. Often she would take them aside and tell them of Christ, and of faith in Him, according as their age could receive it. She would press on them the fear of Him, saying, "Fear the Lord, O my sons! for there shall be no want to them that fear Him. If you love Him, O my darlings! He will give you welfare in this present life, and everlasting felicity with all His saints." Such were her fervent desires, her counsels, her prayers for them night and day. And on the whole they proved not unworthy of such a mother. Three of the sons were kings of Scotland in succession— the amiable Edgar, the fierce Alexander, and the pious David. Of the two daughters the eldest, Maud, as Queen of England, walked in her mother's ways, and the inscription on her monument at Winchester showed the affection with which the Saxons remembered "Mold the god quen." The second daughter, Mary, was married to Eustace, that Count of Boulogne who, with his still more famous brother Godfrey, was among the chiefs of the first Crusade.

Amid cares for her family and household, cares for the kingdom which she shared with her husband, and earnest desire for the reform of the Church, she never neglected her own private study of the Scriptures. Turgot tells how she would often put searching questions about its meaning to the most learned men she could find. He naïvely avers that he himself was often puzzled by them, and wearied with seeking to find fitting answers. As she herself had profound insight, and clear power of expressing it, the teachers often left her wiser than they came.

All this anxious study was not only that she might save her own soul, but also the souls of others. Especially, she was earnest about her husband. He probably knew and cared little for these things at the time when they were married. But he seemed to have been a man of open and noble nature, and unbounded in love and reverence for his saintly queen. There is a story of him, not told by Turgot, but preserved by local tradition. When Malcolm's tower at Dunfermline first became Margaret's home, it was no doubt small and confined enough, and she would often go forth from it and seek retirement in a cave of the glen hard by. Malcolm noticed this, but did not know the reason. So, one day following her, unobserved, he watched to see how she was engaged. Some dark suspicion no doubt haunted him, and he was prepared, if he found it true, to take vengeance. When, however, looking in, he saw her engaged in prayer, all his thought was changed. Returning quite overjoyed, he straightway made the cave be fitted up for the queen's oratory. Marks of chiselling are still visible on its freestone sides, and persons not long dead had heard of a stone table having been seen there with what seemed a crucifix graven on it.

Her influence was, and well might be, great with him, for she drew him, says Turgot, God's Spirit helping, to the practice of righteousness, mercy, almsgiving, and other good works. From her he learned to pray in earnest, and to spend the night watches in pouring out his heart before God. "I confess," says Turgot, "I have often admired the wonderful goodness of God, when I have seen such fervour of prayer in a king, such earnest penitence in a layman." Within his rougher heart there was a central place which love for Margaret had made gentle and pure like herself. What she disliked he learned to dislike, what she loved he learned to love. The missals she used in prayer and the books she read, these he, though he could not read, would turn over, and look on lovingly. If any one book was specially dear to her, he would gaze on it, and press it, and kiss it. Sometimes he would by stealth carry off such a book to the goldsmith, and bring it back to her adorned with gold and gems.

She greatly increased the splendour of Malcolm's court, and caused both the king and those about him to be apparelled with much more costliness than was their wont. She encouraged merchants to bring from abroad wares of price, especially garments of divers colours. These she made the king and his nobles wear, and so greatly increased the pomp of his public appearances. All the dishes in which the king and his nobles were served at table, she caused to be either of gold and silver, or gilt and plated. When she went abroad, she herself was splendidly attired not for the sake of show, but because it was becoming in a queen. In herself, says her biographer, she was full of humility, and felt herself to be, under the gold and jewels, but dust and ashes. She kept ever before her that our life here is as a vapour, and that at the end of it there remains the great account. She would often ask Turgot to tell her when he saw in her any fault, in word or deed. When he did this seldom, she would tell him that he neglected her real good. "Let the just man reprove me kindly," she would say. The reproofs which most would resent as affronts, she desired for her soul's welfare.

Of all her outward works by far the most characteristic was her crusade against the corruptions of the old Scottish Church. What these were we have seen in part, and shall see it yet more. Honest though Turgot evidently is, some deduction may be allowed for his view of a Church, alien, and in some things opposed, to his own. But when this has been made, the fact seems to remain that the Culdee brotherhood were by this time sunk in lethargy and corruption. To awaken this dead Church, she called together from time to time councils of the native clergy. One of these councils is especially eminent, in which for three days alone, or with very few of her own way of thinking, she contended against the defenders of old abuses with the Word of God, which is the sword of the Spirit. Where this council was held is not stated, but it probably took place either at Dunfermline or at St. Andrews, then the chief Culdee establishment in Scotland. Wherever it was held, Malcolm came with her and stood by her side, and, as he could speak both English and Celtic, he acted as interpreter between them. The points at issue do not seem to have been charges of false or imperfect doctrine, but rather of corrupt practices, and carelessness in religious worship.

The first charge which Margaret urged against the Culdees was, that they began to keep Lent, not on Ash-Wednesday, but on the Monday after the first Sunday in Lent. The native clergy pleaded the example of our Lord, who fasted only forty days. "But you fast not forty, but only thirty-six days," replied Margaret, "when you have deducted from your fast the six Sundays in Lent. Therefore, an addition of four days must be made to fill up the full measure of forty days." The Scottish clergy were convinced, and conformed to the Catholic usage. It is impossible for ritualistic persons to conceive how trivial such questions appear to those not accustomed to these observances, and just as little can the latter imagine of what paramount importance such matters appeared to all Christians in early ages, and still appear to many Christians even now.

The next charge the queen brought against the native Church was a graver one. She asked how it came that they had ceased to celebrate the Holy Communion on Easter day. And the reply of those Celtic priests is the same as many everywhere, and especially in the Celtic districts of Scotland, would make at the present hour. They quoted the apostle's words, "Whosoever shall eat this bread, and drink this cup unworthily," etc. etc. : therefore, because we are sinners, we fear, by approaching to that holy mystery, to come under the condemnation. This reasoning would equally, of course, bar them from ever partaking of the Communion. And so Lord Hailes has interpreted their words to mean that they had ceased to celebrate the Communion altogether. But for such an interpretation there is no warrant in Turgot's language. The more probable suggestion is, that they thought there was a peculiar sanctity about the Easter Communion, and were kept from celebrating it by some superstitious fear. It is likely enough that the reception of the Sacrament may have become unfrequent, but not that it was entirely abandoned. The reply of Margaret would do credit to any modern divine. "If all who are sinners are forbidden to communicate, then none ever ought to partake. But if so, why did our Lord command His followers to do so? In the text you quoted, the apostle added, 'not discerning the Lord's body,' that is, not distinguishing the bread and wine of the Sacrament from common food. Those who, with all the defilement of their sins upon them, without confession of sin and repentance, come to the holy table, they fall under the condemnation. But those who, confessing their sins and repenting, in the Catholic faith, come on the day of the Lord's resurrection to His table, they come not to their condemnation, but to the remission of their sins, and their healthful preparation for eternal life." To these arguments of Margaret the Culdees made no reply, but thenceforth conformed in this matter to the rule of the Church.

Again Margaret charged them, priests and people alike, with neglecting the Lord's Day, and working on it just as on other days. She showed that it ought to be kept holy as the day of our Lord's resurrection, and that they should do no servile work on that day, on which we were redeemed from slavery to the devil. She quotes too, Pope Gregory's authority for the strict observance of it.

Other abuses, as the use of certain barbarous rites at masses, and unnatural marriages with stepmothers and deceased brothers' wives, she sternly rebuked, and they were henceforth discontinued. Such was the work done in this three days' council. The authority to which Margaret always appealed, was Scripture, and the opinions of the Fathers. These details are valuable not only as illustrating the character and work of St. Margaret, but as throwing light on the Culdee Church of the eleventh century, or, at least, on the charges which the new Saxon hierarchy brought against it.

But, however much the Culdees, or collegiate clergy, may have departed from old austerity, there were scattered about in secluded places solitary anchorites, who witnessed against the corruptions of the secularised clergy by lives of stern self-denial and devotedness. These probably kept alive the light of Christian faith in remote places, where but for them it would have been lost in surrounding heathenism. In the flesh, but not after it, they lived, says Turgot, an angelic life on earth. Margaret's whole heart went out to these. She used to visit and converse with them in their solitary cells, reverencing Christ in them, and asking earnestly for their prayers. When they refused any earthly benefit which she offered, she would beg of them to tell her some deed of mercy or charity she might do. And she set herself to do whatever they recommended, whether it was to befriend some poor ones in their poverty, or to relieve from their misery some who were down-trodden. The way these anchorites are spoken of shows that neither Margaret nor her confessor was so prejudiced against native Churchmen as not to acknowledge genuine devotion where it really existed.

Whenever she walked or rode abroad, crowds of widows, orphans, and other wretched ones would flock round her as a mother, and none went away uncomforted. When she had given away everything she herself had, she would borrow from her attendants their fine clothes, or whatever else they had, and distribute them. They knew they would receive back their own twofold. She would steal from the king things to give away—a kind of theft which always pleased him. Sometimes he would pretend not to observe such thefts, and then catching her with his stolen gold coins in her hand, would upbraid her jestingly. In that troubled time there must have been no lack of persons in need of such a benefactress. Multitudes of Saxon captives had been driven from England, and were to be found as slaves everywhere throughout Scotland. The queen employed persons to find out such as were in hardest bondage, or most cruelly treated. She paid the ransom of these secretly, and set them free.

St. Andrews was then becoming more and more famous as the resort of pilgrims travelling to the apostle's shrine. For the accommodation of these she caused hospices to be built on either shore where they crossed the Firth, probably at North and South Queensferry, that the foreigners and the poor, when wearied with the journey, might rest there. There she ordered to be kept all the refreshments they would need, and servants to attend them; and those who rowed them over the ferry were not allowed to take any money from them.

But amid all this outward activity, while she zealously cleansed God's temple, she was not less earnest to purify her own soul. "This I know," says Turgot, "for I not only saw her outward works, but knew the secrets of her heart. For she used to open to me her hidden thoughts very unreservedly; not that there was any good in me, but because she thought there was. Many times as she spoke she has melted in tears, and I, touched with her godly sorrow, have wept too. Beyond all mortals I have known she was given to prayer and fasting, to alms-giving and works of mercy." By her excessive abstinence she brought on great weakness and bodily pain. Stern towards herself, she was to the poor so tender-hearted she would have given not only her own, but herself. We now-a-days can hardly enter into the account given of her vigils, church services, fastings, and ministrations to the poor. Always rising early, she spent some time in prayer and psalms. Then nine young orphan children, quite destitute, were brought into her chamber, and these on bended knees she fed, out of the spoons she herself used, with the most delicate and well-prepared meats and drinks. Ministering to these children, she felt she was ministering to Christ. Then three hundred poor were brought into the great hall, and seated in rows all round it. The doors were closed, and none suffered to be present save a few confidential attendants, while the king and queen, beginning at opposite ends, passed round the rows, serving each poor person in turn with meat and drink, so serving Christ in His poor. Then she passed to the church, and there, with prayers and tears, offered herself up as a sacrifice to God. When she came from church she fed twenty-four more poor, and then for the first time that day touched food herself, but that so sparingly, that never even on ordinary days did she satisfy her natural hunger. If such was her common usage, what must her fasts have been? She kept two Lents each year, forty days before Chrismas, as well as the ordinary Lent. During these periods her abstinence was excessive; the number of church offices, the long prayers and vigils, the many times a day she read the Psalter, are hardly credible. To her ordinary ministrations to the poor she added extraordinary ones during her times of fast, herself washing their feet and supplying them with food. But all this austerity was undermining her frame, and bringing on premature decay. As her health declined, she grew more and more weaned from the things of earth. The Psalmist's words express the breathing of her inmost spirit: "My soul is athirst for God, for the living God." "Let others admire in other saints their miracles," says Turgot, "I more admire in Margaret her works of mercy. For miracles are common to the good and bad; pious and charitable works belong only to the good. More rightly should we admire in her those deeds in which consisted her holiness, than those miracles, if she had done any, which would only show her holiness to men." In this passage, so remarkable in a mediæval biographer, Turgot does not ground Margaret's claim to saintship on miracles— indeed implies that she wrought none,—but on the sure foundation of exalted Christian character.

In the year 1093, her health, long declining, began to fail rapidly. Early in that year Turgot had to leave Scotland for Durham, probably to assist at the foundation of that cathedral, of which he was prior. Before he left, Margaret called him to her, and began to review her past life. As she spoke she showed deep penitence, and shed abundant tears. "As she wept I too could not keep from weeping; and sometimes we were both silent, being unable to speak. At last she said, 'Farewell, I have not long to live; you will long survive me. Two things I have to ask of you : one is, that as long as you live you will remember my soul in your masses and prayers; the other, that you take a loving care of my children. Bestow your love on them; above all, teach them to fear and love God, and never cease to teach them this. When you see any of them exalted high in earthly greatness, then in a special manner be to them a father and a guide. Warn them, if need be; reprove them, lest fleeting earthly honour fill them with pride, lest, through covetousness, they sin against God; or, through this world's prosperity, forget the life everlasting. These things, in the presence of Him who is now our only witness, I beseech you promise and perform.'" Turgot promised, bade the queen farewell, and saw her face no more.

What remains Turgot gives from the account of a priest, who, taking his place as chaplain, remained with the queen to the end. This priest, who, for his remarkable simplicity and purity, was much beloved by Margaret, became, after her death, a monk of Durham, and used to offer himself up in prayer for her at the tomb of St. Cuthbert as long as he lived. "Often," says Turgot, "do I ask him to tell me about the Queen Margaret's latter end ; and he is wont to recount it to me with tears." In the autumn of the year Malcolm with his two elder sons, roused by the overbearingness of William Rufus, marched with an army into Northumberland, wasting that district, and laying siege to Alnwick Castle. Margaret, during her lord's absence, had taken up her abode in the Castle of Edinburgh, then known as the Maiden Castle. There, in growing weakness and worn with pain, she awaited tidings from the Scottish army. On the fourth day before her death she said to her attendants, " Some evil is to-day happening to the kingdom of the Scots, such as has not happened for many a day." They heeded not her foreboding at the time. Four days after, on the morning of the 16th November, the last day of her life, feeling some abatement of pain, she entered her oratory to hear mass, and to be strengthened by the holy sacrament for her last journey. The oratory may perhaps have been that small chapel, lately restored, which stands on the top of the Castle Rock. This service over, her suffering returned more intensely than before, and she was laid down on her bed to die. The death paleness was upon her face, and she called on the chaplain and the attendant priests to commend her soul to Christ. She bade them to bring to her the Black Rood, which she had always held in greatest reverence. This was the famous cross known for ages after as the Black Rood of Scotland, for the keeping of which David afterwards founded the Abbey of Holyrood. There was some delay in opening the casket which contained it. "O wretched me!" she cried out, "shall I not be worthy to look once more on the holy cross?" When it was brought she clasped and kissed it, and tried to sign with it her face and eyes. Her body was growing cold, but still she continued to pray, and, holding the cross with both hands before her eyes, repeated the 51st[1] Psalm. At this moment her son Edgar entered her chamber. He had just returned from the rout of the Scottish army. The queen, gathering up all her remaining strength, asked, "How fares it with thy father and brother?" Seeing his mother in her last agony, he hesitated to tell what had befallen, and answered, "It is well with them." With a deep sigh she said, "I know, my son, I know. By this holy cross, by the love you bear me, I adjure you, tell me the truth." He told it all. His father and his brother Edward were dead. No murmur escaped her; but lifting up her eyes and hands to heaven, she said, "I thank and praise Thee, Almighty God, that Thou hast willed to lay on me this anguish at the last, and by this suffering to purge me from some of the stains of sin." And then she began that prayer which is wont to be said immediately after the reception of the sacred elements, "O Lord Jesus Christ, who, according to the will of the Father and with the co-operation of the Holy Ghost, hast by Thy

---

[1] The original Latin has the 50th Psalm, but Hailes and most other modern writers have in their works changed it to the 51st, a change which the probability of the case almost seems to warrant.

death given life to the world, deliver me." As she uttered that "libera me," her spirit passed to the great Deliverer.

Just as she died, Donald Bane, a brother of Malcolm's, who had come from the Hebrides with his wild caterans to claim the kingdom, laid siege to the Maiden Castle. So they had to convey the body of Margaret by stealth from the chamber where she died, which for centuries after was known as "the blessed Margaret's chalmer." They bore it through a postern, called by Wyntoun the "west yhet," down the steep western side of the Castle rock, and so, by her own ferry, to Dunfermline. And there they laid her down in the church of the Holy Trinity, which she had built, before the high altar and the cross placed there by herself. And so, concludes the biographer, her body rests in that spot where she had so often knelt and prayed.

Of that body the subsequent story is too remarkable to be passed over. Malcolm's remains were at first buried in the monastery of Tynemouth, but seem to have been soon after removed thence by his people and laid beside his queen in Dunfermline Church. In 1251, Margaret was, after due scrutiny, canonised by Pope Innocent IV. It had been resolved to translate her remains from their original resting-place, in what is now the nave, to a more honourable place in the choir. On the 13th of June 1250, King Alexander III., with his mother, and many of the clergy and chief nobility, came to Dunfermline. In their presence the relics of Margaret were taken from the tomb of stone, placed in a shrine of silver, and borne by the hands of princes and earls inward towards the choir. When the procession had reached the chancel arch, opposite to the spot where the bones of Malcolm lay, suddenly the shrine, which contained the relics of Margaret, became so heavy that they could carry it no farther. The queen's body refused, so they thought, a more honourable resting-place, unless her husband's remains shared it along with her. On the suggestion of a bystander, according to Fordun, or warned by a voice from heaven, as the Aberdeen Breviary has it, they opened the tomb of the king, placed his bones also in a shrine, and then, without difficulty, carried them both, and laid them in a large tomb at the east end of the choir. That tomb, covered with its ponderous blue grey slab, is still to be seen, but now in the open air, outside of the modern choir. Still visible on it are the sockets in which once burned the silver lamps that for centuries were kept lit above her shrine night and day; but the tomb itself has been empty for three hundred years—type of the oblivion to which Margaret has been consigned in the land which once so greatly revered her. At the Reformation, the remains were thought no longer safe there. The head of Margaret was brought to Edinburgh Castle at the desire of Queen

Mary, but, on her flight to England, it passed through several hands, till at last it found a resting-place in the Scots College at Douay. There for a time it recovered its ancient sanctity, and was exposed to the veneration of the faithful; but it disappeared again, and for the last time, amid the storms of the French Revolution.[1] The rest of the remains of Queen Margaret, with those of Malcolm, are said to have been acquired after the Reformation by Philip of Spain. He placed them in the church of St. Laurence at the Escurial. Attempts have recently been made to have them restored to Scotland; but they, too, had disappeared, or could not be identified.

These details of relic-worship and misplaced reverence it was necessary to give. But these follies, the accretions of later ages, ought not to be allowed to obscure the fair memory of Margaret, or to blind our eyes to her real sanctity. What has been told of her above is enough to show that her wisdom was nearly equal to her devotion. Her whole life was given almost as much to soften and civilise the rude people whom her husband ruled, as to make them more religious. Two objections may be made to the work she did. She strove, it may be said, to Anglicise, and also to Romanise Scotland. With regard to the first, it is curious enough that Margaret is the

[1] [Carruthers saw it at Douay in 1785. Locks of the fine fair hair still remained.]

earliest example of a process which has gone on ever since, and which we see every day before our eyes. For eight hundred years English women have been marrying Scotch husbands and using all their influence to win them over from their national ways to the English feelings and customs. They might be forgiven for this if they were all Saint Margarets. The Saxon infusion which she brought into Scotland must be allowed to have enriched, civilised, elevated the Celtic people. As to Margaret's introducing Romanism, two things only need be said. First, the native Church was well-nigh dead. She may be excused for supplanting its decrepitude by the energetic faith of Lanfranc and Anselm. Secondly, to expect her to be other than she was, to disparage her because she was not a good Protestant in the eleventh century, is to blame her for not being an historical miracle or anomaly. Let us try to see and own essential goodness under all the variety of garbs and even disguises through which in this world it is often forced to reveal itself. Margaret was a partaker of that divine element which links together all the good of all ages. She had in rare measure that faith which pierces through shadows and enters within the veil,—that strong hold on the eternal world which is the only true lever for moving this one.

## III.—BISHOP LAMBERTON AND THE GOOD LORD JAMES.[1]

THERE is perhaps no one spot on Scottish ground which has witnessed so many eventful scenes in the national history as the small but ancient City of St. Andrews. During the six centuries that lie between the reign of Malcolm Canmore on the one hand, and the landing of Dutch William on the other, no great movement took place, one might almost say there happened no great national event, in which St. Andrews did not bear a prominent part. So true is this that to write the history of St. Andrews during the period of its greatness, as it might be written, would almost be to write the history of Scotland. To conceive aright the great panorama of persons and events, as it swept during those six centuries through that ancient place, would bring before us no inadequate picture of all that is most interesting in Scottish annals. Neither were the fortunes of mediæval St. Andrews confined within the narrow compass of merely Scottish history. Its position as the primal Scottish see brought it into such close

[1] [Contributed to *Good Words*, 1874.]

and constant intèrcourse with the Vatican, that this small spot was swayed and shaken by every great current of European politics. So widely ramified were its interests, foreign and domestic, that the annals of no other Scottish city would afford an equal insight into our internal history and our relations with the Continent.

I purpose now to confine our attention to the part which St. Andrews played in one period of Scottish history, but that the most eventful and momentous —I mean the war of Scottish Independence against the First and the Second English Edward. In doing this we shall find the history of St. Andrews resolve itself into the actions of one person—Bishop William de Lambyrton, or Lamberton, who concentrated in himself the whole fortunes of the Church and primacy during his long episcopate from 1298 to 1328; that is, during nearly all the Wallace and the whole of the Bruce period. Of both these heroes Lamberton was the firm friend, and, from first to last, identified himself with their cause. Neither of Lamberton, any more than of his great contemporaries, does any continuous record survive, save only Barbour's "Story of the Brus," if we may accept that as a faithful narrative of the doings of the great king. But in most of the great events, and especially at the chief turning-points of that stormy time, glimpses may be caught of the form of Lamberton moving restlessly to and fro among the principal actors, or standing out as the abettor and counsellor of the champions of Scottish freedom.

Of the parentage and birthplace of William de Lambyrton, or De Lamberton, or William of Lambertoun, or William Lamberton—for in these and other ways the name is written—we can offer no direct evidence. Probably, to argue from the name he bore, he was a native of Berwickshire. Fixed surnames, which arose in France about the year 1000, and came into England with the Norman Conquest, did not reach Scotland till, speaking roundly, the year 1100. But it was already the thirteenth century before they became prevalent north of the Tweed, and it was probably about the middle of this century when William of Lamberton was born. The larger number of Scottish family names, though by no means all, were taken from lands which the family possessed, or from places where they dwelt. The surname of Bishop William would seem to show that he was a native of Lamberton—a tract of country in Berwickshire, the name of which still survives in Lamberton Moor, over which the high road passes about five miles to the north of Berwick-upon-Tweed. Natives of this district, rather than lords of the manor, Lamberton's family probably were.[1]

[1] [Part of the lands of Lambreton, near Berwick, the whole of which had been given by King Edgar, in 1098, to the monks of Durham, was held under them by a manorial tenant, who probably thus adopted the surname "de Lambreton." Adam de

The first time that his name appears in history is in 1292, when he is called William de Lambyrton, parson of Campsey, and chancellor of the diocese of Glasgow. This was five years before William of Ellerslie arose as the champion of Scottish freedom. Ellerslie is not far from Campsie, and it was probably while Lamberton was parson of the latter place that Wallace came to know him, and found in him an ecclesiastic patriot after his own heart. In 1297, when Wallace was at the height of his power and guardian of the kingdom, the bishopric of St. Andrews fell vacant by the death of Bishop Fraser. It was of the first importance that Wallace should have in all the bishoprics, but especially in the primacy, clerics on whose support he could rely. Accordingly he nominated to the vacant primacy his friend the clerk of Campsey. But his nomination was not unopposed. The Culdees, or native Celtic clergy, who dwelt in the monastery of Kirkheugh—

Lambreton, of the county of Berwick, swore fealty to Edward I. in 1296. On the Ragman Roll of that year appear other ten persons of the same surname belonging to various counties. Among these is the future Bishop of St. Andrews, "Mestre William de Lambreton, Channceler del Eglise de Glesca, del counte de Lanark" (*R. R.*, p. 165). The family had thus several important branches in the country. Wyntoun, speaking of him at the time of his election to St. Andrews, says:—

"Wes a nobill and famous man,
That of that Se chosin was than
Master Willame off Lambyrtown,
A lord commendit off renown."

This would seem to imply that he belonged to one of the higher families of the name (*Cronykil*, B. VIII. c. xiv).]

the site of which is still visible between the cathedral
and the sea—claimed the right, from remotest time,
to elect the bishop. When the vacancy occurred in
1297, the twelve Culdee prebendaries of Kirkheugh
put forward as a candidate their own provost,
William Comyn, brother of the Earl of Buchan.
His candidature was strongly supported by Edward I.,
if for no other reason, because Lamberton was the
nominee of Wallace, and because the Comyns were
not reckoned among the partisans of the guardian.
The Augustinian canons-regular, headed by their
prior, on their side elected the favourite of Wallace.
It was enough for them that their rivals, the Cul-
dees, put forward a candidate of their own. When
the election took place in November 1297, Wallace
was in the height of his prestige. It was but two
months before that he had won his greatest victory,
over Warenne, Earl of Surrey, and Treasurer Cress-
ingham, at the Bridge of Stirling. Strange it seems
to find the Augustinian monks, who were compara-
tively a recent importation into Scotland, having
been first brought to Scone in 1114, and thence to
St. Andrews in 1140, siding with William Wallace
and the patriotic cause; while the old Culdees, the
native clergy, are supported by Edward, the invader
of their country. Each party clung to its nominee,
and the result was a disputed election. To the
Pope, as the umpire in all ecclesiastical causes, the
dispute was referred. Comyn travelled to Rome to

plead his own cause. But the Pope, Boniface VIII., after hearing his claims, decided in favour of Lamberton, the choice of the Augustinians. For the Culdees, with their ancient and lax usages, and their freedom from papal interference, had never found favour at Rome. They never afterwards recovered from this defeat. They never again tried to rival the canons-regular of the priory in the election of a bishop. Their monastery, indeed, continued to survive in Kirkheugh, but ever dwindling more and more, till extinguished by the Reformation.

The elect Bishop Lamberton received consecration from the hands of the Pope on the 1st June 1298; but before he returned to Scotland the tide of fortune had turned. The English defeat at Stirling in September 1297 had been avenged by the great victory of Falkirk in July 1298. Broken by this disaster, and harassed besides by the jealousies of the Comyns and the Bruces against him, Wallace resigned his guardianship, and returned once more to the station of a private knight. While Wallace had been in power he had expelled from the kingdom all the English clergy, regular and beneficed, who had been quartered there during Edward's supremacy. Lamberton might well expect that now, when the tables were turned, it would be Edward's turn to expel the churchmen who owed their places to Wallace. On his way through France the new primate busied himself on his country's behalf at the court of King

Philip. From France he wrote to his friend and patron, exhorting him to continued resistance, promising him help from his own episcopal revenues, and encouraging him with hopes of aid from France.

But Wallace was never again in power. Henceforth he became a "wanderer, and almost solitary adventurer." On his resignation, the Scottish barons chose, as governors of the kingdom, John Comyn of Badenoch, and John de Soulis, and afterwards associated with these Bruce, Earl of Carrick, and William de Lamberton. This Council of Regency was to govern the country in the name of Baliol, who was still owned as lawful king. It was in the last year of the thirteenth century that the Regency entered on office. One of their first acts was to send an ambassador to Rome to beg for the intervention of the Pope in behalf of Scotland. During the short government of Wallace, Boniface VIII. had written a letter to Edward, exhorting him to live at peace with his neighbours. At the request of the Regents, he again took up the cause of Scotland more vigorously, and addressed a bull to the King of England almost in the very words which the Scotch ambassador had put into his mouth. It asserted that the kingdom of Scotland neither was nor ever had been a fief of the Crown of England; that it had belonged from ancient times, and did still belong, in full right to the Roman see. He then commanded Edward to cease from his unjust aggressions, to release the prisoners, and surrender the castles he wrongfully held; and if he thought he had any claims on any part of Scotland, to send his ambassador to Rome and plead them before the papal tribunal. This bull was written in June 1299.

During the first two years of the fourteenth century, Edward's attempts against Scotland were much slackened, probably owing to the interference by the Pope and the pending negotiations with France; but in the third, when his commander, Segrave, had sustained a severe defeat at Roslin, by Simon Fraser and Comyn the guardian, Edward arose with all his might, swept Scotland clean from Tweed to Caithness, wintered in Dunfermline till Candlemas, thence marched to St. Andrews. There he "held his court in the regality of St. Andrews," and summoned thither a Parliament of all the chief men of the kingdom. These all made their submission to the English king, swore fealty, and received an amnesty, from which only a few names were, to their honour, excepted, such as Wisheart, bishop of Glasgow, and William Wallace. Among those who swore fealty was Bishop Lamberton. He must have done so at this time with a special grudge, for he saw before his eyes the English soldiers, by the orders of their king, strip the priory refectory of its lead, and bear it away to supply the engines with which the English assailed Stirling after the Easter of 1304.

After this second conquest of Scotland (1303-4), when Edward set about the annexation of the country, he set over it a lieutenant or governor, with a council who should advise him as to the executive government. Of this council Lamberton was one; and when the king went on to arrange for the representation of Scotland in the Parliament at Westminster, there were to be ten Scottish deputies—six laymen and four churchmen. Foremost among the churchmen was the name of Lamberton, so entirely had the versatile prelate recovered the confidence of the English king.

It was in the spring of 1304 that Lamberton swore fealty to Edward, yet on the 11th June of the same year, at the feast of St. Barnabas, we find him meeting with Robert Bruce, the young Earl of Carrick, in the abbey of Cambuskenneth, and entering into a secret indenture or treaty of friendship, by which they solemnly bind themselves to assist each other against all persons whomsoever, and to undertake no business of moment unless by mutual advice. It is the earliest existing specimen of a kind of document afterwards too well known in Scotland, and its issues were momentous.

It was not long before the bishop's fidelity to the indenture was put to the proof. Some rumour of it soon reached the ears of Edward. He took the young Earl of Carrick angrily to task about it; and the same day, when heated with wine, dropped dark words of menace against him. A friend who had heard them, the Earl of Gloucester, sent Bruce a symbolical warning—a pair of spurs and a sum of money. Bruce took the hint, and by next dawn was riding in haste through the snow towards the Border. This bond, therefore, was the immediate cause of that flight which brought Bruce face to face with Comyn in the church of the Grey Friars at Dumfries. It was in June 1304 that the solemn compact had been sworn to in Cambuskenneth Abbey. It was on the 10th February 1306, that, at the high altar of the Church of the Minorites, Comyn fell by the dagger of Bruce. In that crisis of his own and his country's destiny, the friends of Bruce were few; but none were more staunch than the native churchmen who had taken the patriotic side. Lamberton was one of the first to whom the rebel Earl turned in his extremity. Besides the authority of the indenture, and common love of the patriotic cause, other motives may be conceived to have bound Bruce and Lamberton to each other. Bruce knew well the immense aid his cause might receive from the Church. The abbeys could furnish from their own lands about a third of all the fighting men of the kingdom. Besides this material succour, the clergy could intercede daily for him, and invoke Heaven's blessing on his cause. They could rouse the people by enforcing the belief that the divine favour was with him; and preaching, as

David, bishop of Moray, is said to have preached to the men of his diocese, that it was as meritorious to take arms in the cause of Bruce as to join in a crusade against the Saracens. Lamberton and the other Scottish churchmen, on their part, knew that by ranging themselves on the patriotic side they were protecting their own interests as well as their Church's independence, as the King of England would fain remove them, and fill their places with English clerics on whom he could more rely.

Barbour, in his historic poem, "The Story of the Brus," which is on the whole the fullest record extant of the king's life, tells that as soon as the deed was done in the church of the Grey Friars, Bruce

> "Gert men with his lettiris rid,
> To frendis upon ilk sid."

And a letter was sent to the Bishop of St. Andrews amongst others, in which he "tald him all the ded." When that letter was received and read by Lamberton in the old Castle, or it may have been in the priory of St. Andrews, a scene then and there took place, on which I do not dwell now, as I shall return to it in the immediate sequel. In this tremendous crisis the friendship of Lamberton stood Bruce in good stead. A rebel, and a sacrilegious murderer, he had to dread not only the full vengeance of Edward, but also all the thunders of the Vatican, which, indeed, were soon launched against him. But the countenance of the primate of the Scottish

Church, backed as it was by that of other prelates, deadened the edge of the papal excommunication, and disarmed it of half its terrors. From Dumfries to Lochmaben, from Lochmaben to Glasgow, from Glasgow to Scone, Bruce passed with his slender following. At Glasgow, as lying more in his route than St. Andrews, he halted to receive absolution from another churchman friend, Bishop Wisheart. From St. Andrews Lamberton went in haste, and met Bruce and his comrades at Scone, and there bore his part along with Wisheart, his brother prelate, in that memorable coronation. In the words of Lord Hailes, "Posterity ought to remember the chief associates of Bruce in his arduous attempt to restore the liberties of Scotland. They were William of Lamberton, bishop of St. Andrews; Robert Wisheart, bishop of Glasgow; the Abbot of Scone; the four brothers of Bruce, Edward, Nigel, Thomas, and Alexander; his nephew, Thomas Randolph of Strathdon; his brother-in-law, Christopher Seton of Seton; Malcolm, fifth Earl of Lennox; John of Strathbogie, tenth Earl of Athol; Sir James Douglas; Gilbert de la Haye of Errol, and his brother, Hugh de la Haye; David Barclay of Cairns, in Fife; Alexander Fraser, brother of Simon Fraser of Oliver Castle; Walter de Somerville, of Linton and Carnwath; David, of Inchmartin; Robert Boyd, and Robert Fleming." To these may be added, as present in spirit, though detained from actually joining in the coronation, David Moray, bishop of Moray; Nigel Campbell, knight of Lochowe, and brother-in-law of Bruce; and Simon Fraser, lord of Oliver.

The murder of Comyn took place, as we have seen, on the 10th of February; the coronation at Scone six weeks after, on the 29th of March. On the 19th of June befell the fatal battle of Methven, in which Bruce and his followers were surprised, broken and dispersed by that Aymer de Valence, Earl of Pembroke, whose grave may still be seen in the Temple Church in London, covered with a fulllength effigy of dark marble, cross-legged, to mark that he was a Crusader who reposes beneath. The sequel of the battle of Methven all know; how Bruce himself, an excommunicated, outlawed, hunted man, was driven with the few followers who could still cling to him, to hide from cave to cave in the northern and western highlands, among the mountains, first of Atholl and Deeside, then of Breadalbane and Argyll, till at last he found a refuge in the lonely island of Rachrin; how his queen, his two sisters, and his daughter Marjory were taken, carried captives across the Border, and long immured in English prisons; how of the band of barons and knights who gathered round him at Scone, many fell into the hands of the unrelenting Edward, and perished on the scaffold, hanged and quartered: his young brother Nigel, so fair of face, so winning in manners, that even his enemies lamented him; the king's brother-in-law, Christopher de Seton, and Christopher's brother Alexander; John, the Earl of Atholl, and the veteran Sir Simon Fraser. These and many more, knights and warriors, taken captive after Methven battle, perished without pity on the English scaffolds.

The churchmen, who sided with the Bruce, would no doubt have shared the same fate, had not their sacred office protected them. Bishop Lamberton and the Abbot of Scone were found, some time after the battle, clad in mail, and were carried in fetters to England. Bishop Wisheart had laid siege to the castle of Cupar, using, it is said, for this purpose, the oak which Edward had granted him to roof his cathedral with. Having gained the castle, he shut himself up within it, and held it against Aymer de Valence. But, being forced to surrender, he was sent, fettered, in his coat of mail, first to the castle of Nottingham, then to that of Porchester. To Lamberton, also, may be applied the language which Edward II. used of Wisheart, when afterwards he was released; they both "had exchanged the rochet for a shield, the stole for a sword, the alb for a mailshirt, the mitre for a helmet, the crosier for a lance." As Mr. Hill Burton says: "None had been so versatile and indefatigable as these two great prelates, in stirring up the people; and no laymen had broken so many oaths of allegiance to Edward; yet he was content to imprison them, afraid to dip his hands in priestly blood." Rymer's *Fœdera* contains a lengthy document, which minutely details the treatment the two prelates are to receive, and the stages by which they are to pass to their separate prisons. Of Lamberton, it ordains that the sheriff of Southampton shall receive the Bishop of St. Andrews, the betrayer of the king, shall imprison him in the tower of Winchester Castle, and shall defray his daily expenses, which are minutely laid down.

Having got the two bishops safely immured, Edward sent a letter to Pope Clement v., enumerating their heinous offences. Lamberton, especially, he accuses of having sworn fealty to him on the consecrated host, the Gospels, the cross Neyth, and the black rood of Scotland in 1296, while still chancellor of Glasgow; of having broken his oath and joined Wallace, who for this perjury raised him to the see of St. Andrews; of having, when Edward re-conquered Scotland in 1303-4, come voluntarily forward, again sworn allegiance, and again received from Edward the episcopal see and revenues, and the appointment to be one of his lieutenants or governors; of having once more, on the murder of Comyn, violated his oath, and joined Bruce at Scone; of having again after this submitted to Aymer de Valence; and then again sent men and money to aid Bruce at the battle of Methven. For these repeated perjuries Edward requests the pontiff to remove Lamberton from his episcopal seat, and to place there in his stead William Comyn—the same who had been supported by the Culdees and Edward's party, when Lamberton was preferred before him. At the same time he requests that Wisheart should be likewise superseded. With neither of these proposals did Pope Clement comply. And yet the two bishops had not only broken their oaths, they had also thrown the shield of their blessing over the man excommunicated by Rome.

A strange and certainly an unpleasant feature of this age it is, how lightly men, even otherwise of high character, regarded the sanctity of their oaths. Mr. Hill Burton has noted that churchmen were the readiest to break their oaths—that in this war the oaths broken by these were about a hundred per cent. more in proportion than those broken by laymen. And he accounts for it by suggesting that churchmen "knew better than laymen how to get the burden of the offence removed; the affair was in their own way of business—they were sure of what they were about." There may be something in this. Yet it is no sufficient explanation of what seems to us so unaccountable. There was a conflict between two duties—fidelity to an oath extorted by fear, and fidelity to their country's cause. They could not obey both claims, and they may have felt the latter to be the stronger. Still, put it how we will, it is a perplexing subject, one which we cannot understand, unless we can place ourselves in the moral atmosphere of that middle age. It is but one of many questions that make us feel how great and impassable a gulf there lies between us and the men of that time.

Without attempting further to discuss it, I shall leave Bishop Lamberton for a time to quiet his restless spirit in the tower of Winchester Castle, and revert to that moment in his life when he received Bruce's letter from Lochmaben, telling of the death of the Red Comyn. The incident I am about to give is taken and amplified from Barbour's poem, "half-epic, half-chronicle," called "The Story of the Brus." "Scotland," Lord Hailes remarks, "is fortunate in its possession of such a memorial of the great hero." It is neither a mere dry chronicle like Wyntoun's, nor a romance like one of the Arthurian series. It has more the character of a living history or biography. Here and there Barbour has, no doubt, grouped facts together, and disregarded dates, to heighten the artistic effect. Notably so when at the outset of his book he identifies Robert Bruce, the first competitor for the crown, with his grandson, the hero of Bannockburn. But though this is a somewhat daring poetic, not to say historic, licence, I am not aware that he elsewhere ventures on any other like departure from fact. He himself professes at the outset to make truth his aim,—

> "Therefor I wald fane set my will,
> Giff my wit micht suffis thartill,
> To put in writ a suthfast story,
> That it lest ay furth in memory,
> Sa that na tym of lenth it let,
> Na gar it haly be foryhet.
>
> . . . . .
>
> Now God gif gras that I may sa
> Tret it and bring it till ending
> That I say nocht but suthfast thing."

His book has been accepted as historical even by the accurate and doubting Hailes. And since his time it has been the great quarry out of which the historians have dug almost all they have told of Bruce and his adventures.

Barbour belonged to the generation immediately following that of Bruce. Indeed, it is just possible that he may, in early youth, have himself seen the great king. For he appears to have been born only a few years after Bannockburn, and Bruce died in 1329. Barbour completed his metrical life of Bruce in 1375, and died an old man in 1396. Supposing him to have been eighty at the time of his death, this would make him thirteen or fourteen when the king died. From the description he gives of Randolph's appearance, it has been supposed by some, that he had himself seen the Earl of Murray, while his description of Douglas, equally or rather more minute, bears that he had carefully ascertained it from the accounts of those who had seen him :—

> "His body was wele mad and lenyhe,
> As tha that saw him said to me."

And this brings me to the incident with which this paper is to close. In the beginning of his "Story," Barbour tells how King Edward had cast into prison Sir William Douglas, the friend of Wallace, and conferred his lands in Douglasdale on the Clifford. James, the son of Sir William, though then but a lad, taking deeply to heart the indignity done to his father and the loss of his ancestral lands, sought refuge in Paris. There he abode for three years, till tidings of his father's death reached him. Then returning home to see if he might not win back his estates and free his vassals from their bondage, he came in haste to St. Andrews. Bishop Lamberton received him courteously,—

> "And cled him richt honorabilly
> And gert ordane where he suld ly.
> Ane wele gret quhile thar dwellit he,
> All men lufit him for his bounte,
> For he was of full far effer,
> Wis, curtas, and deboner,
> Large and lufand als was he,
> And our all thing lufit lawte."

Bishop Lamberton took young James Douglas with him to Stirling, and there introduced him into the presence of King Edward, and made petition that his lands in Douglasdale might be restored. Edward rebuffed them angrily. The bishop and his young ward returned to St. Andrews, there to bide their time. That time came when the letter from Lochmaben reached Lamberton in February 1306, telling him that Bruce was in arms for the crown and the freedom of Scotland.

The scene here put into verse is taken in its main features from Barbour's narrative. As many of the very words, and as much of the archaic style, as possible, have been retained. A more modern diction seemed less likely to convey the real impression of the whole transaction.

### THE GOOD LORD JAMES IN ST. ANDREWS.

Within his castle-hall the bishop sat,
    That looks down on the sounding sea,
And a "braid letter" he yestreen had gat,
    With eager eyes read he.

And read, and then re-read with anxious heed,
    Then rising, bade his seneschal
Summon the prior and his monks with speed,
    Into the castle-hall.

All met, he read aloud—swift words and brief,
    "I, Robert Bruce, do greet thee well;
This day, John Comyn, Badenoch's perjured chief,
    Beneath my poignard fell.

"And now I rise against King Edward's might,
    This land of ours to disenslave;
The while I battle to make good the right,
    Thy benison I crave."

That hearing, from their chests a deep-drawn breath
    They heaved, those churchmen, every one;
The die was cast, they felt, for life or death,
    And a new act begun.

But straight with voice of cheer the bishop broke
    That pause,—"Good hope I have that soon
Shall be fulfilled the word the prophet spoke,
    True Thomas of Ercildoune.

"This Earl of Carrick, of the ancient breed,
 Is he, that seer foretold would come
To rule the bravest land benorth the Tweed
 In all wide Christendom."

Within that hall a stripling stood hard by,
 Listening the while the bishop read,
And kindling gallant heart and flashing eye
 At the brave words he said.

That was the young James Douglas—lank and tall
 Of frame he was, with coal-black hair,
Great-boned, broad-shouldered, but his look withal
 Mild, sweet, and débonair,

Spoke him true knight and gentle—skilled in lore
 He had brought home from schools of France,
To read the Troubadours, but practised more
 To wield the sword and lance;

And burning Southron foemen to assail,
 Who him had disinherited
Of his own lands and castle in Douglasdale,
 And there held rule instead.

Drew to the bishop's side and spake that youth,
 Soon as the priests the hall had left,
"Thou knowest, sire, how without right or ruth
 These English loons have reft

"Me of my house and lands; and I not doubt
 The doughty Earl of Carrick, he
For yon man he hath slain will be cast out,
 Made landless like to me,

"And have against him every English knave;
 Wherefore, good sire, if so thou will,
I would with him King Edward's vengeance brave,
 And take the good and ill,

"Till from this realm we drive our foes outright;
 And so through him I trowe to win
Once more the lands my father held—despite
 The Clifford and his kin."

The bishop turned on him an aspect kind,
    And answer made, with pity moved,
"Would heaven, sweet son, thou wert with him combined,
    So I were unreproved.

"But this way may'st thou work, and God thee speed,
    In yonder stall doth idle stand
Ferrand, my palfrey,—fleeter, safer steed,
    Or one so well in hand,

"All Scotland holds not. Take him, and be gone,
    But do it as of thine own deed;
And if men ask thee, see thou say to none
    That e'er I gave this rede.

"And if the groom who tends him chance withstand,
    Take thou the steed in his despite;
So shall the deed seem thine own doing, and
    I shall be blameless quite.

"Now do my bidding—haste thee on thy way—
    Say to the Earl of Carrick, soon
I will set forward with what speed I may
    To meet with him at Scone.

"Then God thee bless, and him thou goest to,
    And both from all your foes defend,
And bring the work which ye essay to do
    Unto a perfect end."

Then took the bishop from an oaken chest,
    And gave large moneys for his way,
And in his own right hand the youth's hand prest,
    And bade him fair good day.

Straight to the stable then young Douglas hied—
    In surly wise the groom withstood,
And strove to thrust him from the door aside,
    With churlish words and rude.

But with his sword-hilt Douglas to the ground
    The caitiff felled, and while he lay
In swoon, the saddle on the palfrey bound,
    And lightly rode away.

Forth from the precinct, through the western gate
  He passed out to the open moor,
Alone, with none to guide, but steering straight
  By the Lomonds on before.

To far Lochmaben Castle he was boun,
  For there to find the Bruce he weened ;
But long the road and wild, and tower and town
  With arm'd foes intervened.

Long in forced idlesse he had pined for lack
  Of venture—now 'twas breath of life,
All the spring-day to thread that moorland track,
  West through the How o' Fife.

Beneath the Lomond's northern base he wound,
  Past Leven Loch, and reached the shore
Of Forth's deep flood, and there a boatman found
  To ferry him out o'er.

Up the low Carse for high Torwood, across
  The Carron Water lay his path,
Through mile on mile of weary muir and moss
  Till past remote Carnwath,

Two days, two nights, nor stint, nor stay, he rode :
  The third morn met him, as he clomb
The braes by Coulter Fell, that westward showed,
  Hard by his ancient home,

Cairntable soaring high o'er Douglasdale—
  Him eyeing Douglas—" Soon we'll see,
O native hill ! if we may not avail
  To strike a blow for thee."

Faster he rode the rounded summits bare,
  That cradle springs of Clyde and Tweed,
There of a rout of riders he was ware,
  That forward full in speed

Came on from Annan-head,—thereat perplext,
  One moment Douglas drew his rein,
But one brief moment only, for the next
  Onward he spurred amain.

Straight by his side a knight reined up, and cried,
  "Speak,—whither art thou hurrying?"
"I, Lord of Douglas, for the Bruce do ride,
  As to my rightful king."

"All hail! Sir James, all hail!" the Bruce cried loud,
  And rode to meet him; on bent knee
Down on the bare moor the young warrior bowed,
  To do him fealty.

"Rise up, Sir James, rise up, remount thy steed,
  Of old I know thy noble kind,
When Scotland called her bravest to her need,
  They never were behind;

"And thou of these art worthy." Then they twain,
  Grasping strong hands through gloves of mail,
Plighted their faith where lonely Arickstane
  Looks down o'er Annandale.

That spot beheld their meeting, heard their pledge,
  Broad-chested warrior, tall lithe youth,
The word they plighted on that moorland edge,
  They kept to the end in sooth.

"Now ride, my men, time presses,—forward, on,"
  Bruce slacked his rein, and passed with speed
Along the mountain ridge; soon all are gone,
  Following their chieftain's lead.

That lay through Scone—through Methven's fatal wood,—
  Through outlawed years by land and sea,
On to the field where he a conqueror stood,
  And made our Scotland free.

Through dark and bright, they travelled side by side,
  Comrade with comrade, friend with friend,
In loyal love which nothing could divide,
  Unto that perfect end,

When field of Spain, amid the fiery brunt
  Of battle, shook to that dread cry,
"Now forward pass, brave HEART! as thou wert wont,
  Douglas will follow or die."

Moment! like which none other can succeed,
  When, in one passing blink of time,
The mid-age flowered in that consummate deed
  Of chivalry sublime.

Oh! live for ever these heroic names,
  In noblest friendship intertwined,
The great King Robert and the good Lord James,
  In Scotland's heart enshrined.

# IV.—KING ROBERT BRUCE IN ST. ANDREWS CATHEDRAL.[1]

I HAVE tried to give some glimpses into scenes in the Scottish War of Independence which seem to have been but little noticed; and especially into the part taken in that war by Bishop Lamberton and other Scottish Churchmen. To dwell for a little on these scenes is not merely to con over old-world stories, which have lost for us all meaning or interest. The work that was then done, and the issues of it, are not mere pictures for imagination to feed on. They are living and enduring facts that have influenced and will influence all British history, fruitful of endless blessing. As Mr. Carlyle has it, "A heroic Wallace, quartered on the scaffold, cannot hinder that his Scotland become, one day, united with England; but he does hinder that it become, on tyrannous unfair terms, united with it; commands still, as with a God's voice, . . . that there be a just real union as of brother and brother, not a false and merely semblant, as of slave and master. If the union with England be in fact one of Scotland's

[1] [Contributed to *Good Words*, 1874.]

chief blessings, we may thank Wallace withal that it was not the chief curse. Scotland is not Ireland; no, because brave men rose there, and said, 'Behold ye must not tread us down like slaves, and ye shall not, and ye cannot.'" This from a Scot. And Arnold, veritable Anglo-Saxon that he was, preaching somewhat over-vehemently the right of Anglo-Saxons to rule the world, was yet wont to say, that if England should ever come to keep, as she ought, the anniversaries of her great historic events as national holidays, the day of Bannockburn should be a high festival, and the anniversary of Strongbow's conquest of Ireland a day of fasting and mourning. I therefore make no apology for reverting again to those well-trodden fields, if only I may gather here and there some blade of corn that has been passed over by former gleaners.

We left Bishop Lamberton a prisoner in the tower of Winchester Castle, whither he had been carried when, after the battle of Methven, he had been taken in arms, towards the end of 1306. During his captivity the revenues of the see of St. Andrews were paid to the King of England's treasury, and a small sum out of them was allowed the bishop for his maintenance. While Lamberton was lying a captive in that remote English castle, the king whose cause he had embraced was undergoing endless hardship and danger. In the words of Fordun, "he was tossed in dangers untold, being attended at times by three followers, at times by two; more often he was left alone, utterly without help. Now passing a whole fortnight without food of any kind to live upon but raw herbs and water; now walking barefoot, when his shoes became old and worn-out; now left alone in the island; now alone, fleeing before his enemies; now slighted by his servants, he abode in utter loneliness. An outcast among the nobles, he was forsaken; and the English bade him be sought for through the churches like a lost or stolen thing. And thus he became a byword and a laughing-stock for all, both far and near, to hiss at."

How little has any adequate narrative yet approached that theme! Scott's *Lord of the Isles*, interesting though it be, hardly does full justice to it. The facts as they happened surpass his fiction. No need to lead the wanderer through coasts and islands he never trod. If some young traveller were but to take Barbour's book in his hand, and track Bruce's footsteps all the way from Methven to the Isle of Rachrin, noting carefully the traces of him which tradition still preserves in cave and crag and stream, all through the central Highlands, he might still produce a faithful and living narrative of these wanderings, which would far surpass in interest any that either historian or poet has yet conceived.

It was early in 1308 that fortune once more began

to smile on Bruce. Crossing from Rachrin to Arran, he thence passed over to the coast of Ayr, and retook his own castle of Carrick. Having once more got foot on the mainland, he was never again driven out of it, and though many a chase for life, many hair-breadth escapes, still remained, yet by degrees he gathered the strength, which enabled him finally to make head against all the power of his enemies. On the 16th March 1308 a full parliament was summoned at St. Andrews. In the name of the assembled earls, barons, commons, and all the inhabitants of Scotland, a letter, which is still extant, was addressed to the King of France, asserting King Robert's rights, and calling for aid from their ancient ally. It is not specially stated whether Bruce was present in this parliament. We know, however, that Lamberton was not present in person, though no doubt present in spirit. For it was only in August 1308 that Edward II., who had by this time succeeded his father, released him from his Winchester prison and restored to him his revenues, after the prelate had once more sworn fealty to Edward as his liege lord. So satisfied was Edward with Lamberton's submission, that he wrote to the Pope that he no longer feared any evil from him, but rather looked for much aid from his influence with the Scots, who greatly trusted him.

Lamberton seems to have returned to Scotland in 1309, and from that time forward for many years he contrived to retain the confidence of Edward, though there can be little doubt but that his heart was still with Bruce. No record remains to tell what part he took when, in June 1314, the great conflict culminated at Bannockburn. We may well believe that no man in Scotland more rejoiced in that event than he. Yet his joy must have been well concealed, for in the autumn of that same year he received from Edward a safe-conduct to pass through England on his way to foreign parts.

On his return from abroad he set himself to repair the waste places in his diocese, which the war had so long left desolate. He repaired the Palace of the Bishops—that old sea-fort which, during the war, had been so often taken and retaken, and which since that day has witnessed so many cardinal events in Scotland's history. He made additions to the Priory, built and adorned the Chapter-house, of which a few stone seats are still to be seen; built for himself and his successors sundry fortified manor-houses, in various parts of his diocese. But the greatest of all his works was the completion of the cathedral, a work to which I shall immediately return. At the very time when he was preparing for its solemn dedication, Edward seems to have discovered that Lamberton was a traitor to him. He wrote to Pope Clement v., enumerating all the treacheries of the bishop, denouncing him as "filled with Satanic fury against England," and entreating the Pope to depose him from the primacy. This the Pope refused to do, with moderation yet firmness, and expressed himself leniently towards Lamberton. Such, however, had been by no means the usual attitude of the popes towards the Scottish people during their long struggle. As Mr. Hill Burton has said, "the records of the time are strewn with their fulminations against Scotland," its king and its people. In 1320 Pope John XXII. wrote to Bishop Lamberton, threatening to excommunicate him and his brother bishops of Dunkeld and Aberdeen, for the part they had taken in befriending the excommunicated king. Somehow or other Lamberton contrived to pacify the Pope or to evade his sentence. Once more he appears taking part in public affairs. This was in November 1324, when he accompanied Randolph to York as one of the two Scottish Commissioners to treat for a permanent peace with England. They obtained from Edward II. a truce for thirteen years, which, however, his son did not confirm. This is the last time the name of the busy and versatile bishop appeared in any public transaction. He died in 1328, the year in which was concluded the Treaty of Northampton, by which the independence of the Scottish kingdom was fully acknowledged by England, and finally secured. Whether Lamberton lived to see this consummation for which he had so longed and laboured, does not appear. All we know is what Wyntoun tells, that in 1328 Bishop Lamberton, after having been thirty-three years bishop, died in "the Priory Chamber of the Abbey," and was buried in the north side of the chancel of "the new kirk cathedral," under an arch which he had "gart men work" for himself. His tomb was seen in Wyntoun's time between that of Bishop Gamelin on the east side, and Bishop Walter Trail on the west. Of these tombs, as of the tombs of so many more in that Cathedral, bishops, priors, and canons, and monks, not a vestige now remains. The year after Lamberton's death, the king, for whose sake he had broken so many oaths, died at Cardross, overcome by that "great sickness" which he contracted during his wanderings, and was borne by his sorrowing people to his last resting-place in the choir, before the high altar of Dunfermline Abbey Church.

Let us now turn back to that day when Bishop Lamberton dedicated his now completed cathedral. It was on the 5th of July 1318, the crowning day, we may well believe, of Bishop Lamberton's life, and a high day for all Scotland. A hundred and fifty years that cathedral had been in building, ever since the day when Bishop Arnold, in the year 1160, laid the foundation-stone in the presence of the young King Malcolm the Maiden. The building had begun at the east end with the choir, and proceeded slowly westwards, as each successive bishop could obtain funds and skilled builders for the work. In the eastern gable is still seen the earlier form of architecture in the round arched or Anglo-Norman windows, while, passing westward, we see in the southern wall of the nave—the only wall now remaining—the transition to the pointed-arched windows which came in with the thirteenth century. While the long War of Independence raged, Lamberton could have neither quiet nor money to bestow on the cathedral. But Bannockburn gave both; indeed there is a tradition that Bruce supplied Lamberton with the means of completing it from the abundant spoil of that battle. However this may be, the cathedral was completed within four years after the battle, so that the cathedral might be regarded as in some sort the memorial in stone of the great national deliverance. The cathedral, which took so many years to build, existed entire only two hundred years. And then a few days and an infuriated mob undid the pious labour of a century and a half, and consigned to destruction Scotland's noblest cathedral—a building equal to which none other has since been reared within her borders—in all likelihood never will be reared.

The only authentic record extant, as far as I know, of what passed on the day of its Dedication is that contained in the following lines of Wyntoun's rhymed *Chronicle of Scotland*. As he was a priest of this diocese, and lived within one hundred years after the event, he is likely to have known the truth.

> A thowsand thre hundyr and awchtene
> Fra Cryst had borne the Madyne clene,
> Off the moneth off July
> The fyft Day, full solemply
> The Byschape Willame of Lambertown
> Made the Dedicatyown
> Off the newe kyrk Cathedrale
> Off Saynct Andrewys conwentuale.
> The Kyng Robert honorably
> Wes thare in persown bodyly;
> And sevyn Byschapys ware sene,
> And Abbotis als ware thare fyftene,
> And mony othir gret gentill men
> Ware gaddryd to that assemblé then.[1]

There is no proof, as far as I know, that Bruce was ever in St. Andrews save on this one occasion. The first Parliament of his reign had indeed been convened there in his name on the 16th March 1308, but this does not necessarily imply his presence.

In the verses given below an attempt has been made to revivify the few bald details of Wyntoun's lines, and to set forth how that July day may have actually appeared to an eye-witness, what aspect the whole pageant may have worn, and who were the "mony gret gentill men" gathered with the king to that great solemnity. In fixing on the names of those who, according to historical probability, may have actually been present, we are assisted by the signatures appended to that memorable letter, which "the barons, freeholders, and whole community of

[1] [B. VIII. c. xxi.]

Scotland assembled in Parliament in the Abbey of Aberbrothok," on the 6th of April 1320, addressed to Pope John XXII. That high-hearted address thus concludes:—"Our most Serene Prince, King, and Lord, Robert, for the delivery of his people and his own rightful inheritance from the enemies hand did, like another Joshua or Maccabaeus, most cheerfully undergo all manner of toil, fatigue, hardship, and hazard. . . . To him we are bound and resolved to adhere in all things, both upon the account of his right and his own merit, as being the person who hath restored the people's safety in defence of their liberties. . . . For so long as there shall but one hundred of us remain alive, we will never consent to subject ourselves to the dominion of the English. For it is not glory, it is not riches, neither is it honour, but it is liberty alone that we fight and contend for, which no honest man will lose but with his life."

A duplicate of this document—the Charter of Scotland's freedom—is still to be seen preserved in the Register House in Edinburgh. It opens with the names of at least eight-and-thirty of the chief Scottish barons of the time, and to the bottom of it are affixed the seals of the same, bearing their coat-of-arms, with the name of each appended to his seal. From this document are taken the names of all the companions of Bruce enumerated in the following poem—the "mony gret gentill men" who, we may well believe, accompanied him that day to the dedication of the "Cathedral Kirk." I need only add that Kilrymount is the earlier Celtic name of St. Andrews.

### KING ROBERT BRUCE IN ST. ANDREWS CATHEDRAL, 5TH JULY 1318.

On old Kilrymount all the middle age
    Arose no morning so supremely fair,
As when begirt with baron, knight, and page,
    King Robert entered there.

A day of solemn pomp majestical—
    The minster, building long, was now complete;
And all the land had heard the Church's call
    To Dedication meet.

Ages had watched that fabric slowly climb,
    Priors had toiled, and bishops, many a one,
Their little day—then closed their eyes on time,
    Leaving the work undone.

But William Lamberton, the Bishop good,
    Of Wallace wight and Bruce the steadfast friend,
Who for his country's cause with these had stood,
    Till it found glorious end—

One of the famous few, who, nothing loth,
    At Scone convened to crown the outlawed man,
Then spite of English Edward's tyrant oath,
    Spite of Rome's awful ban,

Forsook him never, till the hard-won close
    Of Bannockburn had crowned the noble toil—
Then Bishop William earned serene repose,
    O'erflowing wealth of spoil—

Spoil that enriched that long majestic nave,
    Still waxing fairer, as it wandered west,
Till groinéd door, and pinnacled gable brave,
    With tracery effloresced.

And there it stood, each key-stoned arch rose-bound,
    Each carvéd niche, and fluted column tall,
Of the best deed e'er wrought on Scottish ground,
        Proudly memorial;

Sacred to that great Saint, they deemed, who brought
    From heaven the strength whereby the day was won,
Clothing his arm with might the while he fought,
        Scotland's anointed one.

Then summons from the Bishop reached the King,
    In old Dunfermline Tower where he lay;
Him bidding come, and his best warriors bring,
        To that high festal day.

All his life through King Robert had respect
    To them who stood by him, the priests at home;
And blessed his work, making of none effect
        The cruel ban of Rome.

And so with earl and baron, squire and page,
    Gladly the King that morning made him boun,
To ride upon a summer pilgrimage
        To old St. Andrews town.

His war-men had just come from laying waste
    The English border, town, and tower, and farm;
And still they rode, their brawny limbs mail-cased,
        Their broad shields on their arm.

For that was all the joy of every Scot,
    Those jubilant days that followed Bannockburn,
To flout the Southron border, thence having brought
        Much store of spoil, return.

Dunfermline forth, down Leven Vale they rode,
    Round Lomond's base, and the green knowes out o'er,
Eastward where lonely Tarvet looks abroad,
        From his far-seen watch-tower.

But when they reached the crown of Magus heights,
  Where first far off the Minster spires they saw,
Down from his in-reined steed the King alights,
  And kneels to earth with awe.

Him following leap, loud clanging, to the ground
  From their high selles the mailed men, one and all
And to their knees in reverence profound,
  On the green sward down fall.

Then rising on they ride ; above their heads
  The July sun shone cloudless ; on before,
Larger the towers grew, gleamed the new roof-leads,
  Beyond, the smooth sea floor

Lay violet-tinted. Ah, me! never came
  Down to the sacred city by the sea,
Nor e'er shall come, all time it hath a name,
  So brave a company.

Foremost the King rode, his broad shoulders mailed
  In coat of proof, but the raised visor gave
Full to the light his noble features paled
  With suffering, calm and grave.

For that broad casque contains the ample brain
  On which hath hung suspended Scotland's doom ;
That mail, the heart that beats to noblest strain
  This hour in Christendom.

Yet bland his look withal ; to them who rode
  On either side, gaily his speech ran o'er ;
The while beneath him his great war-horse trode,
  As proud of whom he bore.

On right and left a knight rode—they, too, mailed—
  Fair-haired, broad-visaged one, large limbed and tall,
Randolph, King's sister's son, who foremost scaled
  Dunedin's rock and wall,

He who o'erthrew the Clifford in hot fight ;
  But now the voice, so dreadful in mid-press
Of battle, soft and low sounds—all that might
  Is sheathed in gentleness.

On the other side there rode a knight well-knit,
    Dark-haired and swarthy, long and lank of limb,
Clean-made and sinewy, for all hardness fit,
    Much talked the King with him.

That was the good Sir James, but whoso scan-
    His face so debonair and sweet to see,
They might not guess in throng of battle-van,
    What other look had he.

The Bishop sent him hence in fervent youth,
    To join the outlawed Bruce in his sore need,
Whom now he hither brings in very sooth,
    King of the land he freed.

That ponderous mace, well-proven in many a fight,
    Lightly and cheerily his right hand wields,
As though impatient to essay its might
    In yet an hundred fields.

And Walter Steward as erewhile in war,
    Rides here in peace by Douglas' side to-day ;
But Marjory Bruce, brief while his bride, sleeps far
    In Paisley's still abbaye.

And many more, the King's own kinsmen leal,
    Who shared his hardship, share his triumph now ;
Young Colin Campbell, son of brave Sir Niel,
    Just come from far Lochowe.

And Donald, Lord of Mar, redeemed at last
    From durance, rides 'mid his glad kinsmen—o'er
His proud head hangs to-day no shadow cast
    From baleful Dupplin Moor.

And hoary Sutherland, long proven in worth,
    And young Ross, from his mountains ocean-walled ;
Sprung these from Mormaers of the rugged north,
    Now earls, not Mormaers called.

And others more, tried comrades of the King,
    Malcolm, old earl of Lennox—he who knew
The Bruce, 'mid Lennox mountains wandering,
    By the bugle blast he blew ;

And then for joy to find his master dear,
   Fell on his neck with weeping, and regaled
The famished company with forest cheer,
     Ere to Rachrin he sailed.

And Angus of the Isles, who, that dark hour
   The King from Lennox mountains forced to flee,
Received and refuged in the grim sea tower
     Of high Dunaverty.

And faithful Andrew Moray, too, rides here,
   From Bothwell towers and 'the bank of Clyde;
Where deep in dungeons mured for many a year
     The Southron captives sighed.

And Keith the Marischal, who broke the flank
   Of England's archers by the famous burn;
With that great Thane of all but kingly rank,
     Earl Malise of Strathearn.

And Magnus, Lord of Orcadie, the heir
   Of grim Vikings who ruled the northern main;
David de Lindsay, Henry de St. Clair,
     And Reginald le Chene.

The men of Bannockburn, the good, the true!
   Shall we not name their honest names with pride?
Shall not to them eternal thanks be due
     Down all the ages wide?

They vowed that they would give their lives to death,
   Or else the land they loved of tyrants rid;
And since has every Scot drawn nobler breath
     For the good work they did.

O to have seen that company as they rode
   Down the long slope to the grey promontory,
Where in sunshine the young Cathedral glowed
     Fair in its pristine glory!

To have gazed one moment on the face of Bruce,
   Supreme amid that lordly chivalry;
The men of simple hearts and iron thews,
     Who made our Scotland free!

But, ere they reached the precinct, a long mile,
  Of a great choir of priests they were aware,
And white-robed singers moving, file on file,
  Whose voices on the air

Floated far off, scarce audible at first,
  But louder growing, as they nearer came,
Till fronting the great cavalcade they burst
  Into full voiced acclaim.

And deep awe fell on each brave heart and face,
  As the priest paced before, their censers swinging,
With the white choristers toward the holy place
  Their chant of welcome singing.

A.D. 730.

This sacred soil hath felt the beat,
Age by age, of kingly feet,
Hither come for prayer and vow,
But of all none great as thou,
Since the day thy great forbear,
Pictish Angus, did appear
O'er yon hill-top, at the head
Of his warriors, vision-led,
Holy Rule to duly greet,
Refuged in his cave retreat.

II.

Fair that dawn for Scotland, when
Met the priests and warrior-men,
Peace-attired. In forefront there,
With his feet and head all bare,
Moved St. Rule, and high in air,
Relics of the apostle held ;
Following him, grey men of eld,
Came the monks, their anthems singing,
With the white-robed children flinging
Up to heaven their choral chant,
Most sweet-voiced and jubilant.
Then barefoot, the King, his proud
War-gear cast aside, and bowed

Low in reverence,—last the throng
Of his warriors, brave and strong,
Men of battle, moved along ;
Seven times from east to west
Compassed they the soil they blessed,
Making all the headlands o'er
Free to heaven for evermore.

### III.—A.D. 943.

But who is this that casteth down
Sceptre, sword, and kingly crown,
For monk's cowl and shirt of hair?
Battle-shout for lonely prayer?
'Tis an aged man and worn
With the weight of care, long borne,
From earth's storms and darkness turning,
Where a purer light is burning,
Fain to find here peace divine,
'Tis the good King Constantine.

### IV.—A.D. 1070.   MALCOLM CANMORE.

Can Kilrymount e'er forget
Her, the sainted Margaret?
The fair-haired young Saxon Queen,
With her lord of swarthy mien,
Standing here amid conclave
Of stoled priests and Culdees grave,
Pleading by God's holy fear
For a purer life austere ;
For a loftier strain of heart,
More from earth and sense apart,
To o'erawe the world and win
The gross people sunk in sin,
Till the coldest needs must feel
Something of her heavenly zeal,
Mother of our royal house !
Fair the crown on thy young brows,
Fairer seal the Church hath set,
Bright and undecaying yet,
Holy, sainted Margaret !

### V.—A.D. 1120. ALEXANDER I.

Whose charger this, so richly dight,
Steed of Araby, silver-white,
Springing stride, and hawk-like head,
To the very altar led ?
Strange these vaulted arches ring
To his proud hoofs echoing,
Trumpet-like his haughty neigh
Shakes yon massy-roofed abbaye.
'Tis the King of Scotland's—there
Stands he on the altar stair ;
While either side a squire doth lead
To the shrine an Arab steed,
Champing bit of massy gold,
Girt with harness jewel-scrolled,
Bearing gorgeous velvet blooms,
Broidery of orient looms,
With a panoply of proof,
Wrought in rings of golden woof,
Silver spear, and silver shield,
Fit for only kings to wield,
Gems might grace an emperor's crown,
On the altar laying down.
So to seal his high intent,
Monarch most magnificent ;
As a dower to render o'er
  To Kilrymount's holy place,
All the lands the famous Boar
  Traversed in his mighty race.

### VI.—A.D. 1130. DAVID I.

Now another Prince is seen,
Meeker, more devout of mien,
Latest-born of Margaret's line,
Kneeling low before our shrine,
Restorer of the Church's rights,
Builder on the ancient sites,
Born to more than reinstate
Holy places desolate,
Ninian's shrine by far Whithern,
Cell of saintly Kentigern,

Raising as with magic wand
Into vast cathedrals grand.
Hither, led by high desire,
Came that Prince with heart on fire,
To reclaim our sacred lands
From the grasp of secular hands,
And to fashion not alone
Fabrics wrought with lime and stone,
But within our primal see,
Spiritual masonry ;
Living temple stones to rear,
Men of holy life severe,
That untiring, night and day,
They for souls sin-soiled might pray,
And to all the land impart
Life from out this central heart.
Kingly labourer! well he wrought,
Till to perfect form was brought,
What his mother had begun,
What his brothers left undone,
Sainted mother! saintly son!

VII.—A.D. 1160.   MALCOLM IV.

But who are these with solemn pace,
On the foam-fringed promontory,
Moving round the sacred place,
Maiden King, with boy-like face,
Mitred Prelate, bowed and hoary,
While behind them, long in row,
Prior, monks, and singers go,
Chanting, "Lord, look down on us,"
"Nisi quia Dominus."

Now with faces fronting east,
Stand bareheaded, king and priest,
And the founding-stone is laid,
And the prayer devoutly made,
Corner-stone of what shall be
Seat of Scotland's central see,
Amen! Benedicite!
Soon from earth that king a priest
Passed, but never since hath ceased

I

Growth of this majestic pile,
Rising through two hundred years,
Choir and transept, nave and aisle,
Till to-day the roof uprears,
Dazzling sheen, far seen to sea,
Joy of mariners, while we
Bear the topmost head-stone forth,
Shouting loud with holy mirth.

### VIII.

Scion of a hundred kings !
Blessèd be the day that brings
Thee and thy companions brave,
'Neath our Minster's holy nave,
Here to hold with solemn glee
This our nation's jubilee.
Come thou, mightiest of thy race,
Enter Scotland's holiest place,
All the virtues of thy line
In thee blended brighter shine,
All their valours rolled in one
Could not match what thou hast done.
Wallace, when in death he fell,
Handed on his sword to thee,—
Thou that sword hast wielded well,
Thou hast made our Scotland free.
Through thy might what marvellous things
He hath wrought, the King of Kings !
Clothing thee with brain to plan,
As the wisest only can,
Patient spirit, and sublime
Self-control to bide thy time,
Then strike home, and stake dear life
On the die of glorious strife.
Vain then England's cavaliers,
Crashing 'gainst our ashen spears,
Vain from morn to noon their toiling,—
Back like broken waves recoiling
From our rock-like ranks that stood
To the knees in Southron blood ;
Till thy voice, O mighty Bruce !
Scotland's Lion-hearts let loose,

## IN ST. ANDREWS CATHEDRAL. 131

Charged then all our battles four—
We were free for evermore.
Come now, Conqueror! take thine own,
Double right upholds thy throne,
Right of heritage and blood,
Right of valour unwithstood,
Thronèd in the nation's heart,
Very king of men thou art;
Alban's far-descended Lord!
To thy people heaven-restored,
Thou who madest Scotland free,
Welcome to her Primal See.

The precinct reached, down from their selles they
    spring;
There at the great Cathedral's western door
The mitred Bishop met the mailèd King,
    And pacing slow before

Led him right on, up the long pillared nave,
    That echoed back the monarch's armèd clang,
While rolling solemn anthems, wave on wave,
    Innumerous voices sang

High mass and requiem for the brave departed,
    Who died on many a field to freedom dear;
And loud thanksgiving for the noble-hearted,
    To-day in presence here.

And heads of convents stoled in long array,
    Abbots and priors stood within the choir,
From Dryburgh, Melrose, Holyrood, Inchaffray,
    And inward rangèd higher,

Six mitred Prelates; for the King's dear sake,
    And for their country's, from his several see,
Each the long way had travelled to partake
    This high solemnity.

Through these, unheeding, calmly the King passed,
    And on St. Andrew's shrine rich offerings rare
Heaped largely; then before high altar cast
    Himself in lowly prayer,

Cleanness imploring, and full pardon free,
  For all the innocent blood that he had spilt;
And rendering thanks that he had lived to see
  This dome so grandly built.

O day august! of solemn joy that thrilled
  The exulting heart of Scotland, when her brave
Deliverers with their glad thanksgiving filled
  That Minster, choir and nave.

They came, they passed, that day, too fleetly gone,
  Like unsubstantial phantom of the mind,
The pageant joined the past oblivion,
  Leaving no rack behind.

Scarce more substantial that Cathedral proud,
  For all its solid frame, to-day doth seem,
From earth long vanished, like a moving cloud,
  Or the fabric of a dream.

## V.—THE EARLIEST SCOTTISH UNIVERSITY.[1]

IT was a favourite saying of the late Dean Stanley that St. Andrews had for him the charm of Canterbury and Oxford combined. Those who are constant residents within it, pressed with the cares or distracted with the frivolities of the hour, might smile at such a comparison. What! they might say, compare these few gaunt and shattered skeletons of ancient magnificence with the vast and still flourishing Cathedral, the seat of England's Primacy, or the two small St. Andrews Colleges, the one still retaining something of cloistral seclusion, the other with no survival of antiquity but its old tower and chapel!—compare these with the grandeur of Christ Church or the serene mediæval beauty of Magdalen!—it is simply ludicrous. To those whose perceptions custom has dulled it may seem so. But one gifted, as Dean Stanley was, with the finest historic eye and the keenest imaginative sensibility, coming fresh upon St. Andrews, sees around him an embodiment of a long and stormy history, in all its

[1] [Contributed to *Fraser's Magazine*, 1882.]

most startling vicissitudes, not perhaps to be equalled on any other spot of British ground. Such an one cannot, doubtless, gaze without pain on those "skeletons of unfleshed humanity," the record of all that is wildest in passion and darkest in fanaticism. But the pain is more than compensated by the crowding memories which thrill him at every turn, as he walks around these ruins, looking down upon him in "all the imploring beauty of decay." There are memories imbedded in almost every stone which he sees, waiting only for the open eye and the receptive heart to take them in.

In this St. Andrews is unique, that the same spot of ground contained Scotland's oldest and metropolitan Cathedral, and also her earliest University, and that the University was the child and nursling of the Cathedral and its monastery. But the wind-swept, foam-fringed promontory had been known as a centre of religion for at least seven hundred years before it became a seat of learning. The earliest sacred place was the cave in the sandstone cliff, close under the Cathedral, known as the Cave of Saint Regulus. It has now so crumbled away as to be almost indiscernible. But thither, probably soon after A.D. 600, came a Columban eremite, and made the cave his abode; and this was, it is suggested, the historic personage who was afterwards transformed into the mythic Regulus. Hard by, there probably soon arose one of those primitive monasteries of wicker-work, in which would dwell a small brotherhood of Columban monks from Iona.

Early in the eighth century the monks of the old Columban foundations were driven out of South Pictland, and among others those of the monastery of St. Andrews would disappear.

The next step was when, in 736, the Pictish king, Ungus or Angus, son of Fergus, placed in Kilrymount a new body of clergy, who had brought the relics of St. Andrew with them. Whence they brought them we know not. From Patras or Constantinople the old legend says; from Hexham in Northumberland Mr. Skene suggests. Kilrymount, afterwards called St. Andrews, thenceforth became the National Church of the Picts, whose royal seat was at Scone; and St. Andrew, superseding Columba, and his successor St. Peter, became their patron saint.

The next important date is A.D. 889, when the Scottish dynasty succeeded to the Pictish throne, and reigned at Scone over the united kingdom of Alban,—when the Pictish and Scottish churches were blended into one,—when Saint Andrew became the patron saint of the United Picts and Scots, —and when the Bishop of St. Andrews became known as the Bishop of Alban. The Scottish line of kings, being established at Scone, brought back with them the Columban monks who had been driven from Pictland early in the eighth century, and these doubtless returned to Kilrymount, whither they had first brought the name of Christ. The Primacy of the whole Scottish Church, which, after the downfall of Iona, had passed for a short time to Dunkeld and then to Abernethy, was, with the sanction of the king, transferred in 908 to St. Andrews, where it remained till the downfall of the mediæval church. It became the policy of the Scottish kings, when they had removed their royal seat from Argyll to Scone, to foster St. Andrews and make it supersede Iona as the chief sanctuary of their people; as Dean Stanley once said, a Cordova to keep the pilgrims from going in search of Mecca, a Bethel to prevent the tribes from returning to Jerusalem.

We read of Constantine, one of the Scottish kings, in A.D. 942, worn out with age and troubles, retiring to the monastery of St. Andrews, and living there as a Culdee, till he died in that "dreary pile"—the pile being the Culdee monastery of Kirkheugh, to the east of the cathedral, and overlooking the harbour. The foundations, after having been for centuries buried out of sight, were within a recent date laid bare, when excavations were being made for a new battery.

On the whole question of the origin and nature of the Culdees, so obscure yet so interesting, much light has of late been thrown by Dr. Reeves and Mr. Skene, but on that enticing subject we cannot linger now.

The first elements of learning were given to Scotland, we know, before the time of the Culdees, through the monks of the Columban Church. They introduced letters and a written language, and were, like their founder, zealous in copying MSS. Whatever education the young received, whatever instruction the people got, came entirely from the Columban monks. When the Columban Church was expelled from South Pictland, and afterwards when Iona was laid waste by the Norsemen, the Culdees, who succeeded the Columban monks in the Celtic monasteries, carried on the work of education. In these monasteries we find in the latter part of the eighth and in the ninth centuries a new functionary taking the place of the Iona Scribhnigh or scribe. This was the Ferleiginn, or lector, or man of learning, whose work was closely connected with education. He was prælector in the monastic school for the training of the clerics. The Culdee Ferleiginn continued in St. Andrews till the beginning of the thirteenth century, after the old Celtic Church had been extinguished.

But the greatest of all the changes which St. Andrews saw before the Reformation was that which was wrought by the Saxon Princess, Queen Margaret, wife of Malcolm Canmore, when she brought to Scotland the Roman clergy and discipline. The Celtic Church she found far gone in decay, partly from external violence, partly from internal corruptions. That saintly Queen herself pleaded in a public Council with the Celtic clergy to convince them of their manifold abuses—their practical neglect of worship, their wide departure from the truth, which with her meant the Roman faith and worship. What she began, her sons Alexander I. and David, when they ascended the throne, completed, superseding the Culdees by Roman clerics and monks, arranging the Church no longer on a tribal but on a territorial basis, and substituting the parochial system and Diocesan Episcopacy for the old tribal church and merely functional bishops.

At the close of the eleventh century—that is, soon after the Norman Conquest—the line of the native bishops ended in the person of Fothad, the last Celtic Bishop of St. Andrews. He died in the last year of Malcolm Canmore's reign, A.D. 1093, and then there was a vacancy for fourteen years, after which the see was filled by a stranger, the first of a line of bishops of foreign descent. This was Turgot, formerly confessor of St. Margaret and author of her biography, whom her son Alexander brought from the Priory of Durham to the see of St. Andrews. The outward visible symbol of this change from the Celtic to the Roman Church is the Tower of St. Regulus. The best architectural authorities give it only a conjectural date, somewhere between the tenth and the thirteenth century. But the late Joseph Robertson, Scotland's most learned antiquary, believed that it must be the "Nova Basilica" of which he found mention in some old chronicle, as erected in A.D. 1127. He conceived that it was built by the Roman clergy, before they had funds for the great cathedral, and that it was raised so high, after the model of the early campaniles of Italy, in order that it might overcrow the humbler Culdee monastery of the adjacent Kirkheugh.

Robert, who was bishop next in succession but one to Turgot, from 1121 to 1159, also a Saxon, founded the Priory, and brought thither from Scone, where he had himself been Prior, the black Canons or Canons-regular of St. Augustine. The site of the monastery was, as all know, immediately to the south of the future cathedral, to which it was attached; and Bishop Robert endowed it with grants from the Episcopal revenues. The Culdees he expressly excluded from being inmates of his new Priory, because they were secular clergy and married men, and could not conform to the strict rule of the Canons-regular.

King David, when he visited St. Andrews, greatly patronised the new Priory. He held a conference in its cloisters with Bishop Robert, and compelled him to relinquish all the lands of the Boar's Chase, which he made over to the Augustinian monks. The Prior of the St. Andrews monastery was of greater dignity than all the other mitred abbots in

Scotland. He was entitled to wear the mitre, the ring, and the pastoral staff in parliaments and councils. Ever since the time of Queen Margaret the Culdees had been dying out by internal decay, and by the establishment of bishoprics and their cathedral staff on the ruins of Culdean monasteries; but in the reign of King David a regular crusade against them was begun, and they were dispossessed of most of their remaining rights. They struggled for a time, and tried to maintain their claim to share in the election of the bishop; but of that they were finally deprived in 1273, after which little more is heard of them.

As Bishop Robert founded the Priory, his successor, Bishop Arnold, founded the Cathedral in A.D. 1160. For 158 years the building of it went on, proceeding and pausing, pausing and proceeding, till at last it was completed and consecrated by Bishop Lamberton in a day of July 1318, in the presence of Robert Bruce, who came hither with all his chivalry to do honour to the dedication. The king further endowed the Cathedral out of his private means, in gratitude for the great victory which the Patron Saint of the kingdom had recently vouchsafed to him at Bannockburn. For only 241 years was that beautiful and venerable pile allowed to stand entire, when, in 1559, it was desecrated by a savage mob, and abandoned to the ravage of the elements, and to the still more relentless hands of the dwellers in St. Andrews. Besides the Cathedral and the Priory, in time there arose two other monasteries, one of the Black-hooded Friars, a remnant of whose church still stands in South Street; the other, a monastery of the Gray or Franciscan Friars, whose foundation has wholly disappeared from its site in Market Street. Besides all these there was the decaying Provostry of Kirkheugh, which continued to dwindle on its old site till the Reformation. This, then, was the order of the sacred places of St. Andrews :—

> The Cave of St. Regulus.
> The Monastery of Kirkheugh.
> The Church and Tower of St. Regulus.
> The Priory of Augustinian Monks.
> The Cathedral.
> The Dominican Monastery.
> The Franciscan Monastery.

Education, which had begun under the Culdees, did not slumber, but rather progressed, under the new order. It must have been fostered more or less by all the monastic foundations I have named, but its chief seat was the Priory. Intellectual activity was greatly stimulated there when, in the twelfth and thirteenth centuries, the Archbishops of York and Canterbury put in their claim for jurisdiction over the see of St. Andrews and the whole Scottish Church. When the independence of the Metropolitan see was thus threatened, it was the monks of the Augustinian Priory who took up the challenge. They were at once the best lawyers and the ablest literary men of their day in Scotland. England's claim for ecclesiastical, was soon followed by a like claim for civil, supremacy. Whenever England put forth one document to support her claim, Scotland answered by another, and those answers were most of them concocted within the walls of our Priory. Columba had to be disowned as the Apostle of the Picts, and the founder of Scottish Christianity, in order to give to St. Andrews a fictitious origin in the fourth century, and thus to antedate St. Augustine and Canterbury. From this sprung the legend of Regulus and his monks coming from Patras. The line of Scottish kings, too, had to be carried back to 443 years before the Christian era, in order to outdo England's claims to antiquity. It was within the Priory of St. Andrews that this tissue of fabulous history was woven, piece by piece, as the needs of controversy required. And at last all these isolated forgeries were woven into a formal history of the kingdom by Fordun, a priest of the diocese of St. Andrews, whose history has passed as authentic almost to our own time. Many as have been the remarkable men who have lived, and many able books as have been written in St. Andrews, it never gave birth to a more important literature than that which then issued from these monastic cloisters. False or true, it was composed for a patriotic interest—to resist the encroachments of England; first, on Scotland's ecclesiastical, then on her civil independence. Whatever falsehood was in those documents does not imply such untruthfulness in the writers as might at first sight seem. Historic certitude and the tests of it are quite a recent growth; historic criticism is not yet a century old. To men living in the 12th and 13th centuries the past was all one confused haze, in which fact, legend and myth passed into each other, and seemed all equally certain.

With the monasteries of St. Andrews, both Celtic and Saxon, schools of some kind were, from the first, associated. If for no other purpose, the monks had to train their successors and the secular clergy. We read of scholars connected with the Culdee community at Kirkheugh, and we know that there were regular schools attached to the Roman monasteries in Scotland, of which the monks were generally the teachers, or at least the superintendents. There existed in St. Andrews, too, from an early date—some say from the twelfth century—a "Schola Illustris," on the site in South Street afterwards occupied by the "Pædagogium." There the youths were taught not only reading, writing, and grammar, but also logic and rhetoric. On holidays the scholars of these schools used to meet in the churches to hold logical disputations, and to make rhetorical declamations. There can be little doubt that this "Schola Illustris" and the school of the monastery were the germs out of which our university sprung. But until the fifteenth century, whenever Scottish youths who had been trained in the monastic schools wished to obtain higher learning, they had to migrate to other countries, some to Oxford perhaps, but far more to Paris. It was to the well-abused mediæval Churchmen that we owe the foundation of our schools, as well as of our universities, and many other blessings. We have remembered their faults; we have forgotten the benefits they bequeathed to us.

To Henry Wardlaw, who was bishop of St. Andrews from A.D. 1403 to 1440, belongs the honour of having founded the first university in Scotland. He seems to have been a man who, besides his general intelligence and public activity, had a turn for educating youth; for in the early days of his episcopate we find the banished Earl of Northumberland coming to St. Andrews, and committing to the bishop's charge Henry Percy, his son; and Robert III. of Scotland intrusted to his care his son, afterwards James I., who spent two years in the bishop's castle as the companion of young Percy, before he (James) was carried captive to England.

It was in A.D. 1411 that the bishop founded the Seminary, and in A.D. 1413 that he received from Pope Benedict XIII. the Papal Bull which confirmed the foundation, and constituted it a university. Benedict XIII., who was one of three rival claimants at that time for the Papal chair, had established his court at Peniscola in Arragon, whence, in one year, he issued six Papal Bulls in favour of the university, of which one is still preserved in the University Charter-chest. It was a day of glad rejoicing when Henry Ogilvy, Master of Arts, "made his entry into this city, bearing the Bull which endowed the infant seminary with the high privileges of a university."

This is the description of it by Tytler, the historian :—

"Ogilvy's arrival was welcomed by the ringing of bells from the steeples and the tumultuous joy of all classes of the inhabitants. On the following day, being Sunday, a solemn convocation of the clergy was held in the Refectory; and the Papal Bulls having been read in the presence of the Bishop, the Chancellor of the University, they proceeded in procession to the high altar (of the Cathedral) when the *Te Deum* was sung by the whole assembly; the bishops, priors, and other dignitaries being arrayed in their richest canonicals, whilst 400 clerks, besides novices and lay brothers, and an immense crowd of spectators, bent down before the high altar in gratitude and adoration. High mass was then celebrated; and when the service was concluded, the remainder of the day was devoted to mirth and festivity."

Such was the high festival which celebrated the day when Scotland's first university was born.

The first Bull says—

"that, considering the peace and quietness which flourish in the city of St. Andrews and its neighbourhood, its abundant supply of victuals, the number of its hospitia and other conveniences for students, we are led to hope that this city, which the divine bounty has enriched with so many gifts, may become the fountain of science, and the nurse of many men distinguished for knowledge and virtue. Therefore, towards these desirable ends, and moved by the prayers of King James, the Bishop, Prior, Archdeacon, and Chapter, we, by our apostolical authority, found and institute a university in the said city of St. Andrews, for Theology, Canon and Civil Law, Arts, Medicine, and other lawful Faculties."

During all the Middle Age, and long after, Scotland, we know, derived most of her civilisation from France, her constant ally. And so when Bishop Wardlaw wished a model for his university he found it in the University of Paris, which was then, and had long been, the most famous in Europe. Following the example of the University of Paris, which divided its students into four nations—France, Picardy, Normandy, and England—St. Andrews divided its students into the four nations of Fife, Lothian, Angus, and Alban. These chose the Rector, who was the chief and most influential officer in the university, and who sat on high festivals in a stall in the cathedral next to the Bishop and before the Prior. The university possessed as its first teachers thirteen doctors of theology, eight doctors of laws, besides other learned men. The students at first were said to be more numerous than they afterwards became, when they were compelled to live within college walls. But, as no record of their number remains, we are left to conjecture on this point. In those first years they lived where they chose, and at their own expense. Let me give *honoris causâ* the names of some of the earliest teachers. These were Laurence of Lindores, abbot of Scone and

Professor of Laws [more probably Theology], who lectured on the fourth book of the famous Sentences of Peter the Lombard; Richard Cornel, archdeacon of Lothian; William Stevens, afterwards bishop of Dunblane; John Litstar, canon of St. Andrews; John Schevez, archdeacon of the same; and, in Philosophy and Logic, John Gill, William Fowlis, and William Crosier.[1] The university, which was at first known as *Studium Generale*, had no local habitation for a time, but private persons lent rooms in different parts of the city, in which the teaching was carried on. The first teachers had no payment for their teaching and no endowments; but, being all beneficed priests, they were, by the Pope and Bishop, exempted from residence on their benefices, and allowed to enjoy their revenues, on condition of providing for the cure of souls under their charge.

Thus for some years, the university continued as a disembodied teaching and degree-granting power, but in 1418, Robert "de Monte Rosarum" granted a certain tenement "on the south side of South Street" to found a College "theologorum et Artistarum," and in 1430, Bishop Wardlaw granted to the Dean and members of the Faculty of Arts the adjoining tenement to serve as "Scholas artium et si opus fuerit grammaticales." The former was known in the early history of the University as the College of St. John the Evangelist; the latter as the

[1] [See Tytler's *History*, vol. iii. p. 155-6.]

Pædagogium. These two tenements with their pertinents form the grounds and site of the present College of St. Mary's. Bishop Wardlaw, in the deed granting this foundation, wills and ordains "that the Dean of Faculty, regents, and masters shall celebrate, in their ordinary academic gowns, and the chaplains in white surplices, the anniversary of his death, in the chapel, with two wax-tapers burning on a covered table, a *placebo* and *dirige* on the eve of the day of his death, and the next day the mass of *requiem cum nota*." Eleven years after the foundation of the university, the accomplished poet-king, James I., returned from captivity with his English Queen, the Lady Jane Beaufort, and visited St. Andrews. His old preceptor, Bishop Wardlaw, had crowned them both at Scone, and soon after this, the king, when he came to be the guest of the bishop in his castle, did all he could to foster the infant university. He invited learned men from Continental universities to take part in the teaching at St. Andrews. He himself used to frequent the public disputations of the students, and he desired the regents to recommend to him for Church preferment only such youths as were of good learning and of virtuous lives.

There is no greater or more honoured name among Scottish Churchmen of the Middle Age, or of any other age, than that of Bishop James Kennedy, the founder of St. Salvator's College. On his father's side he was sprung from an ancient Ayrshire house, and his mother, Lady Mary, Countess of Angus, was a daughter of King Robert III., so that the bishop was cousin-german to James II. Succeeding to Bishop Wardlaw, his tenure of the Scottish Primacy extended from A.D. 1440 to 1466, that is, during almost the whole reign of James II. and half of the reign of James III. He was the last Bishop of St. Andrews, as his successor and half-brother, Patrick Graham, was the first Archbishop. He was without doubt the foremost man of his time in Scotland both for character and ability. All the historians, Pitscottie, Buchanan, Tytler, and Hill Burton, combine in praise of him. As a churchman he lived a life of blameless piety and conscientiousness. His charity, says Tytler, was "munificent, active, and discriminating," his religion "sincere, and as little tinged by bigotry as it was possible in that day to be." Even Buchanan, who has seldom a good word to say of a bishop, is lavish in his praise of Kennedy. Pitscottie mentions that he was unwearied in the work of visiting his diocese. He both kept his clergy to their duty of preaching and tending the sick, and himself visited the churches and preached to the parishioners the Word of God. He set himself vigorously all his life long to reform the abuses which he saw were destroying the Church, and left a bright example to all Bishops and Churchmen. But, besides his work as an ecclesiastic, the necessities of the time called him to be a statesman. His cousin, James II., looked to his wisdom for counsel, and he was twice, without seeking it, appointed Chancellor of the kingdom. In this capacity, Hill Burton says of him, "He was the first Churchman to hold high political influence in Scotland; and his appearance upon the stage affords a glimpse of a more civilised and orderly future for the kingdom—not so much because he was a Churchman, as because he was a man of peaceful and moderate counsels. His is one of the few political reputations against which no stone is cast."

Scottish history contains no more dramatic interview than that which took place between James II. and Bishop Kennedy in his castle of St. Andrews, when the three great Earls—the Earl of Douglas, the Tiger Earl of Crawford, and the Lord of the Isles—had made a "band," and bound themselves by an oath to stand by each other against the king. James, in despair, had all but resolved to fly from his kingdom; but before doing so he took refuge with his cousin, the bishop, within his old sea-fort at St. Andrews. The bishop, seeing that the king was exhausted by fatigue, desired food to be served up to him, while he himself retired to pray for him and for his commonwealth. Returning in a short time, the bishop led the king to his own chamber. There they knelt down and prayed together. After this Kennedy gave the king a sheaf of arrows bound together, and bade him break them as they were.

When the king could not, he then bade him loose the sheaf and break them one by one. By this acted parable the bishop conveyed the counsel, "*Divide et impera.*" The king acted on the advice, and the bishop lent him his aid on carrying it out. The part which Kennedy played in the sequel is full of historic interest; and the result was that the king thus succeeded in dissolving the band of the three great earls, and in crushing the House of those "tremendous earls of Douglas," whose sword for so long had more than counterpoised the sceptre of the Stuart kings.

On the untimely death of James II. Kennedy was appointed guardian of the infant James III., and governor of the kingdom; "*carissimus avunculus noster*," as the young prince styled him. For five years Kennedy by his wisdom kept both Church and State from disorder, but on his death in 1466 there was no man to take his place, and both fell back into confusion. If the righteousness and wisdom of one man could have availed to save a Church rushing headlong to destruction, Kennedy would have saved it.

> Si Pergama dextrâ
> Defendi possent, etiam hâc defensa fuissent.

But it might not be. The ancient church had been for long growing hopelessly corrupt, and the goodness of one man could not avert its doom.

It was in 1456 that the Bishop founded his

college, endowing it with the teinds of several parishes belonging to the bishopric. Out of these he provided for the maintenance of thirteen persons, to recall the number of our Lord and His twelve apostles. These were a Provost, or Principal, a Licentiate, and a Bachelor, who should all be in holy orders and lecture on Theology; four Masters of Arts, and six poor clerics (*pauperes clerici*). The bishop's Foundation Charter, and the Papal Bull of Pope Nicholas, confirming the same, are still preserved in the archives of this college. The first Principal whom Kennedy placed over his college was Althamar, a Scot, who had been educated, first in the Pædagogium, afterwards in Paris. Nothing could exceed the munificence with which the good bishop provided for the furnishing of the college and its chapel—stoles for the priests, dalmatics, copes, chalices, goblets, basins, candelabras, censers, and crosses. An image of the Saviour two cubits long, gold and silver vessels, large bells, small musical bells, and silk tapestry to adorn the church. Of all this magnificence the only remnants which barbarism has allowed to survive are our noble college tower, the shattered and defaced chapel, the bishops' desecrated tomb, and the beautiful mace of silver-gilt, which Kennedy caused to be made in Paris by the Dauphin's goldsmith, A.D. 1461.

In the Bull of Pius II. confirming Kennedy's second Foundation Charter, it is declared that the college is intended for theology and arts, for Divine worship and scholastic exercise, and for the strengthening of the orthodox faith, the increase of the Christian religion, and removing the pestiferous schisms of heretics. Further, the Pope declares that it is his desire that the above thirteen persons shall eat and sleep within the walls of the college, observe the hours which he strictly names, keep matins, vespers, and other canonical hours, that the priests shall celebrate masses and attend exsequies in white surplices, and chant the services. He further ordains that there shall be appointed "pastors and defenders and special conservators of the college, its benefices, and goods, lest ravenous wolves seize thereon." But besides the thirteen persons on the foundation, young men of rank and wealth were allowed to study in the college, but were bound to obey the Provost, and observe the rules of the House, just as the poor scholars were. On the buildings of the college with its endowments, on his own monument, and on the famous Bishop's Barge, which he built for the see and named St. Salvator, Bishop Kennedy is said to have expended a sum which would amount to £300,000 of our present money.

The next academic foundation within the University was St. Leonard's College, the combined work of two very different men, the youthful Archbishop Alexander Stuart, natural son of James IV., and John Hepburn, the prior of the monastery. James had appointed this favourite son to the vacant see while he was still a boy. He studied abroad, and was the disciple and friend of the famous Erasmus, who has left on record a notable eulogy of his genius and his worth. He returned to Scotland and assumed his archiepiscopal duties at the age of eighteen, and when only twenty-one he marched at his father's desire to Flodden, where he died by his father's side. They bore his dead body thence to his own cathedral, and laid it in a stone coffin beneath the high altar. More than fifty years ago that stone coffin was opened. There lay the cloven and now desecrated skull. For it was taken from its resting-place, and to-day, I blush to say it, disgraces the shelves of our museum. Such is the honour we confer on our founders and benefactors. Only three years were granted to Alexander Stuart to fill the archiepiscopal throne, but during that time he helped to found one college and lay the beginnings of another, which his less worthy successors were to complete.

I cannot pass on without alluding to the splendid passage in which Dean Stanley, in his inaugural address as our Rector in 1875—which who that heard it ever can forget?—speaks of Alexander Stuart: "Of all the names of ancient Scottish ecclesiastical history there is none which has a more tragic interest than that of the young Alexander Stuart, who was raised to the archbishopric of St. Andrews at the early age of eighteen, by his father,

James IV. He was the pupil of Erasmus, and that great man has left on record his profound admiration of the Scottish youth, who had been his companion and scholar in the stately old Italian city of Siena. Tall, dignified, graceful, with no blemish but the shortness of sight, which he shared in common with so many modern students—of gentle manners, playful humour—but keen as a hound in pursuit of knowledge, in history, theology, law, above all in the new Greek learning—an accomplished musician, a delightful talker, high-spirited, and high-minded, without haughtiness—religious, without a particle of superstition—born to command, yet born also to conciliate—such was the figure that his master describes; and already the University of St. Andrews had felt the stimulus of his youthful energy; already the enlightened spirits of Scotland were beginning to breathe freely in the atmosphere in which he had himself been nourished. Had that young student of St. Andrews (for so, although archbishop, we may still call him), had he lived to fulfil his wonderful promise; had he, with these rare gifts and rare opportunities, been spared to meet the impending crisis of the coming generation, instead of the worldly, intriguing, profligate Beaton; had he been enthroned, in this venerable see, with the spirit of Colet, in a higher post, the aspirations of More without his difficulties, ready to prepare the way for the first shock of the Reformation, what a chance for the ancient Church of this country! What an occasion of combining the best parts of the old with the best parts of the new! What a call, if its doom had not been already fixed, to purify that corrupt Episcopacy! What a hope, if moderation had in those times been possible, of restraining the violence of the iconoclast reaction! But, alas! he was slain by his father's side at Flodden. Of all 'the flowers of the forest' that were there 'wede away,' surely none was more lovely, more precious, than this young Marcellus of the Scottish Church. If he fell under the memorable charge of my namesake on that fatal day, may he accept thus late the lament which a kinsman of his foe would fain pour over his untimely bier." That kinsman of his foe was Dean Stanley himself. "Thus late," well might he say. For no writer before him had seen or celebrated aright the rare beauty of that character and his tragic destiny. Those, at least, who have had for founders two such men as James Kennedy and Alexander Stuart, have reason not to think ill of bishops. But for many generations no bishop in Scotland has had a chance of having justice done to him. But Scotsmen are, I believe, at length beginning to awake from that irrational delusion, and to see that, as there lived brave men before Agamemnon, so there lived good men in Scotland, and some of these bishops too, before John Knox.

The other joint founder of St. Leonard's College,

Prior John Hepburn, was, I believe, cast in a more mundane mould. But besides building the college, which has now all but disappeared, he has left a monument of himself which still survives in the old towered wall with which he surrounded the whole precinct of the Cathedral and the Priory and the grounds of St. Leonard's College. On the site which was appropriated for the college had formerly stood a hospital, in which lodged the pilgrims, who aforetime came in crowds to adore the relics of St. Andrew, and to witness the numerous miracles wrought by them. In time the relics lost their power, the miracles ceased, and the hospitium was changed into an asylum for old and infirm women. These seem to have proved unprofitable inmates; as the old charter says, "they yielded but little or no good fruit by their life and conversation." We can well believe it. Therefore the young archbishop substituted for these unprofitable inmates others who should yield more fruit to Church and State. He converted the hospitium, with the adjoining Church of St. Leonard, into a college for poor scholars, and endowed it to maintain one principal master, four chaplains, two of whom should say daily masses for the souls of the old founder and the new, and twenty scholars, who were to be well versed in the Gregorian chant. Six of these scholars were to be students of theology.

The statutes of the college, which were drawn up

by Prior John Hepburn, and afterwards approved by Regent Murray, still remain, and are very curious and interesting. No one was to be admitted to the college under the age of fifteen years or more than one-and-twenty. Before admission each student was to ask on bended knees, before the principal master, for the love of our Lord, to be received into this holy society. He was then to be strictly examined as to his knowledge of the first and second parts of grammar, he was to be a good writer, and a good singer of the Gregorian chant; must be poor in this world's goods, and pure in life and morals.

The internal economy and daily life within the college is laid down most minutely. The hour of rising in winter was half-past six, in summer five o'clock. The hours for matins, vespers, and other Church services are laid down, and attendance is rigorously required. Breakfast at eight o'clock, dinner at half-past eleven, supper at eight o'clock. The exact amount of food on festivals, fasts, and ordinary days is specified. Thrice in the week, after dinner, a lecture on grammar, poetry, or oratory, by the Regents in turn.

Before taking the degree of Master the students must perfect themselves in logic, physics, philosophy and metaphysics, and in at least one of the books of Solomon. These subjects, all but the last, were, of course, learned from Aristotle alone, or rather from the scholastic commentaries on him. All members of the college were to converse with each other in Latin, except the cook and his boy. Every Sunday the whole college was to be swept and cleaned by four students in turn. At Christmas and Easter all the students were to sweep the walls, windows, and ceilings clean of cobwebs. No one was to go out of the college without leave, and when they did they must wear gown and hood. Once a week the students, with one of the Masters, shall repair (*ad campos*) to the Links, and having there practised honest games, shall return in time for vespers. If field exercises be allowed more than once a week (which, however, we object to, says the statute), then let the students take to some honest labour in a garden or elsewhere. "The number of students in the college cannot be fixed," says the statute, "but must fluctuate according to circumstances. They may, however, be at present ten, more or less, according to the direction of the principal."

This, however, refers only to the students on the foundation—the *pauperes clerici*. But entrance soon was eagerly sought for by the wealthy; and the statutes provide that the sons of the nobility should be admitted, but only on condition that these shall strictly conform in all things to the same discipline as the poor scholars, shall eat with them, read in their turn at table, and wear the same scholastic dress. Special care is taken to forbid in these sons of the wealthy and noble any kind of extravagance or any eccentricity of dress or behaviour. They are not to wear caps of green, scarlet, blue, yellow, or any showy colour, not to wear a secular dress, or garments too much cut away, not to frequent the town, nor to hold nightly banquets, nor to carry knives or offensive weapons within the college, or play dice, football, or unbecoming games. The course of study is wide enough. Each regent shall teach his pupils grammar, oratory, poetry, or anything else which the principal may direct. The college, though at first provided with but slender funds, rose in time, by the vigilance of its Masters, above these difficulties, and soon attained to great celebrity. Of its outward embodiment all that now remains is a roofless chapel, with its weed-covered monuments.

The foundation of the third college in St. Andrews followed quickly on that of St. Leonard's. Archbishop Alexander Stuart in 1512 changed the original Pædagogium or University schools into a college, and endowed it with the fruits and pertinents of the Church of St. Michael of Tarvet. The two Beatons procured a Bull in 1537 for it from Pope Paul III., and dedicated the College to the Blessed Virgin Mary of the Assumption, and added to its endowments. Archbishop John Hamilton, the last Roman Catholic archbishop, in 1552 obtained a special Bull from Pope Julius III. for re-erecting the College, and he further endowed it out of his archiepiscopal revenues. These two Bulls are, I believe, both still preserved among the archives of St. Mary's College. Hamilton's Charter ordains that thirty-six persons in all shall be maintained on the foundation, four principal professors, called the Provost, Licentiate, Bachelor, Canonist; eight students of theology, three professors of philosophy, two professors of rhetoric and grammar, five vicars pensionary, sixteen students of philosophy, a provisor, cook, and janitor.

The rules of life enjoined were much the same as we have seen in the case of St. Leonard's—life within college walls, meals in common, rules as to dress, strict observance of the canonical hours of worship.

All these three colleges were founded within less than a century before the Reformation; the two younger colleges on the very eve of its outbreak. All three, it was hoped, would protect the Catholic faith against "the schisms and heresies of the pestiferous heresiarchs." By a strange irony of fate two of these colleges became, almost from the first, the foremost agents in working the overthrow of that Church which they were founded to defend. This was especially true of St. Leonard's. Its founder, Archbishop Stuart, was, we have seen, the friend and pupil of Erasmus, and a devotee of that new learning with which the name of Erasmus is identified. It was impossible to drink deeply of that learning, and to continue wedded to the doctrines of the schoolmen and the corruptions of Rome. But probably even Alexander Stuart himself did not dream of the issues which his college was so soon to accelerate. It had, however, caught the contagion of its founder's spirit, and young and ardent minds within its walls were fired with love of the new thought and hatred of the old corruptions. Among the earliest students educated at St. Leonard's were Alexander Alane, better known as Alesius, who graduated in 1515, three years after its foundation; Alexander Seyton, of Touch, who graduated in 1516; and Henry Forrest, who graduated in 1526.

These were all young men studying eagerly in St. Andrews, when Patrick Hamilton, who had graduated at the University of Paris, arrived in St. Andrews in 1527, and was incorporated in St. Leonard's College. Hamilton, the scion of a noble Scottish house, was of a clear-seeing intellect, of a pure life and a devoted heart, and on fire with zeal for the new faith. Alesius, Seyton, and Forrest became his friends and devoted followers. Alesius, who was a Canon of the cathedral, at first had thought to convert Hamilton from his errors, but was himself converted by him. He witnessed the scene in the cathedral when Hamilton was accused, and defended himself before Archbishop James Beaton, his nephew the abbot of Arbroath, afterwards the cardinal, the bishops, and all the Church dignitaries, and he saw him carried thence straight to the front of the gate of St. Salvator's College, and there bound to the stake. The old college tower, still standing, looked down on the fire which slowly consumed the earliest Scottish martyr of the new faith. Alesius at once fell under the suspicion of the Church, and after suffering a year of persecutions, narrowly escaped to the Continent, where he spent the rest of his life, and wrote his record of Hamilton's confession. Seyton, who was of the regular clergy of St. Andrews, and confessor of James v., was even bolder still. He preached in St. Andrews against the evil lives of the clergy, withstood Archbishop James Beaton, and answered him to his face, and then, by a marvel, escaped beyond seas. The third St. Leonard's graduate, who was a disciple of Hamilton, Henry Forrest, was less fortunate. He had listened to Hamilton's teaching, and had seen him die, and the only charge brought against him was that he had said, "Master Patrick died a martyr, and was no heretic." For this he was seized, thrown into the dungeon in the old sea-tower, taken thence and burnt on a rising ground "adjoining the northern stile of the Abbey Church," that the flames might be visible from the shores of Angus. Patrick Hamilton died in 1528, Forrest in 1532. Besides these, Gavin Logie, who was Rector of St. Leonard's, was so zealous in spreading the new tenets, that he was obliged to fly from Scotland in 1533. Well might the saying become proverbial, "He has drunk of St. Leonard's Well," that is, he has imbibed the new Protestant doctrines.

St. Leonard's College was at that time the most active centre of intellectual and spiritual energy in Scotland, and the men just named were the first-fruits it produced.

But there were other students of St. Andrews besides these men of St. Leonard's who worked in the same direction. In the old Parchment Book in our Library, which contains the names of the earliest matriculated students, there occur among the entrants of 1508-9, two names, placed one after the other. These are "D. Lindsay" and "D. Beaton." The first of these became Sir David Lindsay of the Mount, the tutor of the young James V., and the poet and satirist who, by the strong sense, the caustic humour, and the scathing sarcasm of his descriptions, did more than any other writer to fan the growing flame of hatred and contempt for the moribund hierarchy. The other was the Cardinal David Beaton, who by the profligacy of his private life, and the cruelty of his public prosecutions, did more than any other single man to precipitate the doom that was impending over his Church.

We must not pass over another notable figure in St. Andrews during the first half of the sixteenth century, that of John Mair or Major. Educated at the University of Paris, on his return to Scotland he taught first in the University of Glasgow, where John Knox was his pupil. By the year 1523 he appears to have migrated to St. Andrews, where in St. Mary's College he taught the young scholar George Buchanan and John Wedderburn, afterwards author of the "Gude and Godly Ballads." In 1533 Mair became Provost of St. Salvator's. No name in Scotland stood higher in his day as a teacher than that of Mair. He was the oracle of the schools. Though not a Protestant, he held what must at that time have been very advanced opinions—that a general council was superior to the Pope, that the Pope had no temporal supremacy, that unjust excommunications had no force; he censured the avarice, ambition, and secular pomp of the Court of Rome and of the Episcopate, and urged the diminution of monasteries and holidays. But his political sentiments were even more pronounced. To Knox and Buchanan he taught those democratic views which he himself had learnt on the Continent—that the people are the source of all authority, that from them kings derive their power, that kings who rule ill may be deposed, and that tyrants may be put to death. These sentiments Knox and Buchanan greedily took up, and disseminated eagerly among a people no wise averse to receive them.

It is clear even from the brief sketch I have given that the colleges of St. Andrews during the early years of the sixteenth century contained among their members stormy heads and fiery hearts, fitted to do vigorously the work of demolition that had become inevitable.

As to the work of reconstruction, which the same men also as vigorously attempted, this is not the time or place to speak of it. Laudation enough it has already had. Its strong points we all know, its shortcomings we are perhaps less aware of. The hurricane that swept our land in the middle of the sixteenth century, which we call the Reformation, cleansed away much rottenness and corruption, but it took with it also some things which no nation can well spare.

Besides the beautiful material fabrics, some other things disappeared which we cannot but deplore. In the wild work that had then to be done Scotland received some mental and moral wounds from which she is suffering to this day, and I fear long will suffer.

The University of St. Andrews at first existed for some years merely as a teaching and degree-granting institute; that is to say, it confined itself to giving instruction, and attempted nothing more. In a short time three colleges were founded within the university, and these colleges aimed at something beyond mere instruction of the intellect; they aimed at educating the whole man, as they then understood that process, not only informing his understanding, but ordering his life, conduct, and manners, and providing for religious worship. No doubt the conception of life which those Catholic founders held was a cramped and confined one; the worship they provided may have been formal and corrupt; the means they took to carry out their conception may have been poor and faulty. But the root-conception itself—that of moulding not the intellect merely, but the whole man—was, in its essence, deep and true beyond anything we in these modern days dream of. Even after the Reformation, the Reformers still preserved for several generations the old Catholic idea of education as distinguished from mere instruction; and they endeavoured with their new lights to combine the intellectual, the moral, and the spiritual elements; for they believed, and rightly, that thought, life, and worship should go hand in hand, and that they cannot be severed without grievous loss to young souls. But gradually the severance began, and in the Universities of Germany and of Scotland it has long been complete. St. Andrews was, I believe, the latest of our universities to abandon the old idea that we had inherited from Catholic times. England, too, which has so much longer walked in the old way, and has attempted, by the college system in Oxford and Cambridge, to educate the whole man, has for the last twenty years been busy in casting off its old tradition. Men are eager for it, and they call it advance; but they cannot change the nature of things, and it is one of the deepest laws of that nature that the intellectual and the spiritual parts of man are inseparably combined, and cannot be sundered without injury to the whole man. The intellect itself is impoverished or dwarfed when cut off from the spirit—the fountain-light of all our seeing. We may go on keeping up the divorce, and no doubt will do so for a long time to come, but it will be found that we are on a road which leads only to inanition. Perhaps in some far future men may rediscover the true spiritual centre, and after long wanderings may return to make their thoughts, their lives, and their whole education revolve round it. However poor and inadequate may have been the way in which they carried it out, the Catholic universities were right in their ground-conception—in their preference for education over mere instruction, and in their endeavour to order their training according to this conception. We, who boast of our wider views and more scientific notions, have abandoned the attempt to educate the soul, and seek only to instruct the understanding.

When the storm of the Reformation which had been so long impending had burst, no place in Scotland felt the violence of the shock more sensibly than St. Andrews. There were concentrated all the elements that could give fullest force to the collision. On the one hand, the numerous crowd of priests, monks, or canons, proud of their cathedral, and resolute to defend the ancient system, however corrupt, and these led by a prelate, John Hamilton, who, if less able, was not less unscrupulous and cruel than David Beaton. On the other hand, the young regents and teachers and students of St. Leonards, still zealous for the new learning and the new faith, with their ardour not daunted but rather inflamed by the thought of their fellows who had suffered in the cause. And then, to stir the hostile elements and drive them to collision, John Knox, who for nearly forty years kept ever and anon appearing in St. Andrews as the cloud-compeller of the storm.

Knox was not a student at St. Andrews, as once some believed, but at Glasgow University. Wherever he graduated, he is found in St. Andrews as early as 1528 or 1529, teaching the scholastic philosophy with an ability which almost surpassed that of his teacher, Mair or Major. But he was not long held by these trammels. Gradually, by the study of St. Jerome and St. Augustine, he unlearned the Popish theology, and opened his mind to the new faith. If Knox was not in St. Andrews when Patrick Hamilton was burnt (1528), he must have been there very soon after, and must have received the full force of the thrill which that heroic death sent throughout Scotland. The years of Knox's sojourn in St. Andrews—from 1530 till 1542—were those of

Beaton's most violent persecutions. The names of at least ten confessors are preserved who suffered for their faith either at St. Andrews or elsewhere. Numbers more had to fly to the Continent to escape the fury of the cardinal. Knox the while, thrilled by these examples, and stimulated by converse with the society of St. Leonard's College, was pursuing his own thoughts, and by 1542 he had so fully embraced the reformed religion, that his views reached Beaton's ears, so that he had to fly from St. Andrews.[1] Wherever his first university may have been, St. Andrews was to him the birthplace of his new faith. His second coming thither was at Easter 1547, just after the murder of Beaton, when Knox became chaplain to the garrison of the castle, preached his

[1] [It is certain that Knox was a student in the University of Glasgow, under the famous John Major. Knox seems, however, to have left Glasgow without graduating; and there is no evidence from College records of his having been either a student or a regent in St. Andrews. The latter he could hardly have been, seeing he was not a Master of Arts. The incidents of the life of Knox from his entrance at the University of Glasgow in 1522 until 1543,—when he openly joined the Reformers,—are very obscure. It is held by some that during ten years of this period he was a secular priest at or near Haddington, his native place. His minute knowledge of the trials and demeanour of the Protestant confessors and martyrs at St. Andrews, and of the evil lives of the churchmen there during the period referred to, almost indicates some personal acquaintance with the place and time. The absence of University record, while it disproves his connection with the College, does not establish the fact that he was not at St. Andrews during some portion of this decade. It may be added that Knox was also in St. Andrews in 1566, as his name appears, among others, appended to the letter of the General Assembly sitting there, which expressed approval of the later Helvetic Confession.]

first Protestant sermon from the pulpit of the parish church, and confronted at a convention held in St. Leonard's yards the learned men of the Abbey and the University, and confounded their ablest disputants by the power of his arguments in favour of the new doctrines. He was then taken prisoner, along with the garrison of the castle, on the last day of July, and carried off to serve in the French galleys.

Knox's third coming to St. Andrews is that famous one which all men know (June 1559). Archbishop Hamilton, hearing that he meant to preach in the cathedral church, sent him word that if he dared to enter that pulpit the soldiers would have orders to fire upon him. In the face of that threat Knox ascended the pulpit, and, for four successive days, discoursed on Christ's purifying the temple at Jerusalem. The sequel need hardly be told. The purifying of the cathedral was intrusted to the hands of "the rascal multitude," and we know how they purified it. After desecrating the cathedral, and wrecking it of its ornaments, they fell with still wilder fury on the priory, the monasteries of the Black Friars and the Grey, the provostry of Kirkheugh, and the ancient church of St. Regulus, and overthrew them either with partial or total destruction.

Once again—the fourth time and the last—he came, in May 1571. Worn out with age and infirmity, and with harassment in Edinburgh, he sought repose in St. Andrews. That repose he did not find. The Hamiltons and other factions still harassed him. Some members of the University showed their hostility to him, especially Professor Archibald Hamilton; St. Salvator's and St. Mary's Colleges were disaffected towards him. Some of the professors were even suspected of Popery, and soon after returned to it. But St. Leonard's was with him.

James Melville, in his famous *Diary*, says:—

"Our haill Collage, maisters and schollars, war sound and zealous for the guid cause; the other twa Collages nocht sa; for in the new Collage, howbeit Mr. John Douglass, then Rector, was guid aneuche, the thrie uther maisters and sum of the Regentes war evill-myndit, viz., Messrs. Robert, Archbald and Jhone Hamiltons (wharof the last twa becam efter apostates), hated Mr. Knox and the guid cause; and the Commissar, Mr. Wilyeam Skein could nocht lyk weill of his doctrine. The auld Collage was reulit be Mr. Jhon Rutherfurd, a man lernit in philosophie, but invyus, corrupt."

James Melville, who was a first-year student at St. Leonard's when Knox came, further says:—

"Of all the benefites I haid that year (1571) was the coming of that maist notable profet and apostle of our nation, Mr. Johne Knox. I hard him teatche ther the prophecies of Daniel, that simmer and the wintar following. I had my pen and my little book, and tuk away sic things as I could comprehend. In the opening upe of his text, he was moderat the space of an halff-hour; bot when he entered to application he made me sa to grew and tremble that I could nocht hald a pen to wryt. . . . He was verie weak. I saw him, everie day of his doctrine, go hulie and fear (slowly and warily), with a furring of martriks about his neck, a staffie in the an hand, and gude godly Richart Ballanden, his servand, halden upe the uther oxtar, from the Abbay to the paroche kirk, and be the said Richart and another servant lifted upe to the pulpit, whar he behovit to lean at his first entrie ; bot or he haid done with his sermont, he was sa active and vigorous that he was lyk to ding that pulpit in blads, and fly out of it."

Melville tells that during this, Knox's last sojourn in St. Andrews,

" He ludgit down in the Abbay [so that parts of the Abbey must still have been habitable] beside our Collage, and our Primarius, Mr. James Wilkie, our Regents, Mr. Nicol Dalgleise, Mr. Wilyeame Colace, and Mr. John Davidson went in ordinarilie to his grace efter denner and soupper. . . . Mr. Knox wald sum tyme com in, and repose him in our Collage yeard, and call us schollars unto him, and bless us, and exhort us to knaw God and his wark in our countrey, and stand be the guid cause, to use our tyme weill, and lern the guid instructiones and follow the guid exemple of our Maisters."

Soon after this, in August 1572, Knox left St. Andrews and returned to Edinburgh to die, desiring, in his own words, that "I may end my battel ; for, as the worlde is wearie of me, so am I of it."

Such personal incidents as these, interesting in themselves, are almost the only things we know about the University. In 1560, the year when the reformed religion was set up in Scotland, every thing in the colleges of St. Andrews connected with the Roman faith and worship was swept away ; and how violent must have been the shock we can imagine, when we remember how entirely ecclesiastical these foundations were, and how ingrained into them were all the usages of the ancient faith.

Two years before the Reformation very few

students entered the University, "owing to the tumults about religion," says the Matriculation Book; and in the next year, owing to the universal upturning of all things, the graduation ceremonies had to be suspended. When the Reformation was actually established, the greater number of the regents joined the winning side, and became Protestants. Several of the St. Salvator men, however, refused to swim with the stream, and among them William Cranston, the Principal of the college. He and some others preferred to demit their offices, rather than relinquish the ancient faith. But, besides sweeping the colleges clean of everything connected with the Roman faith and worship, the Reformers were minded to make other changes in the University, which, however, they were prevented from then carrying out, as their hands were full of other and more necessary work. When Cranston demitted his office as Principal of St. Salvator's, he was succeeded by John Rutherford. He was a scholar, and wrote Latin in the improved style, acquired by study of the classics. He was still more a philosopher, and published a treatise on the *Art of Reasoning*, which, though strictly Aristotelian in its principles, is said to have "marked a stage in the progress of philosophy in Scotland, and to have been an unquestionable benefit to the University and the nation." At the Reformation John Douglas was the head of St. Mary's, and John

Duncauson the head of St. Leonard's. These both conformed to the new *régime*, and Douglas afterwards became Tulchan archbishop of St. Andrews.

It was twenty years before any effectual commission took the University in hand, and till then, and even after it, the mode of teaching and the academical exercises in philosophy and arts remained much the same as they had been in Mair's time, before the Reformation.

But if the Parliament and General Assembly could not find time to reorganise the Universities, they or their leaders took care that the ablest men of the time were placed in the most prominent academic posts. Two such—the men next to Knox in power of intellect and strength of will— filled the principalships of two of the colleges; the one a contemporary and fellow-worker with Knox, the other his successor, and the completer of his work. The first of these, George Buchanan, was probably the greatest scholar whom Scotland ever produced. After having studied in St. Andrews, under Mair; then having passed to the Continent, where he was knocked from pillar to post, as a poor, almost mendicant scholar; then, after having narrowly escaped the hands of the Inquisition—he returned to Scotland, and received in 1564, from Queen Mary Stuart, his first piece of preferment, a portion of the forfeited revenue of the Abbey of Crossraguel. About this time he became Queen

Mary's tutor, and read Livy with her—it is said in that house in South Street (*domus sumptuosa*) which still bears her name. By Mary's treacherous half-brother, Regent Murray, Buchanan was appointed, in 1566, to the principalship of St. Leonard's, which he held till 1570. While he was still Principal of St. Leonard's, in 1568, he went with the Regent to England, as one of the accusers of his Queen and former pupil, and used his scholarship to compose a Latin "Detection" of her actions, which he laid before her judges at Westminster, and circulated industriously in the English Court. Whoever else might accuse Mary, was it not the depth of baseness in Buchanan to do so? Add to this, that if, as is now by many believed, the casket letters were forgeries, then Buchanan must have been guilty of even a deeper baseness than that of ingratitude. Appointed afterwards to be one of the young king's preceptors, he showed to James the same harsh spirit he had shown towards his mother. Traditions are still rife among the Scottish peasantry how he buffeted his royal pupil; and, as Mr. Hill Burton observes, "the zeal with which these traditions have been preserved, and the zest with which they are still told by the people, show how much fellow-feeling they have for this humbly born and bitter republican." Once it is told that, when Buchanan had been inflicting "dorsal discipline" on the young prince, the Countess of Mar, hearing the cries, entered and asked him how he dared to lift his hand against the Lord's anointed. The grim reply of the sour, coarse stoic was such as may be imagined, but cannot be here repeated. In after years James used to say of some high official that he ever "trembled at his approach, it minded him so of his old pedagogue." No wonder that, when Buchanan tried to impress the young king with his views as to the duty of a constitutional monarch, it only drove James to the opposite extreme, so that in after years he loathed the very thought of Buchanan, and warned his son Charles against his books and opinions as against poison.

Buchanan held the principalship of St. Leonard's for only four years (1566-1570). The only official duty imposed on him was to read occasional Lectures on Divinity. But his great power as a scholar—the best Latinist of his time, unrivalled by any Scotsman since—must, one would think, have done something to promote scholarship in St. Andrews. But the academic cloister was far too narrow a sphere for a spirit busy and turbulent as his. Where the fray was thickest, thither his nature carried him, and from the time he left St. Andrews till his death he was immersed in the stormy politics of the time. Once again he intromitted with his University, when, as a member of the Commission of 1579, which from him is sometimes spoken of as George Buchanan's Commission, he came to reform the

University. There had been various attempts made before this with the same view.

The First Book of Discipline contained a scheme for remodelling the other universities as well as St. Andrews. A Commission for the reform of abuses in St. Andrews followed in 1563, but it came to nothing. The Commission of 1579 went to work more energetically. It found that all the colleges "disagreed in many things from the true religion, and were far from that perfection of learning which this learned age craves," and they agreed on a new form of instruction to be observed in the University. The Report containing this improved plan is written in the Scottish dialect and is still preserved. It was ratified by Parliament. Some credit Buchanan with being the author of this Report, but M'Crie believes that Melville had the chief hand in it. The main practical result was that St. Mary's College was set apart for the study of theology and the languages connected with the books of Scripture, and Melville was appointed Principal of St. Mary's to carry out his own scheme. The two other colleges had new and improved courses of study laid down for them, and it is to be noted that the study of some parts of the Platonic philosophy was enjoined as a counteractive to the Aristotelian philosophy hitherto exclusively taught. It would have been interesting to have followed into detail the improved course of instruction had it ever been carried out. But so far was this from being the case, that throughout the whole of the seventeenth century down to the great Royal visitation of 1718-19, commission followed commission, each new commission complaining that abuses still continued, and that the enactments of the last had failed to be carried out. Each new change in the ecclesiastical *régime* of Scotland was followed by a commission charged to see that the teaching and discipline of the University were brought into harmony with the dominant Church system. When we remember how rapidly these followed each other—that Knox's system of Superintendents lasted from 1560 till 1572; that this was succeeded by Tulchan bishops till 1590; that from 1590 till 1610 Melville's stern form of Presbytery reigned; from 1610 till 1638 the Episcopate, of which Archbishop Spottiswoode was the chief ornament; that from 1638 till 1660 Covenanting Presbytery held its tyranny; then, from 1660 till 1690 the return of the Stuarts and Episcopacy again; lastly, from 1690 onward, the Moderate or non-Covenanting Presbytery;—when we keep steadily in view these rapid changes in the ecclesiastical firmament, and remember that the Universities were as sensitive to these changes as our bodies are to the weather; that they were then the creatures of the Church, whatever form it might take,—the wonder is, not that they made no steady progress, but that they were able to survive such frequent and violent vicissitudes. In this century and a half of turbulence and disorder, when Superintendency, Tulchan bishops, Melville Presbytery, Spottiswoode Episcopacy, the Covenant, restored Episcopacy, and Moderate or non-Covenanting Presbytery, were jostling each other; when the whole kingdom was full of quarrelling, fighting, plotting, convulsions, reactions, and counter revolutions,—the calm pursuit of knowledge was impossible. The strifes that raged without intruded within the walls of the colleges, and made the teachers either strive with each other, or live and teach as they listed, heedless of the commissioners and all their enactments. St. Salvator seems to have been the most obstinately recalcitrant. Here are a few of the charges urged against it by the Visitation of 1588:—That all the masters or regents had disregarded the enactments of 1579, and that each regent continued to teach the class with which he began, throughout the whole course of philosophy. This custom, though forbidden, was continued down till the eighteenth century. Altercations, too, seem to have been rife. The provost asserts that he teaches the Aphorisms of Hippocrates once a week. The masters say that he never teaches, or scantily once a month. Mr. Welwood says that he teaches the Institutions Tuesday, Thursday, and Saturday. The provost says that he "neglectis oft." Mr. Cranston has no class by reason of the pest, and therefore teaches the grammar to the Earl of Cassilis and others privately. A memorial of the Visitation of 1588 opens thus :—

"It is maist difficil in this confused tyme (when all folks are looking for the weltering [overturning] of the warld) to effectuat any gude commoun werk, although men were never so weill willit ; and specially where ye ar not certainly instructit, and hes na greit hope of thankes for your travell."

The memorial concludes with this advice to the Regents :—

"Forbid thair quarelling, . . . albeit it be not altogether prohibit that they may *flyte* (*i.e.* scold), yet forbid fechting or bearing of daggis (pistols) or swerdis. . . . "

Amid such a state of things it took a strong man to hold his own, and to effect any useful work. Such a strong man the University had at the very time of the above memorial, in Andrew Melville, who was Principal of St. Mary's from 1580 till 1607.

Melville had been originally educated at St. Andrews. He entered St. Mary's College in 1559, when he was only fourteen. At that time all the sciences taught in the University were from Latin translations or scholastic commentaries on Aristotle. Melville had learned Greek from a famous schoolmaster in Montrose, the first who ever taught that language in Scotland. His nephew, in his "Diary," says that throughout his course Andrew "used the Greek Logicks of Aristotle, whilk was a wounder to them (his teachers) that he was sa fyne a schollar, and of sic expectation." Again, he says, "All that was taught of Aristotle he learned and studyed it out of the Greek text, which his masters understood not." When he had got all the learning that St. Andrews could give him, he passed to the Continent, studied in the University of Paris, at Poictiers, and finally at Geneva. In these places he perfected his knowledge of Greek and acquired many other things besides. At Paris he made the acquaintance of Peter Ramus, the famed logician, and of Joseph Scaliger, the first scholar of the age; and at Geneva became the friend of the reformer Beza, who had before been the friend of Knox and Buchanan. During all Melville's foreign sojourn France was disturbed by the wars between Catholics and Huguenots, which culminated in St. Bartholomew's day in 1572. The French refugees, who after that dreadful event crowded to Geneva, became Melville's friends. At Geneva, which was then the hotbed of democracy and of Presbyterianism, Melville greedily imbibed both, and became fitted to carry on the work which Knox and Buchanan had begun. In 1574, he returned to Scotland, and was appointed Principal of Glasgow University, which he found in a decayed condition, but did not long suffer to remain so. His nephew says, Mr. Andro entering as principal master, all was committed and submitted to him. To another he left the care of the college, and threw himself wholly into teaching. The account of the labour he underwent in teaching is all but incredible. He himself took the ablest youths, who had been grounded in Latin, read with them Virgil and Horace and other Latin authors, taught them Greek (which till then was little studied), and read with his pupils Homer, Hesiod, Theocritus, Pindar, and Isocrates; taught them Logic, in which he indoctrinated them in the new doctrines of his teacher, Peter Ramus; taught them Moral Philosophy from Cicero's works, Aristotle's Ethics and Politics, and Plato's Dialogues; instructed them in Natural Philosophy from the best extant sources, besides Plato and Aristotle, adding moreover a view of Universal History and of Chronology; introduced them to Hebrew, Chaldee, and Syriac languages, lecturing himself on the different Books of Scripture; and finally introduced them to the Theology of Calvin's *Institutes*. He was in fact in himself an embodied and living university. We might fail to credit it, were not all I have stated, and more, set down in the "Diary" of his nephew, James Melville, who, though a partial, is generally considered a faithful witness. For six years he continued thus to teach twice every day of the week, Sabbath not excepted. Well says his nephew, "I dar say ther was na place in Europe comparable to Glasgow for guid letters during these yeirs, for a plentifull and guid chepe mercat of all kynd of langages, artes, and scienses."

When Mr. Andro passed to St. Mary's College in

this University, he continued with the same energy, only confined within narrower limits by his special duties as a teacher in theology, or by the urgent calls which he thought Church and State made upon his services. His nephew informs us that a great contradiction brake out against him in the University. When the regents of philosophy in St. Leonard's heard that Mr. Andro mightily confuted Aristotle, they "maid a strange steir, and cryed, 'grait Diana of the Ephesians,' thair bread-winner, thair honour, thair estimation, all were gen, giff Aristotle sould be sa owirharled in the heiring of thair schollars." But Mr. Andro, nothing daunted, plied them still more vehemently, so that "he dashit them, and in end convicted them sa in conscience," that he won over his chief gainsayers. He stirred up the theologians from "the coldness and ignorance and negligence" into which, according to James Melville, they had fallen since Knox's day.

"As for Langages, Arts, and Philosophie (he continues), they haid na thing for all, bot a few buikes of Aristotle, quhilk they lernit pertinatiuslie to bable and flyt upon. . . . Bot within a year Mr. Andro, be his delling in publict and privat with everie an of them, sa prevalit, that they fell to the langages, studeit thair arts for the right use, and perusit Aristotle in his awin langage; sa that they becam bathe philosophers and theologes, and acknawlagit a wounderfull transportation out of darkness into light. Bot, indeid, this was nocht done without mikle feghting and fasherie."

We can well believe it.

The above account is that of his nephew, naturally partial to his great uncle. But it would seem that in his engrossment with the affairs of Church and State, Melville had in some measure neglected his academic duties. In the Visitation of 1597 we find these charges against him: that he had neglected his duties as rector for the ruling and ordering of the University; and that neither in the government of the college, nor in teaching, nor in the administration of their rents, had he conformed to the reformed foundation and Act of Parliament. And Spottiswoode further accuses him of teaching, instead of divinity, the principles of republicanism; discussing before his students whether the election or succession of kings was best, how far the royal power extended, and if kings might be censured for abusing the same, and deposed by the estates of the kingdom.

But Melville's "feghting and fasherie" were not confined to the University. Outside and beyond it, he had still more trouble to re-establish and systematise a thoroughgoing Presbyterian system on the ruins of Tulchan Episcopacy, which, always infirm, was by the time of Melville's return to St. Andrews falling to pieces. To touch on this is beside our purpose. His public exertions for his Church must have filled his mind more than his academic labours. In civil and ecclesiastical politics alike, Melville was, as Mr. Hill Burton says, more of a leveller than Knox. There was in him the "fiery fanaticism of the French Huguenots, and the stern classical republicanism of Buchanan, with a dash of the Puritanism then rising in England." When King James was trying to infuse into the stern Presbyterianism of which Melville was the champion a little beauty and Catholic observance, more than once the king and the principal came into severe collision. On these occasions, Melville treated the young king with the same unceremonious rudeness which Knox had shown towards his mother. In 1596, when the king attended divine service in the town church of St. Andrews, the preacher expressed some sentiments of which the king disapproved. He interrupted the preacher and ordered him to desist. "Indignant at this interference, Melville rose and sharply rebuked the king;" and censured the commissioners of the Church for sitting by in silence.

Again, there is the famous scene at Falkland Palace. Thither, in September 1590, four ministers were sent by the General Assembly's Commissioners from Cupar, to remonstrate with the king against the return of the Papist lords, and other changes which he was favouring. James Melville, who was one of the four deputies, narrates the story in his own quaint way: "We came to Falkland, where we found the king very quiet." The others made James their spokesman, alleging that "he could propose the matter in a mild and smooth manner, whilk the king liked best." James accordingly told the king that "to watch for the weal of the kirk in sa dangerous a time, they had convened at Cupar. At the whilk words the king interrupts me, and crabbedly quarrels our meeting, alleging it was without warrant and seditious. To the whilk I beginning to reply in my manner, Mr. Andro doucht nocht abyd it; but brak off upon the king in so zealous, powerful, and unresistible a manner, that, howbeit the king used his authority in maist crabbit and coleric manner, yet Mr. Andro bore him down and uttered the commission as from the mighty God, calling the king God's silly vassal, and, taking him by the sleeve," preached him such a sermon as perhaps never king before or since heard from a subject. The Stuarts may have had many faults, but it can hardly be said to be one of them that they did not greatly love such candid counsellors as Knox, Buchanan, and Andrew Melville. The king could not overpower Melville by force, but when he passed to the English throne he circumvented him by stratagem. He summoned Andrew and some other ministers to London, as it were on public business. When Andrew was there he committed himself by writing a Latin epigram bitterly satirising one of the Church of England services which he had witnessed. For this he was thrown into the Tower, and on being released he was sent into exile, whence he returned no more to St. Mary's. Whatever we may think of Melville's views, ecclesiastical or political, his scholarship and vigour of mind are undeniable. He gave a great impetus to learning and literature not only in St. Andrews University, but throughout Scotland—an impetus which would have been far greater had not the public turmoils of the succeeding century thwarted it. In words that have been applied to him, Melville was "master of a great wit, a wit full of knots and clenches, a wit sharp and satirical, exceeded by none of his countrymen." But his mind was too keen and caustic to be restricted to literature. He was born to be a statesman and ruler of men. A Scottish University, indeed Scotland itself, was too small and narrow a field for him. Burton truly says he was cast in the same mould as Thomas à Becket, or Pope Hildebrand; and Europe, not Scotland, would have been the fitting arena for his marvellous energy.

It would occupy not one paper, but a dozen, were I to go on and describe the other great men who in the seventeenth century followed Melville in the University of St. Andrews. Time would fail me to tell of Archbishop Spottiswoode; of Alexander Henderson, the hero of the Covenant; of Samuel Rutherfurd; of "My Lord Archbishop, His Grace, James Sharp;" each of whom in their own time and way did their best to shape the

University to their peculiar Church views and ends. If commissions, visitations, and rules strictly laid down could have made the University prosper, these men would have done it. But the political turmoil throughout the whole seventeenth century made all efforts of this kind abortive. As one example out of many, take this: Barron, the principal of St. Salvator's, and a regent named Gleg, had approved of the engagement which would have confined the Covenant to Scotland, and did not wish to force it upon England. For this they both were tried and suspended from their offices by a covenanting commission in 1649; no doubt with Rutherfurd's approval, if it was not at his instance.

But if the strife of tongues and the clash of arms that sounded through Scotland in the whole of the seventeenth century left no room for deep study and ripe scholarship, they reared in St. Andrews alone a race of valiant heroes and scholars, who could wield the sword and the pen with equal ease.

Before the Reformation St. Andrews had produced the poets Gawin Douglas, William Dunbar, and Sir David Lindsay; at the time of the Reformation the Admirable Crichton. Early in the seventeenth century James Graham, Marquis of Montrose, studied at St. Salvator's, while a few years before, his rival and adversary Archibald

Campbell — known as Gillespie Gruamach — the Marquis of Argyll, had been a student in St. Leonard's. When these two had taken their sides and played their parts in their country's history, Argyll caused the head of Montrose to be fixed on the Tolbooth of Edinburgh, from which it was taken down only to be replaced by his own. Of the relics still preserved in St. Salvator's College there is none, not even excepting Bishop Kennedy's mace, on which one looks with so much pride as on the silver Archery medal, bearing as its inscription the student name, James Graham, 'Earl of Montrose. Over-against it is the medal of his rival, then Lord Lorne. Other names known to Scottish history are among those medals—Robertson of Struan, the Jacobite chief and poet, who while still a student was present at Killiecrankie; in his mature manhood fought at Sheriffmuir; and in his extreme age met Prince Charles Edward, as he crossed Corryarrick, and plighted to him his fealty, though he could no longer march with him to battle. There, too, is the name of that Marquis of Tullibardine, who as an aged exile unfurled the Prince's standard when the clans in the Forty-five mustered at Glenfinnan. Not among the medals, but one of our students in the middle of the seventeenth century was John Graham of Claverhouse, Viscount Dundee. What thoughts must it have stirred in the hearts of these young cavaliers, to feel themselves students in the university which sheltered Buchanan, Melville, and Rutherfurd, and from which these men had taught doctrines that led to regicide.

That University must have been full of life, which within one century could show on one side such men as Knox, Buchanan, Melville, Alexander Henderson, and Rutherfurd; and over-against them Spottiswoode, Montrose, Struan, Claverhouse, and Tullibardine. Nor must we forget among our students in the sixteenth and seventeenth centuries the more peaceful names, Napier of Merchiston, the inventor of logarithms, and Sir George Mackenzie, lawyer and statesman, founder of the Advocates' Library.

It may be easily imagined that something of prestige was lost by the University at the Reformation, when the old hierarchy went down, and St. Andrews ceased to be the seat of the primacy. This was partially restored during the two periods of Episcopacy, when the city again became for a time the seat of a milder primacy, and the resident archbishop was the Chancellor of the University. With the suppression of Episcopacy and the Revolution of 1688, St. Andrews and its university lost whatever dignity it had derived from its connection with the primacy. The Government of William and Mary appointed, in 1690, a commission which visited St. Andrews with power to purge out and remove all principals, professors, regents, and masters who would not take the oath of allegiance, and submit to the new church-government. I have not been able to find details as to how many of the St. Andrews teachers were then removed, but it is asserted that a tolerably clean sweep was made in all the three colleges. It is recorded that the Earl of Crawford, the head of the commission, treated with great rudeness the aged head of St. Leonard's, James Wemyss, who was forced to resign.

In 1697 an attempt was made to remove the University to Perth, and several of the professors—it is said from motives of self-interest—were urgent for the removal, but the attempt came to nought.

The eighteenth century was a torpid period in most universities, not in Scotland only, but in England also. Oxford and Cambridge continued to drag on a drowsy routine, if we may accept as true the description given of them by Wordsworth and Southey, in the last decade of last century. This drowsiness would seem to have been shared to the full by St. Andrews, which had been exhausted by a century and a half of discord and ever-recurring revolutions. Over all Scotland the loss of her Parliament caused a deep depression, and it was not till the very end of the eighteenth century that the national spirit began to revive. Perhaps no Scottish city suffered more from this depression than St. Andrews did. It had suddenly passed from being the centre of all the stir of ecclesiastical life, to become a remote fishing village, relieved only by a few ruins and an ancient university. But political zeal was not extinct among the students. In "the Fifteen," or Mar's Rebellion, we find certain students of St. Leonard's accused of forcing the keys of the church and steeple of their college from the porter's wife, and ringing the bells on the day when King James was proclaimed. The next commission, which sat in 1718, inquired into this, and ordered that all regents or students who were found guilty of disaffection to King George should be dismissed from the University.

In the "Forty-five," some who had formerly been students at St. Andrews, such as the aged Struan and Tullibardine, were active on the Prince's side. There seems to have been at first no stir within the University, but when Cumberland was returning home from the atrocities of Culloden, the University, I blush to say, sent a deputation to congratulate him on his victory, and inviting him to become their Chancellor. This he did, and we can number the cruel duke among our Chancellors.

In the year that followed Culloden (1747) a grave event in the history of the University took place. This was the union, by Act of Parliament, of the two Colleges of St. Salvator and St. Leonard. The reason for this is said to have been that the revenue of the former college and the buildings of the latter had become dilapidated. By this union the one got better incomes for the professors, the other better buildings for its lecture-rooms and for the residence of the bursars. It may have been necessary, though it is to be regretted that it should have been so. But it was not necessary that they should have merged our two fine old mediæval names in the mean modern appellation of the United College.

When Dr. Johnson paid his famous visit to this place in 1773 two sights filled him with indignation and sorrow. The first was the ruins of the Cathedral; the second, the desolate remains of St. Leonard's College. His anathemas on the "ruffians of the Reformation" all will remember. Boswell asked where John Knox was buried. Johnson burst out, "I hope in the highway. I have been looking at his reformations." This is what he says of St. Leonard's:—

"The dissolution of St. Leonard's was doubtless necessary; but of that necessity there is reason to complain. It is surely not without just reproach that a nation of which the commerce is hourly extending, and the wealth increasing, denies any participation of its prosperity to its literary societies; and while its merchants or its nobles are raising palaces, suffers its universities to moulder into dust."

It is more than a hundred years since these words were written. They continue as true now as then, and as unheeded. The professors of the old College received and entertained the great English literary autocrat respectfully enough. But though he acknowledged that he was entertained "with all the elegance of lettered hospitality," it could not relieve the load of his depression at the sights he saw.

As we look over the lists of the professors during the latter half of last century and the beginning of this, the frequent recurrence of the same family names suggests that nepotism must have been then dominant, and that the professors had learnt the example of their predecessors the old Culdees, who bequeathed to their children the church revenues they themselves held. Yet even during that time neither the old College nor St. Mary's were unprolific in remarkable men. Of St. Andrews students, laymen who were educated here during last century, I find Robert Fergusson, the Scottish poet, the predecessor, and in many respects the model, of Burns, whose poems are coloured with allusions to student life in St. Andrews; Dr. Adam Ferguson, author of the *History of the Roman Republic;* David Gregory, Professor of Mathematics; John Playfair, Professor of Physics in Edinburgh, and one of the first fathers of geological science; Henry Erskine, the famous wit, the ornament of the Scottish Bar; and his brother, the Lord Chancellor Erskine.

It continued to be the custom for the bursars on the foundation to live within the walls of St. Salvator's down till 1820. The change is said to have been made because the old rooms for bursars had become antiquated and ruinous. Yet Boswell had remarked, fifty years before, "We looked at St. Salvator's; the rooms for students seemed very commodious." But besides the few who were on the foundation the unendowed students who formed the majority had for long lived where they chose. It was customary for the more wealthy students to board in the houses of the professors. Among those who thus boarded were many sons of the old noble families, and of the landed gentry, who continued to frequent St. Andrews from the earliest time down till about the year 1830, when the fashion of sending the young Scottish aristocracy to English schools and universities set in. Before that change this University contained among its students representatives of every social grade, from the highest to the lowliest, all gathered in the same class-rooms, and taught by the same professors. You have only to look over the silver Archery medals still preserved, and to note the names of the winners, in order to see how largely the old historic houses were represented. This continued to be the case till the end of the third decade of this century. That this state of things should pass away we may regret as a social loss, but our regrets cannot stop the action of deeply rooted social causes. The change did not come from any deterioration of the professorial staff. Indeed, this century saw a marked improvement in this respect. Not to mention Professors of Divinity, three names among the Professors of Arts stand out conspicuously. These are—first, Dr. John Hunter, who for sixty years taught from the Chair of Humanity. He was known all over Scotland for the accuracy and width of his classical knowledge, and for his power as a teacher. By his instinctive linguistic genius he anticipated many of the results which comparative philology has since made good. There was Dr. Thomas Chalmers, for some time Professor of Moral Philosophy in the United College, who, by his eloquence rather than by deep philosophy, by the width and warmth of his human sympathies rather than by subtlety or learning, did so much to quicken moral and spiritual life not only in this University but throughout Scotland. His successor, next but one in the same chair, Professor James Ferrier, if he had not the moral and practical force of Chalmers, was strong where Chalmers was weak. No Scotsman in this century has done more for metaphysical philosophy. Revolting from the traditional Scotch Psychology, he grappled with questions which it had never dreamt of, and set the idealistic philosophy on a line along which it still is travelling. And then he clothed his subtle speculations in a style that, for lucidity and incisiveness, recalled the charm of David Hume's. Nor must I omit to mention my two immediate predecessors, Sir David Brewster and Principal James Forbes, each, in his own distinct line, a pioneer and a leader in the advance of scientific research. I confine myself to the work of professors who have passed from us. Of the work done by some still living, though of that a good account could be given, this is not the time to speak.

Of former students of St. Andrews who, in public life, were eminent during the middle of this century, I can myself remember three notable men, all living at the same time—Dr. Chalmers, then leader of the ecclesiastical polity of Scotland; Duncan M'Neill, Lord Colonsay, Lord President of the Court of Session of Scotland; John Campbell, Lord Stratheden, Lord Chancellor of England. These three old St. Andrews students were contemporaries, and stood about the same time, each at the head of their respective societies. Nor are our younger men likely to let that succession fail. At this moment one could name several former students of St. Andrews who are among the most eminent ministers, preachers, and leaders in the Church of Scotland; others, but a few years since students or professors in St. Andrews, who are now eminent as professors in the other three Scottish Universities; two, formerly students of St. Andrews, now professors in Cambridge—one of them the originator and organiser of the whole system of university extension, and of affiliated colleges, which now ramifies throughout England; and at Oxford four, whom I can remember students in the United College, as but yesterday, still young men, who, after each obtaining the highest University honours at Oxford, are now fellows or tutors, doing eminent work as teachers, each in a separate college.

These facts are stated, not, I trust, in any spirit of boasting, but as sober truth, which ought to be known and considered when men discuss the public utility of maintaining a small university. If men would measure the worth of a seat of education, not by counting heads, but by estimating the quality of the work done in it, and of the men who are trained by it, then St. Andrews has nothing to fear from the most searching scrutiny.

As to the small number of students in St. Andrews, compared with the crowds who attend Edinburgh and Glasgow University, if that is to condemn it now, it ought to have condemned it equally during any part of its past existence. The numbers who attended it before the Reformation cannot be ascertained. But take each century since the Reformation, and it has been computed that there were in round numbers an average of 180 students during each session of the seventeenth century, of 120 during the eighteenth, and of 160 during the present century. During the last few years there has been a decided tendency to an increase of numbers. Last session there were 187, this session there are 192 students. I assert, therefore, that no argument from paucity of numbers can be brought against St.

Andrews which would not have been equally valid at any time during the last 300 years. I shall not say one word in disparagement of the larger Universities; nor shall I meddle with the controversy as to the merits of large or small professorial classes. That subject has been what newspaper editors call "thrashed out." This only I will say: the system of classes containing from 200 to 300 students has not been proved to be so altogether faultless that it ought to crush out a system where the classes consist of only from 30 to 50 students. If classes in which the students are counted by hundreds have some advantages, those in which they are counted by tens have their own compensations, which are obvious. These are—more intimate knowledge on the part of the professor of the ability and work of each individual student, and the greater amount of personal instruction which each student receives. The classes in St. Andrews are, both in numbers and in mode of instruction, more like those which meet in the lecture-rooms of tutors and professors in Oxford and Cambridge. The charge of fewness of numbers is never brought against these—why should it be made so much of here? were it not that in Scotland educational efficiency has got to be estimated by quantity rather than by quality. Our comparative smallness of numbers gives us the opportunity, which I believe is not neglected, of bringing up the collective students to a higher average of attainment than we could do were the classes quadrupled in numbers.

Add to this, in a small, retired city like ours, in which the University is the chief centre of interest, academic life, with all its associations, is much more vivid and intense than it can be in large and populous towns, where the students are absorbed among the surrounding population. If that academic life is healthy and high-toned, there are few finer incentives to a young man's progress. And from this academic life, spent in such a situation as this, and girt round with such associations, it has come that few students anywhere bear to their university so deep and life-long affection as those of St. Andrews have always borne.

And now let my closing words be those of the same illustrious friend of St. Andrews with whose saying I opened my paper :—

"This secluded sanctuary of ancient wisdom, with the foam-flakes of the northern ocean driving through its streets, with the skeleton of its antique magnificence lifting up its gaunt arms into the sky, still carries on the tradition of its first beginnings. Two voices sound through it. "One is of the sea, one of the Cathedral—each a mighty voice;" two inner corresponding voices also, which in any institution that has endured and deserves to endure, must be heard in unison— the voice of a potent past, and the voice of an invigorating future.—It may still be said of the local genius of St. Andrews, that through all the manifold changes of the Scottish Church —Culdee, Catholic, Protestant, Episcopalian, Presbyterian— its spiritual identity has never been altogether broken, its historical grandeur never wholly forfeited."

## VI.—THE EARLY POETRY OF SCOTLAND.[1]

IF the traveller on Dee-side wishes to reach the sources of the river Dee, he journeys westward along its banks for miles, until he has reached a spot where the beaten road is lost in the open moor, and the river divides itself into two branches. One of these comes leisurely from the western glens, the other descends headlong from the northern fastnesses and the Cairngorm mountains.

The western stream, rising far off in Gaick Forest, flows eastward through mossy glens, which tinge its waters with that deep yet clear amber so beautiful and so characteristic of Highland rivers. The northern stream, born in the deep gorge or hill pass, cloven between Braeriach and Ben Muic Dhui, springs up in great granite basins known as "the Wells of Dee," and after lashing down for miles over a clean bed of grey granite boulders, pours into the western stream a flood of water of the purest crystalline green. For many miles after

[1] [A Lecture delivered in the Museum, Oxford, on Tuesday, 4th June 1878.]

their junction, the two currents flow side by side unblended—the northern current retaining untarnished its clear transparent crystal, the western one as distinctly its deep amber brown. The river Dee, which their meeting makes, has cleared Mar Forest, and reached the pine woods of Invercauld, before the two currents blend into one indistinguishable stream.

These two distinct and unmingling currents are an apt image of the character and history of Scotland's poetry. The amber-coloured stream typifies the literary poetry, the production of educated men, flowing tinged with the culture of other lands, to which it was indebted for its form, its metre, and in some measure for its language and its sentiments. The pure crystal current represents the home-born popular poetry, which springs out of the hearts and habits of the country people, breathes of native manners, utters itself in the vernacular language and in home-spun melodies. It is in this last that the inner spirit of Scotland found vent; this is her peculiar heritage of song; a heritage which, after it had lived on for centuries in the hearts and by the firesides of the people, at last flowered forth into bright, consummate expression in the two great national poets, Robert Burns and Walter Scott.

Before, however, dwelling on this last, the most truly national poetry of Scotland, a word must be said on the early literary or learned poems which have come down to us.

"The Romance of Sir Tristram," if Thomas the Rhymer was indeed its author, the early chronicles —or epics, shall I call them ?—of Barbour's Bruce, and of Blind Harry's Wallace, I for the present pass by, and come to the earliest poems in Scotland which betoken the presence of literary art.

When the light of the Renaissance, after illuminating the Continent and England, at last smote our bleak northern shores, it was by awakening a new style of poetry that it first manifested itself. And it was through a royal poet that this light first visited Scotland. It fell on this wise.

James Stuart, the first of that name, when a boy of eleven years, was by his father sent abroad for safety, to be educated at the Court of France. But the vessel that bore him was treacherously captured on the high seas by an English squadron, during time of peace, and the boy prince was thrown into the Tower, and detained a captive in England for more than eighteen years. But Henry IV. and Henry V., though they kept him so long a prisoner, repaid the wrong by giving him the best education the age and country could provide. And it was well bestowed, for James was by nature rarely gifted, both in body and mind. He soon became an accomplished athlete, a scholar versed in all then known literature, in grammar, in oratory, in Latin and English poetry, in jurisprudence and philosophy. A musician of a high order, he played on eight different instruments, and invented, it is said, a new kind of music, plaintive and melancholy, and quite original. Some suppose that his music still survives in some of the oldest Scottish melodies. In his thirtieth year, James was restored to Scotland, with his English queen. His long captivity of eighteen years he had soothed with poetry, for, as one old writer says, he was "ane natural and born poet;" in the words of another, he "seemed rather born to letters than instructed."[1]

He was the first, and for long the most gifted, poet on whom the mantle of the great father of English poetry descended. It is a remarkable fact that the influence of Chaucer seems to have been deflected by the example of James from England to Scotland, for that influence is much more apparent in Scotland than it was in England for two centuries after the death of Chaucer. The poem by which James is chiefly known is "The King's Quair." In it the young prince describes the circumstances of his capture and imprisonment, and the lighting up of his gloom by the vision of Lady Joanna Beaufort as she walked in a garden under his prison window at Windsor. The king in his

---

[1] Chaucer died in 1400; James was taken captive in 1405-6. It was thus only five years after Chaucer's death that our young Scottish prince passed within the influence of his genius.

poem describes the history of his love with a purity and a delicate grace quite peculiar in that age. A good modern critic has said of "The King's Quair" that it contains "natural description more varied, colour more vivid, a modern self-reflection and a touch of spiritual quality," which are not found even in Chaucer himself. But though this may be true, the whole cast of the poem, the style, versification, and language, are distinctly Chaucerian, and through their employment by this gifted king they became for generations the accepted model of all polished poetry in Scotland.

The influence of Chaucer, which first reached Scotland through King James, was that of his early period, while he (Chaucer) was still under the power of the French and Italian Renaissance, and fashioning his poetry more or less on foreign models. Allegory then plays a conspicuous part, and this in the Scottish followers became rampant. It is partly to this as well as to their archaic diction that they have fallen so much out of our modern reckoning. There is little in them of that realism, that direct portraiture of human character, unalloyed by allegory, which forms the chief charm of the Canterbury Tales.

The style of poetry first introduced to Scotland by The King's Quair was carried on by a long succession of poets, of whom the most illustrious names were—

## THE EARLY POETRY OF SCOTLAND. 207

William Dunbar (born 1460[1]; died 1520). Gawin or Gavin Douglas (born 1474; died 1522). Sir David Lindsay (born 1490; died 1555).[2]

When these and their style disappeared, a new influence arose in William Drummond of Hawthornden (born 1585; died 1649), the only literary or polished poet of any mark who adorned Scotland in the seventeenth century. Taken together, they may be regarded as representative of the learned or educated poets of early Scotland, standing out of a great host of lesser men whom I need not enumerate.

William Dunbar, who lived in the reigns of the fourth and the fifth James, has been styled by Sir Walter "the darling of the Scottish Muses," "the Scottish Chaucer." This is perhaps rather too high praise, but he was a man of wonderful and varied powers. Educated in St. Salvator's College, St. Andrews, he was at first a Franciscan friar, but he soon began to think shame of wandering about preaching and living on the alms of the pious. It involved him, he said, in flattery and falsehood, so he abandoned this trade and became a hanger-on about the Court of the Jameses. From these monarchs he received a small pension, but never a benefice, though in many a line he hinted his desire for it. The kings, it is said, found him too pleasant a companion to part with him.

[1] [Other date, 1450.]     [2] [Other date, 1557.]

His poems are very various in style and subject, and show great versatility of power. In his graver poems he made Chaucer his model, and acknowledged, as James I. had done before him, that he drew his light from his English master.

> "O reverend Chaucer ! rose of rhetors all,
> As in our tongue the flower imperial
> That rose in Britain ever . . .
> Wast thou not of our English all the light,
> Surmounting every tongue terrestrial
> As far as Maye's morrow does midnight ?"

"Our English" expresses faithfully Dunbar's aim. Two of his chief poems, "The Thistle and the Rose" and "The Golden Terge," are framed entirely on Chaucer.

The former is an allegory to celebrate the Union of the Royal Houses of England and Scotland by the betrothal of James IV. to Margaret Tudor. The latter is also an allegory showing how ineffectual is the Shield of Reason against the Shafts of Cupid.

In the former of these two poems there are rich and glowing description of nature, sage advice, and skilful compliments to the royal lovers. His grave poems are full of Chaucerian language, of freshly-coined Latin words, and of that French-English which still lingered. But they were never popular in Scotland, because they were never understood. His satires and other more popular pieces were more in the vernacular language and in the popular vein.

Such is his "Dance of the Seven Deadly Sins," which is a very powerful piece. His poems addressed to the people rather than to the learned, display a force of satire, a rich, if often coarse humour, a vivid description both of nature and human character, such as Scotland never saw again till Burns appeared.

In pathos Dunbar was not a master, yet one of his later poems, the well-known "Lament for the Makars" (poets), shows not a few touches of tenderness. If they were all true poets whom Dunbar there enumerates, Scotland in that age must have been more rich in poets than she has ever been since. After his long catalogue of those who have disappeared before him, he thus concludes :—

> " Since he (death) has all my brethren ta'en,
> He will nocht let me live alane:
> On force, I must his next prey be ;
> Timor Mortis conturbat me."

If Dunbar forfeited popularity by the use of a style and language "not understanded of the people," not so the good bishop of Dunkeld, Gawin Douglas. In his famous translation of Virgil, "the earliest British translation of any Latin poet," he employed the vernacular Scotch of his own time, the Scotch as it was spoken not merely by unlettered people, but by the nobles and the kings at Court.

To this hour that translation remains the purest

well of the Scottish dialect undefiled that exists, the poems of Burns not excepted. For philologists, if not for general readers, that work is still well worth studying. A great Anglo-Saxon scholar of the seventeenth century said that he learned more Saxon by the perusal of Douglas's Virgil than by that of all the old English he could find, poetry or prose, because it was nearer the Saxon and farther from the Norman.[1]

This learned ecclesiastic was the only clerk of an unlettered but warlike race. You all remember Scott's lines—

> "Thanks to St. Bothan, son of mine,
> Save Gawain, ne'er could pen a line."

So Sir Walter makes Archibald Bell-the-cat, Earl of Angus, speak to Marmion in his stronghold of Tantallon. Gawin was Provost of St. Giles, Edinburgh, when he undertook his famous translation. He completed it in eighteen months, he tells us, just

---

[1] See Aytoun, *Ballads of Scotland*, vol. i., lxiv. and lxx., and Small's *Douglas*, i. p. clxii. But the former authority errs in supposing the Scottish language to be so purely Saxon. Later investigations have shown that it contains a very large Scandinavian infusion, and that this is the element that most distinguishes it from the northern Anglo-Saxon. This Scandinavian element, no doubt, Douglas used. He also introduced a number of words straight from the French, besides a considerable sprinkling of Chaucerian terms and usages; for instance, the y prefix to the past participle —"y-back" for the northern "baken," "y-clois" for "closit." This is the more curious as Douglas professes to be "keepand na Soudroun but our awin langage;" which no doubt he did, on the whole, far more than the other early Scottish poets.

two months before the Battle of Flodden, in which so many of his kinsmen fell. That disastrous battle made gaps in the episcopate not less than in the baronage, and Gawin then entered on the scramble for bishoprics, and got immersed in the troubled politics of the time, which at last drove him an exile to the Court of Henry VIII. There he made the acquaintance of Erasmus, but he died soon after his exile began, and was laid in the Savoy Chapel, where the plate that marked his grave was discovered a few years ago.

His later life was too troubled and stormy to give the world any more poetry, translated or original. The translation of Virgil is in the heroic couplet. Vigorous and racy it is, though perhaps in a style more homely than beseems the stately march of Virgil's lines, but his aim was to make his countrymen familiar with his favourite classic. Many of the passages are rendered with great spirit. The death of Priam, the last speech and death of Dido, and the coming of Æneas and the Sibyl to the Elysian fields, have been especially remarked. To each book of his translation Douglas has prefixed a prologue, and these form so many original poems. They discuss Virgil, the heathen religion, the Christian doctrine, as well as describe nature as he saw it before his eyes. The prologue to the seventh book is a vigorous and realistic description of winter. Another prologue describes May-time; another, a summer evening in June. These poems ought to earn for their author a high place among the descriptive poets of his country. But, alas! they are hidden under such a crust of archaic diction, that no one but the antiquary and the philologer now approaches them. To these, if to no others, they are a very treasure-house of old language and idioms. But even judged as a literary production, if it were not for its antique garb, it may be doubted whether any translation of Virgil that England has seen could equal that of Gawin Douglas. The Earl of Surrey—the first introducer of English blank verse—must have estimated it highly; for in the translation which he made of the second and fourth books of the *Æneid*, he in several places copied, almost word for word, the bishop's version.

So competent a critic as the late Professor Aytoun held Gawin Douglas to be the prince of the early and pure Scottish poets.

Sir David Lindsay of the Mount was more a man of the world and a reformer than an imaginative poet. Educated at St. Andrews along with Cardinal Beaton (their names may still be seen together in the roll of students at the opening of the sixteenth century), he lived to see the wild murder of the cardinal in his sea-tower at St. Andrews; to write a poem on his death, called "The Tragedie of the Cardinal," and in a more homely rhyme to say—

> "As for the Cardinal, I grant
> He was the man we weil might want—
> God will forgive it soon ;
> But of a truth, the sooth to say,
> Although the loon be weil away,
> The fact was foully done."

Though Lindsay had no hand in that murder of his old college companion, yet his works must have done much to help forward that rising spirit of discontent with the ancient Church of which that murder was the most startling symptom. Having lived from his youth about the Court, and having been much employed in public affairs, he had seen all the corruption that was among the courtiers, among the nobles, and above all among the clergy. His poems are chiefly occupied with giving vigorous expression to his indignation at the sight of these things. You all remember Sir Walter Scott's description of him in *Marmion* :—

> "He was a man of middle age ;
> In aspect manly, grave and sage,
> As on King's errand come ;
> But in the glances of his eye
> A penetrating, keen, and sly
> Expression found its home ;
> The flash of that satiric rage,
> Which, bursting on the early stage,
> Branded the vices of the age,
> And broke the keys of Rome."

His longest and best-known poem is a play called "Ane Satire of the Three Estates." It is something in the style of the old Moralities ; that is, abstract qualities, virtues or vices, are introduced, such as Rex Humanitas, Diligence, Chastity, and Flattery (*alias* Devotion), Falset, *i.e.* Falsehood (*alias* Sapience), Deceit (*alias* Discretion). These are mingled with real persons, the parson, the abbot, the prioress, the doctor. Under the guise of these abstractions much knowledge of life and character lies hid. The humour is broad, though sometimes coarse, and the vices of all, especially the clergy, are lashed with no sparing hand. There is, I fear, too good evidence that Lindsay's clerical pictures are not overdrawn, but literal transcripts from his time.

This play was acted before James v. and his Court in Linlithgow, and afterwards in other towns of Scotland. Along with his other works it did much to hasten on the Reformation, though he did not live to see that great change completed; so that it has been well said that Lindsay stood to John Knox in much the same relation as Langland, author of *Piers Plowman*, did to Wycliffe.

Tried by range or fineness of imagination, Lindsay cannot be called a great poet. Strong understanding, straightforward if not refined moral purpose, indignation at the abuses of his time, humour broad and telling, often coarse, biting satire, vivid delineation of character, all these expressed in an abundant flow of homely and vigorous verse—these are his chief characteristics. They made him a conspicuous figure in the history of that transition time, and did much to help forward the tide of popular change that was then strongly flowing in Scotland. His works contain more to interest the student of history, manners, and politics, than to attract the lover of imaginative poetry. With Lindsay that wave of Scottish poetry which derived its first impulse from Chaucer may be said to have spent itself.

Drummond, who came a century later, belonged entirely to an English school of another era. I cannot stay to dwell on his work, but must only notice that the polished or literary poetry of Scotland ceased with Drummond, to reappear, after more than a century, in the poet of *The Seasons*, who, though Scotch by birthplace, is in most other respects entirely English.

The chief distinctive notes of the line of poets I have been reviewing are:

1. Minute realistic description of nature, so profuse in detail as rather to approach the inventory style.

2. Broad humour and wit often running into rollicking and coarseness, or losing itself in satire.

3. Intense nationality and individualism. This last a peculiarity which, if we may trust our neighbours, has not yet entirely disappeared from the nature of the Scot. It is not to be wondered at when we remember the fiery ordeal which the country had to pass through, when, for two cen-

turies, it fought at hand-grips with "our auld enemies of England" for its very existence.

The first great current of poetry of which I have been speaking, which came into Scotland coloured with hues brought from the lands of the Renaissance, was, as we have seen, introduced by one of the earliest and by far the most accomplished of the Stuart kings. During the two stormy centuries when this stream lent its influence to brighten and civilise the Scottish people, it was fostered and encouraged mainly by the same kingly race. Each one of the poets I have named, as well as many another poet and minstrel whom I have not named, found shelter and encouragement in the sunshine of the Court of Holyrood. And the poetic genius that was in the kings themselves made some of the best contributions to the national poetry.

When the Stuart kings quitted Holyrood for Whitehall, literature at once almost disappeared from the northern land, and it was more than a century and a half before it returned. The whole of the seventeenth century is almost a blank in Scotland as far as the finer literature is concerned. From George Buchanan till David Hume, as Lockhart has remarked, no name of first-rate mark in scholarship, poetry, or literature, appeared in Scotland. The tide of song may have flowed on obscurely among the people, but it was unheeded till it found vent through Ramsay and Fergusson in the first half of the eighteenth century, and afterwards rose to full tide in Burns and Scott.

Perhaps no royal house in Europe, in proportion to their opportunities, did more to foster literature and all the fine arts than the Scottish Stuarts. This genuine love and patronage of literature might alone plead for their memories against the obloquy which most modern literary men have conspired to heap upon them. But besides this they possessed, as a race, a personal attractiveness, a gracious, romantic, and generous character which, whatever faults they may have had, and however these may have been exaggerated and emphasised by writers of the present day, endeared them to all Scottish hearts, as neither Plantagenets nor Tudors in England, or Bourbons in France, ever were endeared. It was no condescending patronage they bestowed. While maintaining their kingly dignity, they mingled among their people with a grace and ease peculiar to themselves, shared in their amusements, and afterwards turned to poetry the native sights and manners. Hence it has come that every genuine Scot who has not been corrupted by the invectives of English historians has a warm heart to the Stuarts. Burns, half Jacobin as he was, had still a corner in his heart for the Jacobite feeling. And as for Sir Walter, we all know what his sentiments were, how when in his declining health he visited Rome for the first time, the one spot he first sought, over which he latest lingered, was the tombs of the exiled Stuarts in St. Peter's.

I am quite aware that it was not the best side of the Stuarts which England saw, that in some sense they were strangers there. It is true, they could not for their lives learn to appreciate that modern nondescript thing called constitutionalism. But when writers count up their errors, what they call their iniquities, few have remembered to reckon to their credit the fidelity with which they clung to their faith, amid exile and adversity. A change of faith, or even a semblance of it, would have sufficed to restore to them their throne. I heartily wish they could have from conviction and conscience become Protestant. But they could not; and so they refused to sell their faith for a crown—a temptation which, I believe, few other royal houses have been able to resist.

It is now time to turn to that other, greater, more purely poetic current of Scottish song, which I have spoken of as the popular poetry. Popular it was in every sense of the word, the creation of the common people, not of the few or the learned class, breathing the spirit of the people, describing their manners and customs, recording the incidents which most moved their hearts, embalming their emotions of every kind, their sentiments on all that most interested them. And it spoke to the heart of the people as no learned poetry could do, was their literature in a day when books were few or none, was the recreation alike of baron's hall and of peasant's fireside, and was really preserved in the memory of the people, till a time came when the printing-press laid hold of it, and made it a fixed, though, I fear, a less cherished possession.

Scotland's popular poetry naturally falls into three separate kinds or styles. 1. There were, first, poems descriptive of the manners and customs of the peasantry. 2. There were the ballads, heroic or historical—simple and affecting narratives of memorable events,

"Old, unhappy, far-off things,
And battles long ago;"

or ballads founded on the popular superstitions, or lamentations for some personal sorrow. 3. There were the regular songs, not narratives, but short lyrics, embodying some one sentiment, giving impassioned expression to some feeling of love or sorrow or pity, such as naturally finds vent in song.

A few words on each of these.

I. The poems describing rustic manners seem to date from a very early time. Pictorial or didactic, they convey vivid pictures of the manners of past ages, whether as seen in rural life, in general society, or among the clergy. And here is seen a strong characteristic of the Scottish peasantry, that, whether for good report or evil, in a friendly or in a censorious spirit, they can never for long keep their thoughts off the clergy. This seems to have been a marked feature of Scots, not less in Roman Catholic times than it has always been under the Presbyterian *régime*.

The two earliest extant poems of this kind, "Christ's Kirk of the Grene" and "Peblis to the Play," are attributed, with fair probability, but not with absolute certainty, to James I. Some have questioned whether the graceful and refined author of "The King's Quair" could have condescended to such broad humour, and often coarse expressions, as are found in these poems. But it is known that he, like most of his descendants, mingled very freely among his subjects, and took much interest in their frolics and amusements. The king, or whoever the author was, had witnessed a rural holiday at some village in Aberdeenshire, it is supposed, and described what he there saw of the customs of the peasantry in a poem full of sprightliness and humour, which in many parts is too plain speaking for modern recital. The poem must have been well known in England in Pope's time, for he says—

"One likes no language but the Faery Queen,
A Scot will fight for Christ's Kirk o' the Green."

It is in an easy lyric stanza. This is the opening one, somewhat modernised :—

"Was ne'er in Scotland heard or seen
Sic dancing nor deray,
Nouther at Falkland on the Grene,
Nor Peblis at the Play;

> As was of wooers, as I ween,
> At Christ's Kirk on a day,
> There came our Kitties, washen clean,
> In their new kirtles o' grey
>     Full gay,
> At Christ's Kirk o' the Grene that day."

Another poem of the same order, describing a similar scene, only at the town of Peebles on the Tweed, is also attributed to James I., but with the same uncertainty. The language, metre (an unusual one), and humour of both poems are strikingly alike; so much so that they must either have come from the same hand, or one writer must have, on set purpose, imitated the other.

Here is a stanza from "Peblis to the Play," somewhat divested of its antique garb:—

> "Than they come to the townis end
> Withouten more delay,
> He before, and she before,
> To see wha was maist gay:
> All that lookit them upon
> Leuch fast at their array:
> Some said they were mercat folk,
> Some said the queen of May
>     Was come,
> Of Peblis to the Play."

Both poems are full of sympathy with country folk and their frolics, both show a fine descriptive power, and that rare lyric flow that clearly marks the true singer. Many coarse jokes are plainly spoken in them; but that seems almost the necessary concomitant of all realistic description in early times. If these poems were the composition of James I., nothing could better show how intimately he must have associated with his subjects, and what a true eye he had for the picturesque and the human.

His descendant, James V., known as the king of the poor or of the commons, is said to have wandered about the country in disguise, conversing freely with all he met, often passing the night under the peasant's roof or by the farmer's fire-side, and there finding for himself strange adventures. In two poems generally attributed to him, "The Gaberlunzie Man" and "The Jolly Beggar," his adventures, when disguised as a beggar, are described in a lyric strain more like song than pure description. The latter of the two pieces has this chorus, with a fine lyric sound :—

> "And we'll gang nae mair a-roving,
>     A-roving in the night;
> We'll gang nae mair a-roving,
>     Let the moon shine ne'er so bright."

Early in the sixteenth century we have a poem of the same class called the "Friars of Berwick," which represents in somewhat coarse colours the hospitality of the country people, and the laxity of the monks' lives. To the same time also belong "The Thrie Tailes of the Thrie Priests of Peblis."[1]

[1] [This poem is more probably to be referred to the latter part of the fifteenth century.]

But from this time onward, for nearly two centuries, the poetry of rustic manners slumbered in Scotland. Early in the eighteenth century it was revived by Allan Ramsay in his pastoral drama of "The Gentle Shepherd," a poem which, whatever critics may say of it, has great original merits, and has for a century and a half maintained a strong hold on the affections of the Scottish nation. Immediately succeeding to Ramsay, Robert Fergusson carried on the description of rustic manners in his "Farmer's Ingle," "Leith Races," and other poems, from which Burns afterwards took the form and manner of some of his own productions of far higher genius.

II. *The Ballads.*—A ballad is, I take it, a simple direct narrative of some striking action or incident told often in dramatic form, without moralising or reflection, and meant for the common people.

Every country in Europe has, I suppose, had its ballads, or something corresponding to them. We hear of ballads, or something like them, in the early poetry of Spain, Germany, Denmark, Sweden. England, too, had her ballads in early times, clustering round mythic or national heroes, such as Arthur and his knights, Robin Hood, Guy of Warwick. There was the ballad of "The Nut-brown Maid," of "Chevy Chase," and the like. However, of English ballads I speak with diffidence, for it is a subject I have not studied minutely. But I should gather from the contempt with which Shakespeare and all his contemporaries speak of "odious ballads," and "these same metre ballad makers," that the whole trade of ballad-making had fallen into disrepute by the sixteenth century, and the fine heroic ballads of an elder day been buried under the mass of ephemeral broadsheets that were worthless, scurrilous, and contemptible. No poet of any name in that day would have intermeddled with ballads. It may have been partly that the genuine old work was discredited by the more modern rubbish which bore its name—partly also the great growth of more artistic literature put out the vernacular poetry. For one effect of the spread of civilisation and literature is to crush the rude but genuine poetry of the people. And long before the national taste has got so far advanced as to appreciate those songs, "the precious music of the heart," they have all but disappeared.

You will not, therefore, imagine that I claim for Scotland any exclusive possession of a ballad literature. But this may be truly said, that she has been very rich in ballads, that these have entered largely into the texture of her literature and coloured it distinctively, and that her ballads have some peculiarities about them worthy of being noted.

What are these peculiarities? Chiefly these two, I think. (1.) That owing to the later survival of primitive manners in Scotland, her ballads were orally preserved till a much later date, that their committal to printing is comparatively recent, and that many of them can be more distinctly localised than elsewhere. (2.) The features of the country, the genius of the people, and their eventful history, have impressed on them a very marked character of their own.

The preservation of ballads is a curious chapter in literature, which, however, I cannot now enter on. Collections of ballads, made by curious investigators as early as the sixteenth century, had long lain neglected in some of our great libraries. Early in the eighteenth century Addison's comments on "Chevy Chase," and the publication of collections of ballads for popular use, showed that the tide was turning in their favour.

But the great epoch-making books—those which established the ballad for ever as a great national inheritance—were (1) Percy's *Reliques of Ancient English Poetry*, first published in 1765; many of its finest treasures were, however, Scottish ballads communicated to the bishop by the eminent Lord Hailes; (2) Scott's *Minstrelsy of the Scottish Border*, first published in 1802-3.

These two great works wrought quite a revolution in English thought and sentiment. They not only restored the long-despised and almost forgotten ballad to its rightful place, as the most native and genuine kind of song, but, like fresh springs let into a stagnant lake, they changed and revivified the whole body of England's poetry.

Later in Scotland than in England the ballads had lingered, and later among the Border hills than elsewhere of Scotland. It is not true that the Borders were in any exclusive sense the home of the ballads, but it is true that the nature of the Border country and its historical circumstances combined to make them cling to those green hills with a peculiar tenacity. In old English songs every eminent bard is said to have come from the North Countrè; in Scottish song he belongs to the South Countrè. One and the same district is meant by both expressions.

That vast line of multitudinous hills that sweeps across Scotland, from St. Abb's Head on the east, to Galloway and Loch Ryan on the west, with their softly moulded outlines, their mammy bosoms, their unnumbered dales, each flowing with its "water" so clear and musical that Mr. Ruskin's ear overhears in them a peculiar melody of their own—the greenness of the hills, their gentleness, their lonesomeness, their "pastoral melancholy," how these things soothe while they awe the solitary wanderer! Other mountains are in outline far more striking; indeed, to many these seem tame and featureless; but there is that about them which melts into the heart—a charm, an enchantment more than the eye discovers.

How many a time, as I have wandered among them, have I paused to ask myself, what it is makes the charm, the enchantment of that delightsome land? Beautiful the green hills are, with a silent unobtrusive beauty, but some power there is upon them that is more than this. It is the atmosphere of tradition and minstrelsy with which the whole face of the land is overspread, so that there is not a dale, scarcely a side mountain-burn which does not give name to some grand old melody. And then, lying in the centre of all, like their pathetic heart, the lonesome and lovely vale of Yarrow, hallowing all the rest with that immemorial but nameless sorrow which wails itself down through centuries of song.

As you gaze on the green silent pastures, with here and there a solitary ash-tree or thorn, remnants of the Forest that once overhung them, with the crumbling peels or Border towers which once sheltered famous fighting men or song-renowned ladies, you feel that here is something more than sense takes in, even a whole world of foregone humanity —you feel that here still lingers some shadow from that old Cymric people and their kingdom of Strathclyde, through which swept King Arthur with his twelve great battles;—whither Merlin, the crazed and despairing seer, fled when all was lost, to find a refuge, and at last a grave, by Tweed.

Some influence, too, there is of that later seer,

Thomas of Erceldoune, who, after pouring forth his prophecies and his "Romance of Sir Tristram," passed from his Border keep to sleep within the shadowy Halls of Faery, beneath the green slopes of Eildon. These things have left on the Border hills a glamourie that has not yet forsaken them.

Memories, too, are all around you, not only of the shadowy world of faery, but also of veritable battles, well known to history, when the line of Border hills became the wall between the two rival kingdoms, and the Border men were called to man the mountain rampart and stem the tide of southern invasion. A grandly exciting time it must have been when, soon as the beacon-fires warned the water, or the dish of clean spurs served up on the board, told the chief that his cattle-stalls were empty, he sprang to horse for midnight foray, and rode into England to drive a prey, more gleefully than his descendant to-day rides forth to the hunting-field. These were the men who stood foremost, and suffered most at Neville's Cross, Otterburn, and Flodden Field, and on whose remembrance these sore battles engraved themselves most lastingly. All these things are in the old Border ballads :—

"The weird under-world, and the wild battle-time."

Nor less the tender tones of wives and children left behind them in the old peels, to wail their heart-broken lamentations over their fallen ones.

Who may have been the authors of the old ballads we still possess is wholly unknown. Many of the oldest were probably composed by those wandering minstrels who abounded before the Reformation, welcomed by the king and nobles, the delight of the common people, but represented by more sober writers as intruders, profligates, and low buffoons. These minstrels absolutely swarmed about the Court of James V. Dunbar, in his "Lament for the Makaris," mentions two poets recently dead as ballad-makers. He says that death has taken Maister Johne Clerk and James Afflek "fra ballat-making and tragedè."

Neither can we fix more definitely the age when the ballads were produced. Some of the romantic ones may have been adapted by the minstrels from the elder metrical romances for singing or recitation before the people. Others, the historic ones, we can hardly doubt, were struck out immediately by some great event, from the popular heart and imagination, breaking spontaneously into song. Till last century they were handed down orally, and preserved in the memory of the people, especially those in sequestered districts whose chief literature, after the Bible, they were. At the close of last century Sir Walter gathered some of the most precious from the recitation of old women in Ettrick Forest, and of farmers like Dandie Dinmont in Liddesdale. It is not to be supposed that they have come down to us wholly unchanged. "They represent the changes and additions, the suggestions and passing touches of many generations. They are, in fact, the growth of ages, the continuous expression of the national heart, rather than individual productions."

My friend Professor Veitch, whose words I have just quoted, and whose recent work on *The Poetry of the Scottish Border* I commend to the careful study of all who care for such things—Professor Veitch proposes a threefold division of the ballads proper into the following orders:—

1. Under the head of romantic he would range both those ballads which deal with extraordinary events and characters, such as mainly have come down from the Arthurian time, and also those which introduce powers of the unseen world as interfering with the affairs of men, whether those powers be Fairies from Elfland, or other spirits, or reappearances of the dead.

2. Ballads on historic events, whether great national battles like Otterburn and Flodden, or forays across the English border, or feud fights between clan and clan.

3. Ballads which refer to some tragic or pathetic incident in the life of a person or district, calling forth emotions of love, sorrow, tenderness, and pity. Of this kind are most of the ballads that were cradled in Yarrow.

An instance or two of each of these kinds before I close.

Of Elfinland, and the old feeling about it, the ballad of Thomas the Rhymer is the finest example. That ballad is said to have the oldest MS. authority, being found in MSS. as far back as 1430 or 1440. This half-historic, half-mythic personage lived about the middle of the thirteenth century, in his Tower of Erceldoune on Leader Water. The poet-seer and visitant of "another countree"—that is, the land of Fairy—has left his prophecies scattered all Scotland over, and some of them have had strange fulfilments. His gift of prophecy he got from intercourse with the Elfin Queen. His first meeting with her the ballad thus describes:—

> "True Thomas lay on Huntlie bank,
>   A ferlie he spied wi' his e'e;
> And there he saw a lady bright
>   Come riding down by the Eildon Tree."

After some parley, in which Thomas, by kissing the Queen of Fairy, becomes bound to serve her for seven years,

> "She's mounted on her milk-white steed,
>   She's ta'en true Thomas up behind;
> And aye, whene'er her bridle rung,
>   The steed flew swifter than the wind.
>
> O they rade on, and further on,
>   The steed ga'ed swifter than the wind;
> Until they reached a desert wide,
>   And living land was left behind."

She then shows him three paths—the first the path of righteousness, the second that of wickedness, and a third thus:

> "'And see ye not that bonny road,
>   That winds about the fernie brae?
> That is the road to fair Elfland,
>   Where thou and I to-night maun gae.
>
> But, Thomas, ye maun hauld your tongue,
>   Whatever ye may hear or see;
> For, if ye speak a word in Elflyn land,
>   Ye 'll ne'er get back to your ain countrie.'
>
> O they rade on, and further on,
>   And they waded through rivers aboon the knee,
> And they saw neither sun nor moon,
>   But they heard the roaring of the sea.
>
> It was mirk mirk night, and there was nae stern-light,
>   And they waded through red blood to the knee;
> For a' the blood that 's shed on earth,
>   Rins through the springs o' that countrie."

Thomas, on reaching the Elfin world, serves the queen for seven years, and receives from her his wages.

> "Syne they came to a garden green,
>   And she pu'd an apple frae a tree;
> 'Take this for thy wages, true Thomas,
>   It will give thee the tongue that can never lee.'"

Thomas thought this a rather inconvenient gift, if he was to carry on business on earth again.

> "'My tongue is mine ain,' true Thomas said;
>   'A gudely gift ye wad gi'e to me;
> I neither dought to buy nor sell
>   At fair or tryst where I may be.

I dought neither speak to prince or peer,
  Nor ask of grace from fair ladye.'
'Now hold thy peace!' the lady said,
  'For as I say, so must it be.'

He has gotten a coat of the even cloth,
  And a pair of shoes of velvet green;
And till seven years were gane and past,
  True Thomas on earth was never seen."

On his return he uttered those prophecies which were deemed infallible, many of which are remembered in Scotland till the present day.

As one snatch from the heroic ballads, take this description of a fray between the Scotts of Buccleuch and an English freebooter. It is from the ballad of "Jamie Telfer of the fair Dodhead." The Scots caught up the English reivers, retreating with their prey at the fords of Liddel Water. "The Dinlay snaw" mentioned in the passage is the snow on the top of the Dunion, a mountain of the Cheviot range, standing conspicuous to the south of Jedburgh.[1]

"Then til't they gaed, wi' heart and hand,
  The blows fell thick as bickering hail;
And mony a horse ran masterless,
  And mony a comely cheek was pale.

But Willie was stricken owre the head,
  And thro' the knapscap the sword has gaen;
And Harden grat for very rage,
  When Willie on the ground lay slain.

But he's ta'en aff his gude steel cap,
  And thrice he's waved it in the air;
The Dinlay snaws were ne'er mair white,
  Nor the lyart locks of Harden's hair.

[1] [More likely the Din Fell or Dinlay Hill, in the Hermitage Water.]

'Revenge! revenge!' auld Wat 'gan cry;
'Fye, lads, lay on them cruellie!
We'll ne'er see Tiviotside again,
Or Willie's death revenged shall be.'"

Wat Harden, with his snow-white hair and steel cap in hand, cheering on his men, what a subject for a painter!

Then for the ballad of personal incident and emotion, take this. James V., intent on putting down the marauders of the Border, made one of his dashing rides over the southern hills, came suddenly down upon one of them, Piers Cokburne, a noted freebooter, and hung him up at once over the gate of his own Tower of Henderland.[1] The ruins of that tower may still be seen standing on Yarrow side, near where Meggat Water falls into St. Mary's Loch. In a deserted chapelry hard by Sir Walter found the broken head-stone that covered his grave, and could still read the inscription: "Here lyes Perys of Cokburne and his Wyfe Marjory."

This is the lament of Marjory, his widow, over him :—

"I sewed his sheet, making my mane;
I watched the corpse, myself, alane;
I watched his body, night and day;
Na living creature came that way.

I took his body on my back,
And whiles I gaed, and whiles I sat;
I digg'd a grave, and laid him in,
And happ'd him with the sod sae green.

[1] [It is now certain that Piers Cokburne was not the subject of the king's summary justice. William Cokburne of Henderland was convicted of theft and beheaded in Edinburgh in May 1530.]

> But think na ye my heart was sair,
> When I laid the moul' on his yellow hair;
> O think na ye my heart was wae,
> When I turned about, awa' to gae?
>
> Nae living man I'll love again,
> Since that my lovely knight is slain;
> Wi' ae lock of his yellow hair
> I'll chain my heart for evermair."

Is there anything in the whole compass of poetry that for pathos surpasses that?

The passages I have just given belong to Scott's *Minstrelsy of the Border*. But Scotland's ballad poetry is not confined to these. Donibristle is an ancient home of the Earls of Moray, on the north side of the Firth of Forth, about twelve miles from Edinburgh. The young Earl of Moray was said to be the handsomest man then in the kingdom. King James VI., who had some grudge against Moray, had given commission to the Earl of Huntly to pursue Bothwell and his followers with fire and sword. Huntly, under cover of that commission, took occasion to revenge a private quarrel he had with the young Earl of Moray. Huntly laid siege to Donibristle, fired the castle, and slew the young earl while gallantly defending himself. The ballad begins with "Ye Highlands and ye Lawlands," because Moray had large lands and many vassals, both in the Highlands and in the Lowlands.

> "Ye Highlands and ye Lawlands,
> Oh, quhair hae ye been?
> They hae slain the Earl o' Moray
> And hae laid him on the green.

> Now, wae be to thee, Huntly!
>   And wherefor did you sae;
> I bade ye bring him wi' you,
>   And forbade you him to slay.
>
> He was a braw gallant,
>   And he rid at the ring;
> And the bonnie Earl o' Moray
>   Oh! he might hae been a king.
>
> He was a braw gallant,
>   And he play'd at the ba';
> And the bonnie Earl o' Moray
>   Was the flower amang them a'.
>
> Oh! lang will his lady
>   Look owre the Castle Doune,
> Ere she see the Earl o' Moray
>   Come sounding thro' the town."

Here is another fragment, belonging to no one knows what time or what actual event. Some have imagined that it is a lament for one of the followers of Argyll, who may have fallen in the battle of Glenlivat, "stricken on Thursday, the third day of October, 1594 years." But this is mere conjecture, and the few verses that are left, are they not all the more impressive for the utter uncertainty as to time, place, and person?

> "Hie upon Hielands,
>   And low upon Tay,
> Bonnie George Campbell
>   Rade out on a day.
> Saddled and bridled
>   And gallant rade he;
> Hame cam' his gude horse,
>   But never cam' he!

> Out cam' his auld mither,
>    Greeting fu' sair;
> And out cam' his bonnie bride
>    Rivin' her hair.
> Saddled and bridled
>    And booted rade he;
> Toom[1] hame cam' the saddle,
>    But never cam' he!
>
> 'My meadow lies green,
>    And my corn is unshorn;
> My barn is to big,[2]
>    And my babie's unborn.'
> Saddled and bridled
>    And booted rade he;
> Toom hame cam' the saddle,
>    But never cam' he!"

III. There is a third form of poetry in which the national heart of Scotland has expressed itself, I mean her songs—her songs as these are distinguished from the ballads. Of these I had intended to speak to-day, but I find that I must reserve what I have to say on this subject till my next lecture, when I hope to speak of Burns.[3]

Meanwhile if there are any of my younger hearers present who care for these things, may I be allowed to hint to them that the ballad literature both of Scotland and of England also, is really worthy of their mind's regard; not merely of such passing regard as most educated men have at some time of their lives cast upon it, but worthy of close, careful, discriminating study. In these old songs of the

---

[1] Empty.     [2] Build.
[3] [See "Scottish Song and Burns" in *Aspects of Poetry*, c. vii. 1881.]

people they will find no unreal sorrow, no fantastic love, no fine-spun subtleties, either of thought or sentiment, but the direct warm throb of strong human hearts, in the presence of the great simple facts of life and death, under the pressure of the primal emotions. The open air, the free breath of the moorland, is all about them, as Professor Veitch says, "not the stifling atmosphere of morbid feelings and artificial fancies." When I turn from these to most of the poetry one meets in the present age, highly wrought, but eminently unhealthy as this is, what a weariness and loathing one feels!

Were any young man to make a serious study of but two books, Percy's *Reliques* and Scott's *Minstrelsy*, taking them ballad by ballad, and trying as far as he could to master all the history, legend, and incident that clusters round each; and if he would further compare and illustrate them by the Iliad and the Odyssey—I do not ask him to go into all the ballad literature of Europe, for here concentration is everything—he would give himself the finest, freshest, most inspiring poetic education that is possible in our age. So furnished he might well neglect more than half of modern poetry.

For those of you who have still youth and leisure on your side, I can imagine no more instructive and delightful way of passing a summer long vacation than to take Scott's *Minstrelsy* alone, and with it in hand to traverse on foot the whole range of the

Border hills, both the Scottish and the English side of them, from Cheviot to Hartfell and Queensberry—visit the spot to which each ballad refers, search out each name, and localise each incident, making shepherd after shepherd, from day to day, the companion of your wanderings. I could wish no pleasanter or wiser companion for a long summer day than I have found among these men, when one knows how to approach them and get their confidence. From their lips you will best learn whatever of tradition still lingers about each locality. To do this thoroughly would be the work, not of one summer only, but of several summers, in which mind and body alike would find full exercise and refreshment.

Do not suppose that the ballads are an exhausted field. Most persons have skimmed them, few have been at pains to know them thoroughly. He who would make such an open-air hillside study of them as I have suggested would come into actual contact with the scenes where much of the best poetry was born, and would learn more of lonely nature, of his country's history, and of the human heart, than he would by perusing at his desk a whole library.

I should be sorry to speak heresy against this place and its studies, but am I wrong in believing that one who could make such a study as this would educate his own nature more largely, more richly, than by reading for a first class in every one of the Schools?

# VII.—JAMES I. OF SCOTLAND AND THE KING'S QUAIR.[1]

SOME of my hearers may probably remember the scene in the *Fair Maid of Perth* in which Sir Walter has depicted King Robert the Third and his brother the Duke of Albany meeting in the large chamber of the Dominican Convent at Perth. The king, full of amiable feelings and good intentions, but feeble-minded, irresolute, beloved not feared, no match either for the haughty Barons and fierce people he was born to rule, or for his brother the calm, cool, crafty Albany, who, with eye fixed on far-off dark designs, was able to conceal them under the cloak of desire for the king's and the country's good. Both royal brothers, unlike as they were in their inner man, were outwardly alike "noble and majestic in stature and countenance." And then the Council of State which followed in that same chamber, when

[1] [Oxford Lecture, October 22, 1883. Not before published. *King's Quair* is King's Book—sometimes written *Quhair*, but the proper spelling is *Quair*, as in the only MS. of the poem in the Bodleian Library at Oxford (about 1475). *Quh* is equivalent to our *wh*, but *Quair* has nothing in it corresponding to this form, being derived from old French *quaier*, and represented in English by *quire*.—Cf. Skeat, Int. p. xxxvii.]

Rothesay, heir to the Crown, gay, graceful, open-hearted, but giddy, pleasure-loving, and dissolute, regardless of his father's presence, insults both by deed and word Archibald the Grim, that tremendous Earl of Douglas, whose daughter he had married and neglected, and lays himself open an easy prey to the deep-plotting Albany, who works calmly on; while George Dunbar, Earl of March, whose daughter Rothesay had loved but been forced to forsake, leaves the Council-table in anger, with the prophetic words, "Farewell, my Lords of Albany and Douglas; you are playing a high game, look you play it fairly. Farewell, poor thoughtless Prince, who art sporting like a fawn within spring of a tiger!—George of Dunbar sees the evil he cannot remedy—Adieu all."

The sequel foreshadowed in these words followed quickly. Soon after this Council the king lost his best adviser and Rothesay his guardian angel, when the wise and good Queen, Annabella Drummond, died. On her death, Rothesay became more than ever reckless, and Albany all-powerful with the king. Wearied out with age and infirmity, and saddened by his son's misconduct, King Robert retired to his castle in the Isle of Bute; and there in an evil hour put his hand to "an order under the Royal Signet," empowering Albany to arrest and confine the prince, with a view to his improvement. No time was lost in carrying out this order. Albany had bound to himself by a close alliance the most powerful of the Scottish nobles, and amongst them Archibald the fourth Earl of Douglas, the hero of Shrewsbury field, "where, fighting side by side with his old antagonist Percy, he is said to have felled Henry IV. to the ground." These two conspired to bring about the death of the heir to the throne, who was nephew of the one and doubly brother-in-law of the other. They caused the ill-fated prince to be arrested near St. Andrews, and thrown into the dungeon there. Thence they themselves hurried him to Falkland Castle, which was a stronghold of Albany's. There, in a few days, the ill-fated prince died, as was generally believed, of starvation, and was buried far from the royal tombs, in the Abbey of Lindores. Tradition still points to the deep dark dungeon in the Castle of St. Andrews and to a broken vault in Falkland as the scene of these horrors. There are not wanting at the present day some who are disposed to take the part of Albany, as though historians had conspired to malign him, but I see no grounds for reversing the general verdict of history.

But one more son remained to the king, James, who, sixteen years younger than Rothesay, was only eight years old when his brother died. James was cast in a wholly different mould from Rothesay. In mind and character he resembled his mother rather than his father, and from her inherited a sagacious intellect and a firm will. Him his father committed to the care of Henry Wardlaw, primate of Scotland

and bishop of St. Andrews, a man of wisdom and cultivation, at a time when these qualities were rare in Scotland. Under Wardlaw's roof in the old sea-fort, James had for companion Henry Percy, son of the banished Earl of Northumberland. There Wardlaw imbued the young prince, even at that early age, with something of his own love of letters. But after the tragic fate of Rothesay, the bishop felt that no Scottish stronghold, not even his own sacred precinct, could keep James safe. He therefore advised the aged king to send his boy to the court of his old ally, the King of France, "in order that," as the old *Chronicle* says, "he might there be instructed in manners and virtue, and be the more safely kept."[1] Probably safety, rather than education, was the object of his father. James, who was then just eleven years old, embarked at the Bass Rock, in the Firth of Forth, in February 1405-6, and sailed for France. But, as the vessel coasted along Yorkshire, it was attacked off Flamborough Head by an English merchantman. James and his attendants were captured, and carried to London, though at that time there existed a truce between the two kingdoms.[2] There, when James was brought

[1] *Book of Pluscarden*, vol. ii. p. 262.
[2] [The date of the capture of James at sea has been variously given as the 12th April and the 30th March 1405-6. He could not have set sail before the 13th of March, as, from his own account, the sun was in the sign Aries, which, according to the *Scottish Kalendar*, it enters on that day.—See *Quair*, stanza 20. Mr. Skeat, Introd. p. viii, dates the capture March 12th.]

into the presence of Henry IV., the latter exclaimed with sarcastic joy, "Had the Scots been grateful, they ought to have sent this youth to me to be educated, for I understand French well." Henry then ordered the Scottish prince and Orkney to the Tower, and fully nineteen years were to pass ere the captivity of the former came to an end.

Whether the capture of James had been preconcerted with the English king, by his uncle Albany, is uncertain, but it is one of the many suspicions that attach to him. When the news of it reached his poor father, it filled up his cup of misery. He never again held up his head, but drooped and died within less than two months, and was laid in front of the altar of Paisley Abbey, the burial-place of his Stuart ancestors. Albany at once assumed the reins of government, and for thirteen years ruled Scotland as though he were its king, till he died in 1419.

For the King of England to imprison and detain as captive the son of a neighbouring monarch with whom he was at peace was, no doubt, an act of high-handed injustice. But Henry IV., and his son who succeeded him, Henry V., did their best to repair the wrong, by providing for the young captive as good an education as if he had been their own son —such an education as Scotland could not have afforded him. Sir John Pelham had the charge of the young prince and his education, and he was trained in the best learning of the time. Literature in the vernacular was then for the first time coming into vogue. Chaucer had died just five years before James was brought to England, and his poetry, which was then popular in his own land, found no more appreciative student than this stranger prince, who, during his long captivity, fed his imagination upon it, and was destined in due time to prolong so well the strain which Chaucer had begun.

The confinement of the prince was rigorously carried out, but his places of imprisonment were frequently changed. First, it was the Tower of London; then, in 1407, it was the Castle of Nottingham. In 1412 he was at Croydon, as we know from the charter, still preserved, which he wrote, in his native Scotch, with his own hand, granting to William Douglas the lands of Drumlanrig, Hawick, and Selkirk.

In 1413 he was taken again to the Tower, but was in the same year transferred to Windsor Castle. There, to preserve his health of body and mind, as he himself tells us, he rose early, and

"Took a book and read therein a while."

The result of that early rising we shall see by-and-by.

Rigorous though James's imprisonment was, it was relieved from time to time by visits from some of the most influential Scottish nobles, who had free access to the English court and to their own young king as long as the peace between England and Scotland lasted. They made him acquainted with the condition of their country under Albany's rule, and they returned home, firm friends of James and of his cause.

In 1416 a treaty was all but concluded for his restoration, when, suddenly, by some mysterious influence, it was broken off. We cannot wonder, even if without direct proof, that Albany's hand was suspected in this.

But the chief and most exhilarating break in the monotony of James's long captivity was when Henry v. resolved to take him with him in his last expedition against France. Henry's reason for doing so was that the Scottish auxiliary force had been doing wild work against his own troops.

In 1421, John Stewart, Earl of Buchan, had gone with 7000 chosen Scots, and the flower of the Scottish nobility, to aid the Dauphin, at that time sorely pressed by his English foes. The Earl had just severely defeated the English in the battle of Baugé, in which he slew the Duke of Clarence, Henry's own brother, and made prisoners of many English nobles. Henry conceived that the presence of the Scottish king in his own army would counterwork this evil and detach the Scots from the side of the French. With this view, having entered into an agreement to restore James to his own people within three months, after the return of both to England, he took him with him to France. But Henry had miscalculated. When he requested James to command his subjects to leave the service of France, the Scottish king replied, "that as long as he remained a prisoner it neither became him to issue, nor them to obey, such an order;" but that he would gladly attend the English king "as a private knight, and learn the art of war under so great a captain."[1] So he served in the English army, had command of that division which laid siege to Dreux, and pressed it so vigorously that in six weeks the town surrendered. But this visit to France afforded James other advantages beside an apprenticeship in the art of war. His own subjects who were in France freely visited him; he himself conversed with the best soldiers and chief statesmen of England, and at the coronation festival of the French Princess Catherine, whom Henry V. made his queen, he, the young king of Scotland, sat next her, on her left side.

Whether Henry V. would ever have agreed to restore James to his own kingdom we know not, but on his sudden death in 1422, the way was open for James's deliverance. All things conspired towards it. Bedford, Henry's brother, who was appointed Protector of England, had his hands so full of troubles both at home and in France, that he would gladly be rid of the guardianship of a foreign prince.

[1] Tytler's *History of Scotland*, vol. iii. p. 166.

Scotland, too, weary of the weakness and misrule of Murdoch, the second Duke of Albany, longed more than ever to see her king again. Even Murdoch himself is said to have helped forward the negotiation. We know Scott's story about Murdoch's son wringing the neck of his favourite falcon.

In the autumn of 1423 a large Scottish embassy passed to England, met James with the English deputies at Pontefract, and agreed on the terms of James's restoration. These were, that a sum of £40,000 was to be paid by Scotland to England, not as ransom-money, but in defrayment of the cost of the young king's maintenance for nearly twenty years; that a truce of seven years was to be concluded between the two kingdoms, and that James was to marry an English princess. The marriage, however, was no mere diplomatic arrangement, but the result of a romantic affection. Indeed, there are few royal marriages on record that will compare with this one for the romance that surrounded its origin, and the happiness and fidelity which attended it till its close. The lady was Joan (Joanna) of Beaufort, daughter of John, Earl of Somerset, and granddaughter of John of Gaunt—she who continued James's helper and comforter in good and evil fortune, and stood by him at the dismal close of his life.

The story of this romantic attachment King James has himself related in his poem, *The King's Quair;*

indeed this is the main subject of that poem. James had steeped himself, during his long captivity, in the poetry of Chaucer, and now, when love impelled him to sing, it was Chaucer's metre and manner that he employed. *The King's Quair* consists of 200 stanzas, each of seven lines, the same stanza in which Chaucer wrote his *Troylus and Creseyde* and his *Parlemente of Foules*.

The keynote of the whole poem is the love kindled in his breast by the first glimpse he had of Joan Beaufort. This is how it befell, according to the story. James had passed a sleepless night reading Boethius *De Consolatione Philosophiæ*, a book much prized through all the middle ages, translated into Saxon by Alfred, and afterwards into English by Chaucer. From his musing and sombre thoughts, he is aroused by the sound of the matin bell.

> "Soon I heard the bell to matins ring,
> And up I rose, no longer would I lie."

Still, even after rising, he continues to muse over his forlorn estate—goes back over the incident of his wrongful capture, and the hardness of the captivity he had now for nineteen years endured. Wearied with the burden of these sad thoughts, he looks forth from the window of the tower at Windsor into the freshness of the morning. The nightingale and all the birds are singing, awake to love. The king then begins to think, if love be so delightful and so universal, what guilt have I, what offence have I done,

> "That I am thrall, and birdis gone at large."

> "And therewith cast I down mine eye again,
>     Where as I saw walking under the tower
> Full secretly, new cumyn her to pleyne,[1]
>     The fairest or the freshest youngë flower
>     That ever I saw, methought, before that hour,
> For which sudden abate,[2] anon astert
> The blood of all my body to my hert.
>
> . . . . . . . .
>
> No wonder was, for why my wittis all,
> Were so o'ercome with pleasance and delight,
>     Only through letting of mine eyën fall
>     That suddenly my heart became her thrall
> For ever of free will, for of menace
> There was no token in her suetë face.
>
> And in my head I drew right hastily,
>     And eft-sonës I lean'd it forth again,
> And saw her walk, that verray womanly,
>     With no wight mo, but only women tweyne,
>     Then gan I study in myself and seyne,
> 'Ah! sweet, are ye a worldly creature,
> Or heavenly thing in likeness of nature?'"

Wondering whether she be of heavenly birth or a creature of earth, he asks himself—

> "If ye be worldly wight, that doth me sike,[3]
>     Why list[4] God make you so, my dearest heart,
>     To do a seely[5] prisoner this smart,
> That loves you all, and wot of nought but wo?"

When the lady passes out of sight, her lover falls into a half dream, half swoon, in which he has a strange experience.

[1] Play.   [2] Surprise.   [3] Cause me to sigh.
[4] Pleased it.   [5] Miserable.

The sequel cannot be given more clearly or briefly than in the words of Mr. Ward in his *Selections from the English Poets*. He seems to be carried from sphere to sphere to the empire of Venus. He wins her favour; but, since his desperate case requires the help of "other mo than one goddesse," he is sent on with Good Hope for guide, to the Palace of Minerva. The Goddess of Wisdom receives him with a speech on free will, and, finally, after an interview with the great goddess, Fortune herself, he wakes to find a real messenger from Venus, "a turtuse quhite as calk," bringing him a flowering branch, joyful evidence that his suit is to succeed.

> "'Awake! Awake! I bring, lover, I bring
> The newis glad that blissful bene, and sure
> Of thy comfort; now laugh and play and sing,
> That art beside so glad an aventure,
> For in the hevyn decretit is the cure.'
> And unto me the flowers fair, present:
> With wyngis spread, her wayis forth she went."

With this, and with the poet's song of thankfulness, *The King's Quair* ends.

> "Go little treatise, naked of eloquence,"

he says, commending it very modestly, with all its "defautis," to the reader's patience, and in the last stanza of all unto—

> "My maisteris dear,
> Gower and Chaucer, that on the steppis sate
> Of Rhetoric, while they were lyvand here,
> . . . . . .
> I recommend my book in lynis seven
> And eke thair saulis unto the blisse of heaven."

The stanza "in lynis seven," from the king's use of it, came to be called "the Rhyme Royal." The traces of Chaucer's influence are visible, not only in the general structure but in the minute details of *The King's Quair;* not only incidents, but single stanzas, and even lines recall Chaucer. The setting of the poem is the common allegorical filagree work of the time, the mixture of allegorical romance and pagan mythology with the actual facts of life, which Chaucer, and all other poets of the Renaissance revelled in. Love and Fortune, as heavenly powers, are each striving to wield the destiny of man.

But the central part round which all this is gathered —the real love-story of the king, described by himself —thus has a prominent and historic value. As it has been well expressed, "the dress is the common tinsel of the time, but the body beneath is real and human." The sonorous rhythm and sweet flow of his verse bespeak James to be a real poet, and it is no small merit to have been the first poet to appreciate and reproduce the power of Chaucer, and to have deflected the stream of his influence for more than a century from England to Scotland.

The stanza and manner which James introduced to his own country, he handed on to two native poets—Henryson and Dunbar;—something of them is still present in the rougher vernacular of Gawin Douglas, and their last echoes are heard in "The Dreme" of Sir David Lindsay.

But greater and more interesting than this or almost any poem is the great drama of the King's life. The bare facts themselves are greater than any fiction, and their absorbing human interest comes out more directly when they are left to speak for themselves, without any attempt at comment or theory or philosophic interpretation.

The lady whom James had wooed in this poetic fashion he married in the Church of St. Mary Overy in Southwark, on the 2d February 1423-4, and straightway left his poetic musings behind and set face towards Scotland with his young wife. To Durham, many Scottish nobles, knights, and squires crowded to meet their restored sovereign and his queen, and to conduct them across the Border. His rejoicing people received them with loud acclamations, and conveyed them to the Monastery of Melrose, where the king ratified and signed the treaty with England, which had set him free.

James had left Scotland a boy of eleven years. After a captivity of nineteen years, he returned home, at the age of thirty, a scholar, a poet, and an artist, skilled too in every knightly accomplishment. In the art of war he had been trained under the greatest general of the age, and he had learned the art of politics by studying the institutions of England and by conversing with her best statesmen.[1] But poetry he had now to leave behind for more stern

[1 Burnett, *Exchequer Rolls*, vol. iv. p. lxxxvi.]

realities. A man of cultivated and refined mind, yet vigorous and lofty of aim, with what feeling must his eyes, accustomed to England's well-ordered monarchy, have looked on the spectacle which his own land presented—the anarchy, the barbarism, the lawless and savage oppression. Meditating, no doubt, many things, he for the most part kept his own counsel, and waited his time.

Once only, it is told, as he crossed the Border and heard from some nobles of the fearful disorders under which his country groaned, he, in an unguarded moment, exclaimed, "Let God but grant me life, and I shall make the key keep the castle, and the bush the cow through every spot of my dominion, though I myself should lead the life of a dog." These words are the key-note of his whole after-life.

After keeping Easter festival at Edinburgh, James with his queen passed to Scone, the immemorial seat of the coronation of the Scottish kings. There, on the 21st of May, he and Queen Joan were crowned with all the ancient solemnities. His cousin, Murdoch Stewart, Duke of Albany, but lately Regent, in virtue of an old hereditary right, as Earl of Fife, placed the king upon the throne, and Henry Wardlaw, bishop of St. Andrews, his former tutor and friend, anointed him with oil and set the crown upon his head.

In a few days he held his first Parliament in Perth. The king proceeded cautiously, yet in all the Acts are visible traces of a legislator, and hints of a policy he did not think fit yet fully to reveal. To keep down rebellion, to restrain private wars among nobles and chiefs, to remove the many forms of oppression, to improve agriculture, these were the aims of the laws then passed. Inquiry was ordered into all lands alienated from the Crown, and the owners of such lands were required to produce their charters. To quell the overgrown and rebellious aristocracy, to strengthen the Crown, and for this purpose to befriend the small lairds, and to raise the despised burgesses, and to make the Law be respected by all alike, these were the objects which he set resolutely before himself and never lost sight of. But mingled with these objects was a personal feeling of a darker hue. He would not forgive his kinsmen of the House of Albany, who had, as he believed, sought to supplant himself and extinguish his race. And this vindictive feeling is said "to have been stimulated for selfish ends by his uncle, Walter, Earl of Athole, who was secretly cherishing more hostile purposes than the Albanys had ever done."

In a country so disordered and lawless as Scotland then was, in which the nobles warred with each other at will, plundered the revenue, and laid violent hands on the customs, for their own use,—the most powerful nobles the most defiantly,—there were, as it has been well put by the latest and best authority, "but two ways in which it could be ruled at all. One was to secure the persons and confiscate the estates of the nobles who acted as if they were above all laws ; the other was to purchase the support of these magnates, so as to restrain them as far as possible, and to connive at injustice and oppression when it could not be restrained. The latter was the course pursued by Albany, the former was adopted by James, but at the cost of his life." When he had been seated on the throne for ten months he felt himself strong enough to show his hand.

He summoned his second Parliament to meet at Perth in March 1424-5. For the first eight days he confined himself to carrying through routine business, regulations about States and Customs, Statutes against Lollards, warnings to abbots and priors to put their houses in order. Suddenly, on the ninth day, he astounded the whole country by ordering the arrest of Murdoch, Duke of Albany, lately governor of the kingdom, and his son, Alexander Stewart. These were thrown into prison, and the Parliament was adjourned, to meet again in two months at Stirling. When it reassembled, the king, clad in all the pomp of royalty, seated himself upon the throne, as the supreme judge of his people. Gathered around him was an assize or jury, consisting of one-and-twenty nobles and barons, among them the greatest of the realm—the Earls of Douglas, of

Angus, and of Dunbar, along with the King's uncle, Walter, Earl of Athole. These men had lately been friends and supporters of the House of Albany, and were now met to sit in judgment on the members of that House (for they could be tried only by their peers). On the first day of the assize, Walter Stewart, Murdoch's eldest son, was brought before the tribunal, tried, condemned, and immediately beheaded. Next day, Murdoch himself, his son Alexander, and his father-in-law, the aged Earl of Lennox, were brought forth from their prison-houses, and met the same fate. Murdoch was beheaded on the Heading Hill, an eminence before the Castle of Stirling, from which, as Walter Scott has noted, he might clearly descry the battlements of his own Castle of Doune, which he had built for himself with great magnificence, and in which he had but lately kept royal state. Of the charges on which they were condemned, no record remains. "We know only from an ancient chronicle that the heir of Albany was tried for robbery, 'de Roboria.'"[1] But James had in memory a long score of crimes against his family and himself, from the murder of his brother Rothesay onward, which must have seemed to him to cry aloud for righteous vengeance. Of palpable offences on which to found a charge of treason, there were: the connivance at his long captivity, the usurpation of kingly power and of

[1] Tytler, vol. iii. p. 191.

all but kingly title, and the appropriation of royal lands. In the case of the first Albany, indeed, his title of Regency had been guaranteed by the Three Estates, but in Murdoch's case it had no such sanction. Yet this swift justice, however righteous it may have been, was far from popular. The first Albany had always courted and generally secured popularity, and Murdoch, if weak, had been courteous and kindly. He and his son had that commanding bearing and those graceful and dignified manners which always win the people. And now, when they beheld them led forth to execution, these men of almost gigantic stature, and of most noble presence, none could look without emotion on "that elevation and that fall." The white hairs and venerable aspect of the Earl of Lennox, now in his eightieth year, awoke a throb of pity in the hardest heart.

Other executions of adherents of the House of Albany followed, marked by the ferocity of the times, if not of the king. Other nobles were made to feel the king's hand—as the Earl of March, who, by a sentence of Parliament, which, if just, was yet harsh, was stript at once of his title and his lands.[1]

From the Lowlands, overawed, not conciliated, James cast his eyes across the mountain rampart called the Highland Line, within which lay the clans, now as always, in still wilder disorder. These

[1] See Tytler, vol. iii. pp. 247-8.

had never yet been really subject to the Scottish king. Him they regarded only as a distant and nominal suzerain, whom they might obey or defy at will. The only real power which each clan acknowledged was its own head, and thus they fought, chief with chief, clan with clan, "an inextricable fray;" yet feudal tenure and baronial pomp were blended strangely with Celtic usage. Scoto-Norman barons, who had intermarried with families of the Gael, were in alliance or conflict with fierce aboriginal Celtic chiefs of uncouth name, and all alike hung loosely by the king and refused to pay taxes or bear any additional burdens. Pre-eminent among these was the Lord of the Isles, who, ruling the Islands and the Western Mainland, regarded himself as a separate sovereign, and often transferred his allegiance to the king of England at the very crisis of the contest between the two kingdoms. James resolved that it should be so no longer, but that those ferocious chiefs should feel the weight of the hand which had crushed the House of Albany. In this mind he summoned a Parliament to meet at Inverness, commanded the most powerful of the Highland chiefs to attend it, and himself, with his queen riding by his side, marched thither, surrounded by his principal Lowland nobles and barons, and with an armed force that could quell all resistance. The Highland chiefs obeyed the summons, but as soon as they entered the Hall of Parliament forty of them were at once arrested and thrown into irons.[1] Among these was the Lord of the Isles, also Angus Duff, leader of the Sutherland Mackays, who could then bring into the field 4000 men from Strathnaver, and many more of equal power. Of these the most murderous were at once executed; the rest, after a brief imprisonment, were set free. But the mercy thus shown had little effect on the Lord of the Isles. Scarcely had James turned his back on the Highlands, than that Ocean chief, half prince, half pirate, gathered all the strength of Ross and of the Isles, wasted the whole country, especially the Royal lands, and razed to the ground the royal burgh of Inverness, in which he had suffered so great indignity. With a small force, James flew back to the mountains, and with incredible suddenness came upon the Island chief and his disorderly host of chieftains and caterans in a moss of Lochaber, dispersed them utterly, and hunted Alexander himself from isle to isle. He, as though he were an independent prince, sent ambassadors to treat with the king. James, incensed at this insolence, scorned to receive them, but sent his officers to hunt down the rebel chief still more relentlessly, and himself returned to his capital. There, while the king and queen were keeping Easter Festival surrounded by their court and nobles, as they stood before the high altar in

[1] Tytler, vol. iii. pp. 215-6.

Holyrood Chapel, there appeared a miserable-looking man, his legs and arms bare, and his body covered only with a plaid, and holding the naked sword by the point, he offered the hilt to the king, and threw himself on his knees before him. This was none other than Alexander, the mighty Lord of the Isles.[1] Accepting this proof of unreserved submission the king gave him his forfeited life, but immured him in the stronghold of Tantallon, while his mother, the Countess of Ross, who had shared in his rebellion, was sent to the ancient Nunnery of Inchcolm in the Firth of Forth. Both, after a time, were released, restored to their Highland dominions, and remained quiet for the rest of their days. Their kinsmen and clan did not cease from troubling, yet the swift vengeance, mingled with mercy, which the king had shown, struck a terror into the Highland chiefs which was long remembered.

In spite of these violent strifes with his nobles, James never slacked in urging on the work of legislation. He reigned thirteen years, and each year he summoned a parliament. The record of the laws, passed year by year, bears witness to the wisdom of his guiding mind. To clench all this legislation, however, one thing was wanting, that is, a living law, which should ensure the carrying out of those which were placed in the statute-book.

[1] *Exchequer Rolls*, vol. iv.; Tytler, vol. iii. p. 219.

The king's strong right hand alone could supply this. No wonder therefore it was sometimes violent in its action.

In the parliament or general council that met at Perth in 1427-28, James introduced a principle which had a great future before it in Scotland, and a still greater elsewhere. That was the principle of parliamentary representation, as it has since been called. He enacted that the small barons should be exempted from attendance on parliament, which they regarded as a burdensome duty, on condition that in each shire these small barons should elect two or more wise men to represent them in the national council. The commissioners so elected were to have their costs defrayed by the barons who elected them. In this enactment James was following the example of England, which he had, while a captive, seen in full force under the fourth and fifth Henries. But this legislation, however wise, was before its time. Scotland was not ripe for it. It was not till the reign of James VI. that the representation of the small barons in Scotland actually began.

There is nothing which speaks more for the character of James than his anxious efforts to befriend the poor, to alleviate their miseries, and to provide for them open and equal justice. He did what he could by influence and exhortation to make the nobles consider their labourers, and not to remove them from the lands which they tilled.[1] He instituted the court known as the Session, which was the first rudiment of Scotland's supreme court of justice. He exerted himself to obtain capable and upright judges, and he enacted by law that the poor man's cause should be heard before a judge, and that justice be dispensed to the poor as well as rich, without fear or favour. "And gif there be ony pur creatur that for defalte of cunnynge or dispens, can nocht, or may nocht folow his caus, the king, for the lufe of God, sall ordane that the juge before quhame the causs suld be determynt, purway and git a lele and wyss advocate to folow sic creaturis caus," etc. Humaner legislation than that it would be hard to find.

During his short but energetic reign—what between reducing the overgrown power of his barons, quelling the renewed outbreaks of the savage Highland clans, and urging on reformatory legislation—the king, we may believe, had small leisure to give to the cultivation of the muses. That way, however, lay the real bent of his nature. In this he found little sympathy among his turbulent nobles. Rude themselves, caring only for war, the chase, and life out of doors, they did not care to have their sons educated, and despised the pursuits of the scholar as fit only for clerics. One sympathetic cleric, at least, James had in Bishop Henry

[1] Tytler, vol. iii. pp. 232-3; *Exchequer Rolls*, vol. iv.

Wardlaw, the friend and teacher of his boyhood. It is the bishop's glory, that while James was in captivity, he had founded at St. Andrews the earliest Scottish University. James, though absent, was able to co-operate with the enlightened bishop. From his prison he sent to the Pope an urgent entreaty that he would grant a papal bull which should endow with all the privileges of a university Wardlaw's infant foundation. James being still a captive, could not share in the joy of that high festival (3d February 1413), when Henry Ogilvie, Master of Arts, made his entry into the city, bearing the papal bulls; when to welcome his advent the bells from all the towers clashed forth rejoicing peals, and the great procession of prelates, priors, and priests sang *Te Deum* for thanksgiving at the high altar of the cathedral, and the citizens for the rest of the day feasted with tumultuous joy. But the king, as soon as he was restored to his throne, made it, we are told, one of his earliest cares to resort with his queen to St. Andrews, and lodge with Henry Wardlaw in his episcopal residence in the old sea-fort.[1] He visited, accompanied by the bishop, the rising schools, and was present at the disputations held there by the students. He did all he could to encourage the growth of the university. He invited from foreign universities many learned theologians to come and teach in the young Pæda-

[1] Lyon's *History of St. Andrews*, vol. i. p. 208.

gogium, and especially monks of the Carthusian order. And he ordered the regents or professors to recommend to him for ecclesiastical preferment none but students of proved capacity and learning and of virtuous life.

But James, though a lover of letters, and a patron of learning, had, unlike his descendant, the sixth James, nothing of the pedant in him. His breadth of human nature and his range of imagination required a freer field than the pursuits of a university. Tradition asserts that he was wont to hide his kingship, and stroll about in disguise, mingling freely with the poor people and the small farmers, that he might enjoy their humorous talk and hear what they thought of himself, of the nobles, and of the country.[1] In these excursions, in which he was imitated by his great-great-grandson James V., he often met with strange adventures among the peasantry. But, besides his disguises, the king betook himself to the Border dales for hunting and pastime. Professor Veitch, in his delightful book on Border History and Poetry, tells us, "that the face of James was as familiar in the border town of Peebles, and in the valleys of the Tweed, the Manor, and the Meggat, as is the presence of Queen Victoria in Braemar and on Deeside."

[1] Boethius, *Scot. Hist.*; Lesley, *De Reb. Gest. Scot.*, as quoted in a note of Irving's *History of Scotish Poetry* (Carlyle), p. 146.

A record of the scenes which James witnessed on those ramblings is preserved in the very ancient vernacular poem called " Peblis to the Play." The author of this poem is generally supposed to have been James I., though it is not quite beyond dispute. The poem, written in the Tweedside dialect, redolent of rustic life and manners, is a "picture of rural customs and festivities, and of the humorous and grotesque incidents of a mediæval Feast-day in an old provincial border town. There is here for the first time the humorous painting of rude social manners lit up by gleams of genial laughter, and by shrewd common sense," which became a characteristic feature of subsequent Scottish poetry.

Although the language is so archaic and vernacular as to be a little difficult to follow, yet the verse has such a merry ring, that it carries every heart along, and makes us join in the feeling of holiday merry-making.

This is the opening stanza :—

> " At Beltane, when ilk bodie bounis
>     To Peblis to the Play,
> To heir the singin and the sounds,
>     The solace, suth to say ;
> Be firth and forest furth they found,
>     They graythit them full gay ;
> God wot, that wald they do, that stound,
>     For it was their Feist-day
>         They said,
>     Of Peblis to the Play.

. . . . . . . .

If in *The King's Quair* James introduced to Scotland

the Chaucerian strain and the descriptive poetry which lasted in that country for centuries, in "Peblis to the Play" he set the example of another style—a style which, after being renewed from age to age, culminated in one of Burns's happiest poems—his Hallowe'en.

There is another poem of the same order which is often attributed to James I., but perhaps with less certainty; this is "Christ's Kirk o' the Grene." George Bannatyne, the earliest authority who mentions it, was born about 80 years after the death of James I., and he attributes it to that king. Other later authorities make James V. the author of it. However this may be, it has much resemblance to "Peblis to the Play." In subject, in tone and style, and in the peculiar metre, the two poems are alike.

I cannot take upon me to assert that this poem was actually the work of James I. But if "Peblis to the Play" was his, as seems most credible, then he has this claim at least to "Christ's Kirk o' the Grene," that he was the first to employ the stanza, and to set the tone to which it and other subsequent Scottish poems of the same order were set. But besides these vernacular poems, one or both, it seems probable that James composed more in the same kind, which have either been entirely forgotten or absorbed into the body of popular Scottish song.

James was then, as we have seen, a king, a statesman, a soldier, and a poet; but he was more.

It is difficult to believe in such universality of genius as is attributed to him, yet we cannot doubt it, unless we reject all the most direct contemporary evidence. Judging by authentic accounts of him which have come down to us, there seems hardly an accomplishment of body or mind with which he was not endowed. Though short of stature, his muscular strength was great; a good walker, fleet of foot, a fine horseman; the sword, the spear, and the bow he handled with equal skill. "His leisure hours," we are told, "were alternately dedicated to such hardy exercises, and to the pursuits of gardening, painting, music, and poetry."[1] He was a good architect, and planned many castles, and built or repaired the royal palace of Linlithgow, and the castles of Stirling and Edinburgh. On the royal residence of Linlithgow he lavished much care and expenditure. It had long been a royal manor, and the two first Stuart kings, James's father and grandfather, had frequently resided there.

Next to poetry, music was the art he most excelled in. Bower, his contemporary, tells that James not only sang sweetly himself, but could play deftly on every instrument then known, but especially the harp. Tassoni, an Italian writer, who lived in the time of James VI., mentions him as a distinguished musical composer. He says that he not only composed sacred music, but also invented a new kind of

[1] Irving, pp. 133-4.

plaintive melody, different from all others. Many indeed suppose that the peculiar and plaintive pathos that haunts our native melodies may have been first breathed into them by this royal musician.[1]

Though none of his descendants ever equalled himself in powers of mind and in range of accomplishments, yet to many of them he handed on some of that grace of manners, that refined sensibility to art, and that winning character, which gave to the Stuarts a deeper hold on popular affection than any royal race in Europe ever won. His daughters inherited not a little of that love of letters which distinguished their father above all other crowned heads. The eldest, Margaret, was betrothed while still an infant to the young Dauphin, afterwards Louis XI., of France. At the age of eleven she sailed from her native land, and in a few months was married, at Tours, to the Dauphin, then only twelve, by a papal dispensation. But Louis was a man of dark malignant nature, as is pictured in *Quentin Durward*, and neither the prudence of his young wife, nor her wit, or love of learning, or her poetic accomplishments, could save her brief life from misery. She died at Chalons, in her twenty-second year, lamented by all who knew her, a beautiful lady, and a good, says the old French Chronicler; she was a "patroness of men of letters, and herself a proficient in French poetry." She would sit up all night, it

[1] Irving, p. 158.

is said, composing rondeaux and ballads. A story is told of her, that one day, while passing through the gallery of the palace, she saw the French poet, Alain Chartier, lying fast asleep. As she passed, she stooped down and kissed him. When her ladies in attendance expressed some surprise that she should have done so, the princess replied, "It was not the man I kissed, but the mouth which had uttered so many fine things." "That kiss," says the reciter of the incident, "will immortalise her."[1]

Isabella, her second sister, who was married to the Duke of Bretagne, wrote in French a lament for her sister, the Dauphiness. Eleonora, the fourth daughter, translated into German a well-known French Romance of the time [*Pontus und Sidonia*], for the amusement of her less literate husband,[2] Sigismund, Archduke of Austria. Indeed, the stories and the fates of the six daughters of James would form a Romance in themselves; but over these I may not linger.

No history of any nation is more deeply indented by tragic incidents than that of Scotland. One of these has furnished Shakespeare with the subject of one of his most powerful dramas. But there are many more events in the Scottish annals of tragic interest equal to, if not greater than Macbeth, which no tragedian has ever touched. Among these is the

[1] See *Proceedings of Antiq.*, vol. iii. p. 91.
[2] *Antiq.*, vol. iii. p. 95.

death-scene of the first James. Though it has never that I know been dramatically described, it has been made the subject of the best and the most elaborate of Dante Rossetti's historic ballads, under the title of "The King's Tragedy."

Among historians, some regard the dark conspiracy which overwhelmed King James as the recoil upon his head of the wrath of feudal earls, exasperated beyond endurance.[1] Some trace it mainly to a dynastic plot, hatched by a hidden claimant of the Crown. Perhaps both elements combined towards the great tragedy. James had, as we know, broken up and annexed to the Crown many feudal earldoms, but in none of these annexations does his conduct seem to have been more questionable than in the case of the earldom of Strathearn, on the pretext that it had been inherited through the female line, whereas it was a male fief only. The uncle of the disinherited Earl, Sir Robert Graham, a man violent in character and implacable in revenge, rose in Parliament, in presence of all the barons, and denounced James to his face as a tyrant and oppressor. He had the audacity even to approach the royal seat, and lay his hand on the king, and say, "I arrest you in the name of all the three estates of your realm, here now assembled in this present parliament."[2]

[1] *Exchequer Rolls*, vol. v., Preface by Burnett, p. xl.
[2] Pinkerton's *History of Scotland*, vol. i. p. 135. *The Dethe of the Kynge of Scotis*, p. 50 (Maitland Club).

The king caused him to be imprisoned, forfeited, and banished, but soon released him. How he ever allowed so bold a rebel to go free seems inexplicable.

Graham retired to the country of the Wild Scots, as the Highlands were then called. Thence he sent a letter to the king, branding him as a tyrant and the ruiner of his family and house, and warning him, that, wherever he should find him, he would slay him as his mortal foe. Graham regarded himself, not only as the avenger of his family's wrongs, but as the champion and vindicator of the outraged nobles, who, though they secretly hated, were too craven-hearted to join in striking down, their oppressor. In the Highland fastnesses to which he had fled, Graham found one who lent a ready ear to his dark designs. This was the aged Walter Stewart, Earl of Athole and uncle of the king. He was the son of Robert II., and the representative of his second family by his wife Euphemia Ross. It is a fact well known and important in the history of that time, that the younger branch, this second family of Robert II., had always secretly held the elder branch, the children of Elizabeth Mure, to be illegitimate, owing to some irregularity in the marriage. James was the representative of the elder branch, and, wholly unsuspicious of his uncle's designs, had placed in him implicit confidence, and heaped on him many benefits. Walter, Earl of Athole, however, had long been a dark plotter, working as he could to remove, one after another, all members of the royal line who stood between him and the throne.

He had a hand in the plot which ended in the murder of his nephew Rothesay. He had been the king's chief adviser to extirpate his other nephew Murdoch and all his house, and had assisted at his condemnation. Such a man Graham would find little difficulty in persuading to join in the conspiracy to remove the king himself. Strange, is it not, that James, for all his knowledge of human nature, should never have suspected this hoary traitor? Whether Graham was the tool of Athole, or Athole the tool of Graham, is a matter of dispute. Mr. Burnett, the most recent authority, takes the first view. Tytler, Pinkerton, and Sir Walter Scott adopt the second. As the earl was himself too old ever to hope to reign, it was hoped by Graham that the Crown should be placed upon the head of Robert Stewart, Athole's grandson. This Robert Stewart the king loved and trusted as his own son, and promoted him to be his chamberlain, and to be much about his person.

Of no event in Scottish mediæval history have we a more minute and exact contemporary record than that which is preserved in the Chronicle entitled "The Dethe of the Kynge of Scotis." The incidents of that great tragedy are well known, but they are of so surpassing interest that they must again be told.

While Graham and Athole were preparing their

S

dark plot within the fastnesses of Athole, James, as if led by fate, went unwittingly straight into the midst of the meshes they were weaving for him. He resolved to hold the Christmas Festival in St. John's Town, as the city of Perth then was called, which was within a few miles of the mountains in which the traitors lay, waiting for his coming. Forth from Edinburgh he rode with his queen and a great retinue of nobles. When they reached the ferry, by which they were to cross the Scottish Sea, as the Firth of Forth was then called, a Highland woman, who was deemed a prophetess, rose before him, and standing by that same Scottish Sea, cried aloud, "My Lord King, an ye pass this water ye shall never return again alive." The king, struck with her wild looks and earnest manner, and remembering a prophecy he had read that a king should, in that year, be slain in Scotland, paused for a moment, and bade one of his knights stay and ask what she meant? He then passed the Firth of Forth with his queen and nobles, and rode on to Perth. There he took up his quarters in a cloister of the Dominican Convent or Abbey of the Black Friars, which lay without the town, hard by the North Inch. In that abbey he held a great feast at Christmas, and day after day passed in every kind of feudal delight and revelry. During those weeks his squires and James himself were visited by doleful dreams of a cruel serpent and horrible toad that assailed the king furiously in his chamber. Still, nothing dismayed, he lingered on far into the month of February. The fatal night fell between the 20th and 21st of that month. The traitors had been allowed full time to mature their plans, and that night Graham, with 300 Highlanders, had descended from the mountains and was already at the Convent gates.

He had induced Robert Stewart, the chamberlain, after dark, to lay planks across the moat that environed the garden of the monastery. He also "bruised and blundered" the locks of the doors of the king's chamber, so that no man might shut them.[1] While this was being done, Robert Stewart and his grandfather Athole, both before and after supper, were passing freely out and in to the king's presence. Three times that night, Christopher Chambers, one of the minions of the conspirators, drew near to the king, intending to warn him that danger was at hand, "but either his heart failed him, or he was prevented by the throng of knights and ladies who filled the presence-chamber."[2] The night was spent, says the old Chronicle, "att the playing of the chesse, att the tables, in redyng of Romans, in syngyng and pypyng, in harpying, and in other honest solaces of grete pleasance and disport."

While the "gamyn and the glee" were at their height, there was heard a loud knocking at the door.

[1] *Chron.* p. 55.   [2] Tytler, voL iii. p. 262.

The usher at length opened it, marvelling to see there the same woman that stood by the Scottish Sea. He asked what she would at that hour. She answered, "I have somewhat to tell the king," and implored earnestly to see him. The usher went in and told the king. He, "busy in playing," bade her "come again upon the morrow." "Well," said the old woman, "it shall repent you all that ye will not let me speak now with the king," and with that she departed sorrowfully, while the usher laughed at her as one who was demented. Within an hour the king called for "the Voidee" or parting cup, and drank, and all departed to rest. The last to leave was Robert Stewart.

The king, half unrobed, was standing before the chimney, talking to the queen and her gentlewomen before retiring to rest. Just at that moment he hearkened, and heard a great noise without, clattering of harness and tramp of armed men, and saw a great flare of torches through the convent windows. At once he bethought him of his deadly enemy Robert Graham. The queen and her ladies rushed to barricade the doors, but the bolts were gone. The king tried the windows, but they were fast with iron bars, soldered with molten lead into the stone. Graham was now at the outer door while the queen and her ladies were feebly trying to barricade it. One of them, Catherine Douglas, for lack of a bar, thrust her arm into the staple, but it was instantly broken by the brutal violence of the assassins. The king, in despair of other refuge, seized the tongs from the fireplace, and burst open a plank of the chamber floor, and went down to a vault underneath, closing the plank above himself. There was but one outlet from the vault, by which the king might have escaped beyond the reach of his foes, but this had been closed a few days before, by the king's order, because when he played there at tennis ("the pawme"), the balls went into it and were lost.

There was therefore nothing he could do but remain in that dark vault as quietly as he could. By this time the traitors and their armed followers had broken their way with levers and axes into the innermost chamber. There the ladies, shrieking with terror, had fled to the uttermost corner of the room. The queen stood speechless, petrified with horror. One of the murderers attacked and wounded her as she stood there "astonied," and he would have slain her had not a son of Graham commanded him to hold his hand, saying, "She is but a woman; let us go and seek the king himself." And they sought him everywhere, "in the withdrawing chambers, in the litters, under the presses, the forms, the chairs, and all other places," but in vain. Then they passed to search for him in other parts of the precinct.

The king for a long time hearing no noise or stir, thought that they had all gone from the Convent, and raising the plank, cried to the ladies to bring sheets and "draw him out of that unclean place." As they were helping him up, one of the ladies, Elizabeth Douglas, fell into the vault beside the king.

Whether attracted by the noise of this fall, or by a sudden thought, one of the accomplices, Thomas[1] Chambers, who was familiar with the king and all his ways, remembered the secret vault, and that they had not searched it. Returning thither, he looked and saw that the plank of the floor had been broken up. He raised it, and looking down with a torch exclaimed, "Sirs, the spouse (or bride) is found for whom we have come, and all this night have carolled here." Straightway one of Graham's minions, Sir John Hall, leapt down into the vault, and with his dagger assailed the unarmed king. But James, such was his strength, seized the miscreant by the throat, and dashed him to the ground beneath his feet. Hall's brother followed, but the king threw him down above his brother. So strong was the king's hand that the marks of his grip were said to be visible on their throats when, a month afterwards, they were brought out for execution.

The arch-traitor, Robert Graham, seeing that the two Halls were unequal to the work, himself sprang down upon the king with a drawn sword, "an horribill and mortall wepone," as the Chronicle has it. Faint and weary with the struggle, weaponless, "the more

[1] *Robert* in the Chronicle, p. 57; *Thomas* in Tytler. [The latter is correct. See *Exchequer Rolls*, vol. v., Introd. p. xliv.]

peté was," says the Chronicle—his hands bleeding with the wounds from the Halls' daggers, the king called on Graham for mercy.

"Thou cruel tyrant," answered Graham, "thou hadst never mercy on lords born of thy blood, nor other gentlemen that came in thy danger, therefore no mercy shalt thou have here." "Then I beseech thee, for the salvation of my soul, let me have a confessor." "Thou shalt never have other confessor but this same sword," answered Graham, and with that he thrust it through the body of the king. Seeing the king lying bleeding at his feet, and still faintly imploring mercy, even the iron heart of Graham relented, and he would have turned back, leaving the bloody deed half done. But the other traitors called to him from above, that if he did not at once complete his work he should die by their hands. Graham then, with the two Halls, fell upon the king with their daggers and slew him with many stabs.

There were sixteen deadly wounds in his breast alone. There lay dead the flower of the Scottish kings, one to be compared with his great ancestor the Bruce, in the 44th year of his age and the 13th of his real reign. By this time, but too late, the town of Perth was aroused, and the king's household and the citizens of Perth with torches and weapons were hurrying to the rescue.[1] But through the darkness, the assassins, all save one, escaped and

[1] *Tales of a Grandfather*, chap. xix.

fled back to the mountains. No event ever so struck the heart of the whole country, or aroused such resentment in all, from the greatest earl to the humblest peasant. But cruel and dastardly as the murder was, hardly less cruel was the vengeance that followed it. The queen and all the nobles urging on the pursuit, within a month every one of the murderers died on the scaffold with the most hideous tortures which barbarous ingenuity could devise.

The king who thus died in the Dominican Convent of Black Friars' Abbey near the North Inch was buried in the Carthusian Monastery or Charter House, near the South Inch, which he himself had founded. His heart, like that of his great ancestor Robert Bruce, was taken from his body before interment, and sent on a pilgrimage to the East, probably to the Holy Land. But, like the heart of Bruce, it never reached it, but was sent back in 1443 from the Isle of Rhodes, in the keeping of a Knight of St. John, and presented to the Carthusian monks at Perth. We may hope that they laid it with his body in the tomb in this precinct. That tomb was attended and adorned with much care, and the doublet which the king wore on the fatal night was long preserved by the Carthusian Brotherhood. But both tomb and doublet disappeared in that whirlwind which swept away so many venerable things at the Scottish Reformation.

The work of bringing order out of chaos, which James had so vigorously begun, was renewed age after age, by each successive James, when their turbulent minorities were past. But it was still unaccomplished when the Reformation came, and when the sixth James passed to the throne of England.

## VIII.—THE SONGS OF SCOTLAND BEFORE BURNS.[1]

THERE was a time, long since gone, when poetry and music were one. If there was instrumental music without poetry, there was no word-poetry without either vocal or instrumental music, or both. But in time the twin sisters were sundered, "not without tears." If the separation brought some gain to each, it brought also some loss. In one kind of poetry alone has the divorce not been effected—in those vocal melodies which now monopolise the name of song. In all the other forms of modern poetry it is complete; only some hint of the former union still lives in the words "lyre," "harp," and such like, applied to the poet's work—words now so wide of the reality as to have become trite and meaningless. Yet, notwithstanding this long divorce, there is a kinship between the inward swell of all emotion and musical sound, which nothing can destroy—a subtle connection to which no form of merely read words, however perfect, is adequate, but which forces those who

[1] [Contributed to *Macmillan's Magazine*, 1861.]

feel it deeply to give it utterance by not reading, but chanting all high poetry. No man ever yet felt the power of a fine poem without being tempted to intone it. Every poet, I suppose, chants, not reads, his own poetry, thus unconsciously vindicating the old name of singer, or ἀοιδός. It is as if poetry, even after centuries of separation, still remembered the home of her childhood, and went wandering back in search of her long-lost sister. An interesting subject of thought this kinship between poetry and music, on which, however, I cannot linger, but must turn to the one kind of poetry in which they are still combined. And nowhere is that union more perfect than in the national songs of Scotland.

It is not, however, on their musical so much as on their poetical side that I shall now regard them. While they interest us by representing, in the best sense of the word, the poetry of the people, they win our admiration by their literary excellence. Often, the songs or poems which have found most favour with the poor are not excellent, while those which are excellent have not pleased the poor.

The greatest poets of our country, Milton, Spenser, Wordsworth, even Shakespeare—these require at least some education for their appreciation. However wide be their audience, it is still limited. As you descend in the social scale, you reach a class, and that numerically by far the largest, into which they have never penetrated. How many a worthy artisan and field-labourer has there been in England to whom Shakespeare was a name uncared for, perhaps unknown! But in the songs of Scotland we meet with words, which, while they thrill the simplest, most untutored bosoms, as no book-poetry can, find a scarcely less full response in hearts the most educated and refined. This, then, their catholicity, their power of commanding a universal sympathy is their first strong claim on our regard.

Akin to this is that other characteristic of them—their transparent truthfulness. No other poetry I know keeps so close to life and nature, giving the fact as truly as a photograph, yet idealising it. Veritable Pre-Raphaelites these old song-makers must have been, without knowing it. It would almost seem as if there was no art, no literature, in them; as though they were the very words, as they fell from the lips, of actual men and women. These are the true pastorals, by the side of which all pastorals and idylls, ancient and modern, look artificial and unreal. The productions, many of them, not of book-learned men, but of country people, with country life, cottage characters and incidents for their subject, they utter the very feelings which poor men have felt, in the very words and phrases which poor men have used. No wonder the people love them; for never was the heart of any people more fully rendered in poetry than Scotland's heart in these songs. Like the hodden-grey, the cotters' wear in former times, warp and woof, they are entirely home-spun. The stuff out of which they are composed,

> "The cardin' o't, the spinnin' o't,
> The warpin' o't, the winnin' o't,"

is the heart-fibre of a stout and hardy peasantry. Here are no Arcadian lawns nor myrtle bowers, but the heathery "knowes" and broomy "burnsides," the "bught," the byre, the stackyard, and blazing "ingle"—no Damons or Chloes, but Willie and Jeanie—the Allans and Marions of our villages and heather-thatched cottage-homes. Every way you take them—in authorship, in subject, in sentiment, in tone, in language—they are the creation and the property of the people. And, if educated men and high-born ladies, and even some of the Scottish kings, have added to the store, it was only because they had lived familiarly among the peasantry—felt as they felt, and spoke their language—that they were enabled to sing such strains as their country's heart would own. For the whole character of these melodies, various as they are, is so peculiar and pronounced that the smallest foreign element introduced, one word out of keeping, grates on the ear, and mars the music.

Note also their power to unite past with present, blending ancient with modern life. Laying such a hold on the far past, they so bring it down into the present, they have such antiquity of style, yet such continuity, that in them old things are new, and new old. Homeliest occurrences of to-day are rescued from vulgarity, and take new interest and dignity, when touched with their mellowing light. Rising far back in the warlike centuries, they come down through all changes of Scottish life, even till the present hour, full of the rugged manhood, the drollery, the humour broad or sly, the light-hearted merriment, the simple tenderness, here and there the devout pathos, of the men who first sang them; letting in, with a word or two, the whole scenery of a countryside for back-ground; condensing into a line a whole world of Scottish manners and character —heart-music as they are, of many generations of its people. They have a strain for every season of life, for every mood of soul—seed-time and harvest, bridal and burial, childhood's mirth, manhood's strength, mellow evening of age, the fair and the rocking, house-heatings and harvest homes, the burnside tryst, married fellowship of joy and sorrow, jest and laughter, lamentation and tears.

Lastly, as they faithfully represent the peasant life of Scotland, so they throw back on it that consecration which only song can give. There is not a moss-thatched cottage and kail-yard from Tweed to Tay but looks more beautiful for these songs. Blended with the lives of men and women, how many else unknown localities have they made dear, even to eyes that never looked on them

When the Canadian of Scottish descent returns, after the second or third generation, to visit the land of his ancestors, the names of these melodies are his guides. They come to us, in many tones but one harmony, from Border streams whose very names are songs, Annan, Tweedside, Yarrow—from dusky moorlands, where the shy whaups are screaming; from Lothian furrows, with their sturdy ploughmen; from "hairst-rigs" of Ayrshire, blithe with shearers' voices, mingled with wilder Celtic cadences from "out-ouer the Forth." The Braes of Athole and Balquhidder are in them, Lochaber, and Moidart, and the far blue Hebrides.

But, though the Highlands have lent some glorious gleams to these songs, they are but gleams, such as the far-off Highland Bens cast down on the plains or lowlier hills of the Lowlands. The Highlanders have their own Celtic music and Celtic songs, of a character entirely distinct. The songs I speak of belong wholly to the Scottish Lowlanders, though they may have caught some of their wildness from the Highlands—a fact I need not have mentioned, but that so many English men and women confound the Scottish Lowlands and Highlands, as if they were all one, knowing not how wide apart they have been and still are, in their history, their character, and their language.

A like confusion is often made between our ballads and our songs. Though there are a few which might be ranked indifferently under either head, such as are "The Bonnie Earl o' Moray," and "Bonny George Campbell," yet, as a general rule, they are easily distinguishable. Let those who may be ignorant of the difference compare any of the ballads collected by Scott in his *Border Minstrelsy* with the best-known songs of Burns—"The Outlaw Murray," or "The Douglas Tragedy," for instance, with "O' a' the airts," or "John Anderson, my Jo." He will at once see that, in the ballad, narrative is the main element, and the effect is produced by the undercurrent of power or pathos with which the story is told and the incidents are selected; that the song, on the other hand, is the embodiment of an emotion or sentiment, which is simple, direct, all-pervading; what narrative or reflection there may be is quite subordinate, and is used as the mere framework on which the inspiring sentiment is hung. The moment that narrative predominates, you have a ballad; that thought becomes prominent, a reflective lyric; but in either case the pure song is gone—for emotion or sentiment is song's vital air, in which alone it lives, removed from which it dies. Lastly, the song must be composed of the simplest, most familiar, most musical words, with that native lilt in them which is melodious feeling become audible—which, coming from the heart, goes straight to the heart.

It is believed by many in the south, and even by some natives of the north, that Scotland's song began with Burns, that he is the creator of it, and that all else there is of it is but an echo of his primal melody. This opinion is contrary to all analogy, is disproved by abundant facts, and would have been disclaimed by no one more indignantly than by Burns himself. It might be truly said that Burns stands to our song, as Shakespeare does to the English drama. What centuries of mystery-plays, popular legends, stories from English history, acted in rude fashion to village audiences, must have pioneered the way ere the English drama could culminate in Shakespeare! And for how many generations had Scotland been warbling her native songs ere she uttered herself in the perfect melodies of Burns! To each of these belongs, not the creation, but the ripe glory of his own peculiar art. None knew better, or felt more deeply, than Burns how much he owed to these old nameless song-makers of Scotland. He never alludes to them but with the kindliest affection, and fain would have rescued their names and memory from oblivion.

But though, no doubt, the lineage of the words of these songs is old, yet older than them all, and behind them all, lies that great background of native music, which has been the true inspirer of the words, which has come down to us a heritage unidentified with any personal name, but sounding like the far-heard music of nature and time and foregone humanity blending in one. The origin of these tunes, whether

T

they be the remains of the old Roman plain chant, surviving in the people's memory long after it has been banished from their worship; or whether, as some have vainly thought, their seeds were first sown by foreign Court-musicians, such as Rizzio; or whether they came to us through our Norse forefathers, as their likeness to the Norwegian tunes and to songs still sung by the lone Faroe Islanders would perhaps indicate, no one has as yet determined. Mr. Chappell, in his *Popular Music of the Olden Time*, has lately claimed for England several tunes which have long been held native to Scotland; but we may leave it to Scottish antiquarians and musicians to maintain the nativity of our tunes, as well as to explain their genius, the sudden transitions from scale to scale, the omission of certain sounds common in other music, the peculiar tonality, which are said to form their most marked characteristics. This only I know—they are like no other tunes. Simple, wild, irregular, yet with a marked, dignified, expressive character quite their own, "caller" as the mountain air, yet old as the mountains over which it blows—strong and full of purpose, yet with a pleasing vagueness that carries you far away into solitary places, or back into a dim antiquity, or deep down to the child's heart long buried within the man's—often humorous and droll, lively and light-hearted, with the skylark's tones in them, yet earnest as nature's own light-heartedness—oftener sorrowful, with a sadness deepening into profoundest pathos, yet always manly — always, whether in joy or lamentation, truthful, kindly, human-hearted!

The mystery that hangs over the first composers of our oldest airs and words, much as we may long to pierce it, adds I know not how much to their imaginative charm. As we read or hear them, there mingles with their cadences a vague feeling of sympathy with those old nameless song-makers, lying in their unknown graves all Scotland over, "buried," as Wilson beautifully says, "centuries ago in kirkyards that have themselves perhaps ceased to exist, and returned to the wilderness—lonesome burial-places, such as one sometimes sees among the hills, where man's dust continues to be laid after the house of God had been removed elsewhere." Whatever charm there may be in this unknown authorship, there is little fear of its being broken by any results of inquiry. The oldest extant songs cannot be proved, at least, to have existed before the year 1600. Before that, none of our present ones, even if they may have had an oral life, had any existence in print. Nor is this wonderful. What little printing there was in Scotland during the foregoing century was employed on other documents than the songs of the people. Naturally, these are always the last kind of literature to find their way to the printing-press. But though no individual songs can be identified before A.D. 1600, the lineage of the race can be traced three centuries further back.

Almost the earliest scrap of our national song that survives is a snatch of a triumphal song for the victory of Bannockburn—

> "Maydens of England, sore may ye morne,
> For your lemmans ye have lost at Banokysborne;
>    With heve a lowe.
> What! weneth the kynge of England
> So soon to have won Scotlond?
>    With rumbylowe."

"This song," says the English chronicler who preserved it, "was, after many days, sung in dances in the carols of the maidens and minstrels of Scotland, to the reproofe and disdayne of Englishmen, *with dyvers other*, which I overpass." Some other snatches of song have come down to us from the same age, all in the same strain, jeers and gibes of the Scots against "their auld enemies of England." About a century later, the first James, the ablest of all his race, and one of the most accomplished princes of Europe in the middle age, is well known to have been eminent both as a poet and a musician. During his English captivity, he composed *The King's Quair*—a poem which Ellis, a good judge, and no Scot, thinks will stand comparison with any like poem of Chaucer. After his return to Scotland, notwithstanding his lifelong strifes with his untamed barons, he still found time to compose other poems and songs, and among them a highly humorous poem, called *Peblis to the Play* which contains the first lines of two songs then sung by the country people. "There fure ane man to the holt" (there went a man to the wood), and "Thair sal be mirth at our meting zit." His two long poems still remain; his songs have all either perished, or perhaps, having become blended with others of later date, are now unidentified.

From the death of James, A.D. 1437, down to the opening of the seventeenth century, the thread of song has been traced by such facts as these: that a rude comic poem, called "Cockleby's Sow," of the middle of the fifteenth century, in the description of a rustic merrymaking, gives the titles, or first lines, of about thirty tunes and songs, sung or danced to by the peasantry—titles which, if not exactly the same as, are entirely in the style and tone of, our oldest extant songs; that Gawin Douglas, bishop of Dunkeld, in the prologues to his translation of the *Æneid* into "Scottish metir"—a book which is a regular mine of the Scottish language, mentions the first lines of several "ring-sangis, dances, ledis, and roundis," commonly sung by the country-people of his day; that Wedderburn's *Complaynt of Scotland*, the first original work printed in Scottish prose, 1549, has imbedded in it a whole layer of fossil songs, some of which are perhaps the same as individual songs still well known, while of the greater part the first lines prove them akin to those we still have; lastly, that before the seventeenth century, while an English traveller in Palestine was passing through a village not far from Jerusalem, he overheard a woman, as she sat at her door and dandled her child, singing to herself, "Bothwell bank, thou blumest fayre." The Englishman addressed her, and found that she was a Scotch woman, who had married an officer under the Turk, and gone with him first to Venice and thence to Palestine, where she was now soothing her exile with this song from her own country. These and many more like facts serve to mark the existence and course of our national songs before they come down to the age of written evidence, like the thin silver thread among black mountain precipices by which the eye traces the headlong torrent up where distance still keeps it silent and inaccessible.

The seventeenth century is, as has been said, the earliest to which we can with certainty trace back any of our still extant songs, though some of them may be of older date, or may incorporate in themselves older strains. The ground for fixing the opening of the seventeenth century as the birth-time of our oldest is, that when men began early in last century to collect the most popular songs, there were many which they put down as of unknown antiquity, and which, therefore, cannot be of later date than the time I have named. Shakespeare enables us to fix the date of one of them, or, at least, the time later than which it cannot have been made. Iago quotes, with some striking variations from our set, two verses of the well-known Scotch song, "Tak your auld cloak about ye"—a song, by the way, with which the great Duke of Wellington was so taken, when he heard it sung at a Scottish dinner in London, that he asked to have it sung a second time. The occurrence of two verses of this song in the play of *Othello*, first published 1602, and the variations from the Scotch set, suggest one or two interesting questions, which, however, I cannot now stay to consider. There were many things going on in Scotland during that seventeenth century which might have been expected to have driven song-making out of men's heads. Among the educated classical learning had just come in, and much of the best wit of the time spent itself on writing Latin verses. There were educated poets, too, in Scotland then, such as Drummond of Hawthornden, and Alexander, Earl of Stirling; but they disdained their homely mother tongue, and wrote their sonnets in the best English they could achieve. As the century wore on, the people were busy with the Covenant, first maintaining and enforcing it, then suffering for it. And the ministers of that age, it is well known, discouraged all song as profane—not without some reason, it must be owned, from the coarseness and looseness of many that were then most popular. But neither modern learning nor religious wars could drive out of the people's heart the love of their native minstrelsy. From out-of-the-way nooks, here and there, came true snatches of the old strain, genuine outpourings of the old spirit, still pure from the mixture of modern classicalities which a little later nearly put an end to our native melodies. Such are—

1. The gaberlunzie man.
2. The auld gudeman.
3. Todlen but and Todlen ben.
4. Andro' and his cutty gun.
5. Although I be but a country lass.
6. O gin my wife wad drink hooly and fairly.
7. Here awa, there awa, wandering Willie. (Old set.)
8. My love, he's built a bonnie ship, and set her on the sea.
9. A cock laird fou cadgie wi' Jennie did meet.
10. On Ettrick banks, ae simmer nicht,
    At gloamin, when the sheep gaed hame.
11. Fy! let us a' to the bridal, for there will be lilting there.
12. O saw ye Johnnie comin', quo' she.

It were easy to go on multiplying the names of songs like these, of undoubtedly the old time; that is, which were reckoned so 150 years ago, when men first began to collect the country melodies which till then had only an oral existence. They are born of a kind of life, once universal in Scotland, which has now nearly disappeared before large sheep-walks and high farming with its bothy-system, or, at least, has retired into the most out-of-the-way moorlands, whither these twin products of modern times have not yet penetrated. They bring before us the "theekit" green moss-roofed farms, with their old-fashioned "buts" and "bens," in which dwelt the gudeman, farmer, or bonnet laird, wearing the antique broad blue bonnet, and clad in home-spun hodden-grey, who tilled the "mailen," or, maybe, small lairdship, with his own labour and that of his family. In such a life, master and servant, if servant there was, lived on a footing of equality and kindliness; dined on the same homely fare, at the same board; sat when work was over by the same ingle-cheek. It was a healthful state, in which wants were few, life was strong, and if, in some respects, coarse to our apprehensions, it was full of a kindliness and neighbourliness, such as is always most marked in early times, and in a retired narrow country. The occurrence of a wedding between a "neibur" lad and lass, a dispute between a "gudeman" and his "kimmer," a harvest "kirn," or a curling "bonspiel," was enough deeply to excite the neighbourhood, and to draw forth the fun and broad drollery latent in a whole country-side.

Here is one specimen, called "The barrin' o' the door." Tradition reports the scene of it to have lain in Crauford Muir, a high upland district, near the springs of Clyde, between Lanarkshire and Dumfriesshire; and those who in coaching days may have travelled over it in winter-time, on the top of the Glasgow or Carlisle mail, will enter feelingly into the situation of the wedded pair, with their door open to a Martinmas moorland wind on a winter night in such a place :—

"It fell about the Martinmas time,
    And a gay time it was then, O,
When our gudewife had puddins to mak,
    And she boiled them in the pan, O.
And the barrin' o' our door, weil, weil, weil,
    And the barrin' o' our door weil.

The wind blew cauld frae north to south,
    And blew into the floor, O ;
Quoth our gudeman to our gudewife,
    'Get up and bar the door, O.'
       And the barrin', etc.

'My hand is in my hussyfskip,
    Gudeman, as ye may see, O ;
An it shouldna be barr'd this hunner year,
    It's no be barr'd for me,' O.

They made a paction 'tween them twa,
    They made it firm and sure, O,
The first that spak the foremost word
    Should rise and bar the door, O.

Then by there came twa gentlemen,
    At twal' o' clock at nicht, O ;
And they could neither see house nor ha',
    Nor coal nor candle licht, O.

'Now, whether is this a rich man's house,
    Or whether is it a puir, O ? '
But ne'er a word wad ane o' them speak
    For barrin' o' the door, O.

And first they ate the white puddins,
    And syne they ate the black, O ;
And muckle thocht our gudewife to hersel',
    Yet ne'er a word she spak, O.

Then said the t'ane unto the t'other,
    'Hae, man, tak ye my knife, O,
Do ye tak aff the auld man's beard,
    And I'll kiss the gudewife,' O.

  'But there's nae water in the house,
   And what shall we do then, O?'
  'What ails ye at the puddin' broo,
   That boils into the pan, O?'

  O up then startit our gudeman,
   And an angry man was he, O;
  'Wad ye kiss my wife before my face,
   And scaud me wi' puddin' bree, O?'

  Then up and startit our gudewife,
   Gied three skips on the floor, O:
  'Gudeman, ye've spoken the foremost word,
   Get up and bar the door, O.'"

Of probably the same age, though in a far other spirit, is that heart-broken strain, beginning—

  "O, Waly, Waly, up the bank."

Let no Englishman read it, "Waily, Waily," as they sometimes do, but as broadly as they can get their lips to utter it—"O Wawly, Wawly."

Chambers, following Motherwell, supposes the subject of it to have been a Lady Barbara Erskine, married in 1670 to the second Marquis of Douglas, who, having had his mind poisoned by the foul slander of some former lover of his wife's, deserted her, while she was confined in child-bed, and never saw her more. However this may be, poetry has nowhere anything more forsaken and heart-lorn,—

  "O, Waly, Waly, up the bank,
   And Waly, Waly, down the brae,
  And Waly, Waly, yon burnside,
   Where I and my love wont to gae!
  I lean'd my back unto an aik,
   I thoucht it was a trusty tree;
  But first it bow'd, and syne it brak:
   Sae my true love did lichtlie me.

> O, Waly, Waly, but love be bonnie
>   A little time while it is new;
> But when it's auld, it waxes cauld,
>   And fades away like mornin' dew.
> O wherefore should I busk my heid?
>   Or wherefore should I kame my hair?
> For my true love has me forsook,
>   And says he'll never love me mair.
>
> . . . . .
>
> 'Tis not the frost that freezes fell,
>   Nor blawing snaw's inclemencie;
> 'Tis not sic cauld that makes me cry,
>   But my love's heart's grown cauld to me.
> When we came in by Glasgow toun,
>   We were a comely sicht to see;
> My love was clad in the black velvet,
>   And I mysel' in cramasie.
>
> But had I wist, afore I kiss'd,
>   That love had been sae ill to win,
> I'd lock'd my heart in a case o' gowd,
>   And pinn'd it wi' a siller pin.
> Oh! oh! if my young babe were born,
>   And set upon the nurse's knee,
> And I mysel' were dead and gane,
>   And the green grass growing over me!"

These two samples fairly represent the style and range of our oldest extant songs. The name of no author claims them—indeed, few authors' names have come down to us from earlier than the eighteenth century. Two of the seventeenth, however, may be mentioned: Semple of Beltrees, reputed author of "Fy! let us a' to the bridal," and "Maggy Lauder," though his claim to these is not beyond question; and Lord Yester, maker of the oldest and best set of words to the air of "Tweedside."

But the most marked epoch in the history of song before Burns was the advent of Allan Ramsay and the publication of his *Tea-table Miscellany*, 1724. Allan was born and lived, till his fifteenth year, among the Lead Hills, by the springs of Clyde, a pastoral district, rich in native song and music, the love of which clung to him throughout his life, which was spent in very different scenes. When he was only fifteen he left for good his native hills, and came to Edinburgh, where he was apprenticed to a peruke-maker, then a flourishing trade, as this was the age when perukes roofed all fashionable skulls. But as soon as his time was out, Allan quitted the wig-making trade, lucrative though it was—a good wig then cost from twenty to fifty guineas—and opened a bookseller's shop; choosing rather, in his own words, " to line the inside of the pash, than to theek the out." From this shop issued, from time to time on single sheets, Ramsay's songs and other productions, which were greedily bought up as they appeared. In 1724 they were all given to the world in the *Tea-table Miscellany*, a collection of songs containing four distinct kinds—(1) Old characteristic songs, which had floated among the people "time out of mind;" (2) Songs of the same kind, but changed and recocted at the discretion of the editor; (3) About sixty songs by Allan himself, with thirty by "some ingenious young gentlemen, who were so well pleased with his undertaking that they generously lent him their assistance." These are generally headed by, and bear the names of, very old tunes, and were probably substituted for others of the antique stamp, which Allan may have deemed too homely, or, it may be, sometimes too coarse for publication. (4) A number of English songs.

The appearance of this miscellany was remarkable in many ways, but it was not for the excellence of the majority of its contents. In truth, we should not lose much if, of the four divisions, the last two were utterly expunged. For Allan himself no Scot but must entertain a most kindly feeling. He was an honest, social, blithe-hearted "chield," not without a strain of his country's humour, and every way a patriotic Scot. But while we thank him for what of our songs he has preserved, we are provoked that he should not have preserved more while he might. As for his own songs, not to mention those written by his friends, not one of them is of the highest order. I am not sure that there is one of them all which a critical editor, intent on culling only the flower of Scottish melody, could admit into his collection. With a natural line, sometimes a genuine verse here and there, there is not one that has the ring of the true metal from beginning to end.

It must be said, however, that Burns never speaks of him but with warmest gratitude. In his poem on "Pastoral Poetry," after lamenting the scarcity of true pastoral poets, he breaks out into this hearty strain—

> "Yes! there is ane; a Scottish callan—
> There's ane; come forrit, honest Allan!
> Thou need na jouk behint the hallan,
>         A chiel sae clever;
> The teeth o' Time may gnaw Tamtallan,
>         But thou's for ever!
>
> In gowany glens thy burnie strays,
> Where bonnie lasses bleach their claes;
> Or trots by hazelly shaws and braes
>         Wi' hawthorns gray,
> Where blackbirds join the shepherd's lays
>         At close o' day."

But this applies rather to his pastoral drama, *The Gentle Shepherd*, than to his songs.

The fact is, that Allan had a genuine love of our native songs, but his town life, and the literature then fashionable, were too much for him. From his fifteenth year he lived solely in Edinburgh, with only brief glimpses of the country, so that there is in his would-be pastoral songs an unreality and a mawkishness, along with a coarseness and obtuseness in the sentiment, if not in the words, very unlike the directness and heartiness of the old. Then he lived among the classicalities and frigidities of the Queen Anne poetry, than which can anything be imagined more alien to our old minstrelsy? Can we wonder that Ramsay could not set at nought its influence, but tried to engraft some of its refinements on the old stock? But the result was a very deluge of vapid classicalities, which had nearly extinguished the native fire—Scottish lads and lassies appearing as Damon, Phyllis, and Chloris, calling the sun Phœbus, and the moon Cynthia, and vowing fidelity by Jove and Pallas.

But even in its greatest obscuration, during the first half of last century, the ancient lyrical inspiration never failed. However those who were exposed to the then nascent literature of Edinburgh, and to the Pope style of poetic diction, may have had their finer sense of song dulled, the springs of it were still running clear in country places, south and north, remote from such contagions. In the very time that Ramsay's "Miscellany" was in its first access of popularity, the north country gave birth, among other songs that might be named, to that well-known and most sweet melody, both air and words, "O Logie o' Buchan, O Logie the laird." It was composed about 1736, by George Halket, schoolmaster of Rathen, in Aberdeenshire, known in his day for a most devoted Jacobite, who let loose many a strain and squib in favour of the exiled family to float about, to the delight of the country people and the danger of his own head. There is another as genuine strain, born a little later, in the north country, too, "My daddie is a cankert carle." Its author, James Carnegie, was laird of Balnamoon on the slopes of the Grampians, to the north-west of Brechin, and was remembered long after as "a curious body." He, too, was a staunch Jacobite, was out in the Forty-five, and, after Culloden, had to live for some time under hiding, as a shepherd to one of his own hill farmers. As Carnegie's song is less known than "Logie o' Buchan," though of not a less genuine stamp, it may be well to give it here—

Tune—"*Low doun i' the brume.*"

"My daddie is a cankert carle,
　　He'll no twine wi' his gear;
My Minnie, she's a scauldin' wife,
　　Hauds a' the house asteer.

　　　But let them say, or let them do,
　　　　It's a' ane to me,
　　　For he's low doun, he's in the brume,
　　　　That's waitin' on me:

　　　Waitin' on me, my love,
　　　　He's waitin' on me:
　　　For he's low doun, he's in the brume,
　　　　That's waitin' on me.

My Auntie Kate sits at her wheel,
　　And sair she lichtlies me;
But weel ken I it's a' envy,
　　For ne'er a Joe has she.
　　　But let them say, etc.

My Cousin Kate was sair beguiled
　　Wi' Johnie o' the Glen;
And aye sinsyne she cries, Beware
　　O' fause deluding men.
　　　But let them say, etc.

Gleed Sandy he cam' wast yestreen,
　　And speir'd when I saw Pate;
And aye sinsyne the neebors round,
　　They jeer me air and late,
　　　But let them say, etc."

U

Let this show how the north country could still sing through its Jacobite laird, while the ingenious young gentlemen of Edinburgh were coquetting with their Chlorises and their Chloes. But the south, if anything, outdid the north in the exquisiteness of the songs it gave birth to during the same age.

How could it but sing—that delightsome Border land, with its hundred dales, not a stream of which but has lent its name to some immemorial ballad or familiar melody—with, midmost of all, Yarrow—the very sanctuary of song—lying there like a pensive, feeling heart, and sending through all the land its own pathetic undertone, to mellow whatever in our songs and character might else have been too robustly shrewd or too broadly humorous. In the early years of last century, that Border land gave birth to three ladies, of three of its oldest families, whose names come down to us, each linked to and immortalised by a single song. These sweet singers were Lady Grisell Baillie, Miss Jane Elliot of Minto, and Miss Rutherford, of Fairnielee, afterwards Mrs. Cockburn.

These were hearts in which nature was too strong to be chilled by the fashion of the hour. The old peelhouses in which they were born looked out on the Border hills, and they themselves spent their youth in closest and kindliest intimacy with the dwellers of the scattered hamlets and "farm-towns" among them. For this is one of the facts these songs bear witness to—the close interchange of feeling between the laird's family and that of the humblest cottar round about, long after feudalism had ceased. But for this, these ladies of gentle blood never had sung those strains that ever since have lived in all Scottish hearts, "gentle and semple" alike. It was the " owerword," or refrain, of an old lament for the foresters who fell at Flodden that Miss Elliot caught up and wove into the oldest of the two sets of *The Flowers of the Forest* which we now have—a song so beautifully pathetic as almost to make up for the original dirge, hopelessly lost in our day, perhaps lost even in hers. Only a little less good, if indeed they be less, are Miss Rutherford's later words to the same air. They sang themselves through her heart, doubtless, while she lived at, or when in after life she recalled, the old enlarged peel of Fairnielee, the home, so blithe and beautiful, in which she was born and passed her childhood; from which she must so often have gazed over the Tweed and the woods of Yair up into the bosom of the Forest Hills. That now forsaken mansion, not yet roofless, but soon to be so, standing on the braeside among disappearing terraces, holly hedges run to waste, trees few and forlorn with decay, hearing now no music but the Tweed far below, or the owlet's cry, or the wind soughing through its cobwebbed rooms, what an affecting commentary on the song first sung there !—

"I've seen the smiling of Fortune beguiling;
I've felt all its favours and found its decay."

The other lady singer I have mentioned was of an earlier day than these two, and her youth was cast on stormier times, which put her heart to proof, and showed it heroic. Grisell Hume was daughter of Sir Patrick Hume of Polwarth, a staunch Presbyterian, when it cost something to be one, and, notwithstanding Lord Macaulay's unfavourable estimate, seemingly a true patriot and friend of freedom. In the Scottish Parliament, all through Charles the Second's reign, he withstood that king's despotisms, and for his free speech more than once suffered imprisonment. He was one of a small band of Scotsmen who entered into negotiations with the English Whigs to prevent a Popish succession—a cause for which, in England, Lord William Russell lost his life, and in Scotland, Robert Baillie of Jerviswood. Baillie was an intimate friend of Hume's, and when he was thrown into prison it was time for Sir Patrick to look to his own head. But before he could find his way beyond seas, his first place of hiding was the family burial vault underneath the parish kirk of Polwarth. In that ghastly concealment, where, even by day, no light could enter, he passed many weeks of the autumn of 1684, with no attendant but his daughter Grisell, then only twelve years old, who each night, after dark, made her way, all alone, from the family home to her father's retreat, bearing his food and what news she had been able to gather. It is said that, in order to avoid the suspicions, even of the household, she used to save off her own plate, at family meals, the food she bore him. During this time, her father wished to send a letter to his friend Baillie, in his cell, and to receive back some tidings from him. His daughter was the messenger. And it was during this visit to the Tolbooth that she is said to have met, for the first time, George Baillie, the son, who afterwards became her husband. As much for the character of the authoress as for its own worth, her single song is here given :—

> " There was anes a may, and she loo'd na men ;
> She biggit her bonnie bouir doun i' yon glen ;
> But now she cries, Dule, and a well-a-day !
> Come doun the green gate, and come here away.
>
> When bonnie young Johnie cam ower the sea,
> He said he saw naething sae lovely as me ;
> He hecht me baith rings and monie braw things ;
> And were na my heart licht I wad dee.
>
> He had a wee titty that loo'd na me,
> Because I was twice as bonnie as she ;
> She raised sic a pother 'twixt him and his mother,
> That were na my heart licht I wad dee.
>
> The day it was set and the bridal to be ;
> The wife took a dwam, and lay down to dee ;
> She maned and she graned, out o' dolour and pain,
> Till he vowed that he ne'er wad see me again.
>
> His kin was for ane of a higher degree,
> Said what had he to do wi' the like o' me ?
> Albeit I was bonnie, I was na for Johnie :
> And were na my heart licht I wad dee.
>
> They said I had neither cow nor caff,
> Nor dribbles o' drink rins through the draff,
> Nor pickles o' meal rins through the mill-e'e ;
> And were na my heart licht I wad dee.

His titty she was baith wylie and slee,
She spied me as I cam ower the lea;
And then she ran in, and made a loud din,
Believe your ain een an ye trow na me.

His bonnet stood aye fou round on his brow;
His auld ane looked aye as weel as some's new;
But now he lets 't wear ony gate it will hing,
And casts himself dowie upon the corn-bing.

And now he gaes daundrin' aboot the dykes,
And a' he dow do is to hund the tykes.
The live-lang nicht he ne'er steeks his e'e
And were na my heart licht I wad dee.

Were I young for thee as I hae been,
We should ha' been gallopin' doun on yon green,
And linkin' it on the lilie-white lea;
And were na my heart licht I wad dee."

The third last and final stanza were once on the lips of Burns on an occasion first recorded by Lockhart, and since repeated by Carlyle. Late in his life, when, owing to suspected Republicanism and other things, the respectables had begun to turn their backs on Burns, one fine summer evening a friend of his, riding into Dumfries to attend a county ball, was surprised to see him walking alone on the shady side of the street, while the opposite side was thronged by gentlemen and ladies, drawn together by the ball, none of whom seemed willing to recognise the poet. The horseman dismounted, joined Burns, and proposed to him to cross the street with him. He replied, "Na, na, my young friend, that's all over now," and then, after a pause, quoted the two stanzas above mentioned. But "it was little in Burns's character," adds Lockhart, " to let his feelings on certain subjects escape in this fashion. He immediately, after reciting these verses, assumed the sprightliness of his most pleasing manner; and, taking his young friend home with him, entertained him very agreeably till the hour of the ball arrived." This incident, which gives an extrinsic interest to the song, was first recorded by Lockhart, and drew forth from Carlyle a characteristic comment.

During Ramsay's time, then, it would seem that our sweetest singers—those who kept truest to the pure Scottish vein of song, when the men with a smattering of literature were doing their best to deprave it—were ladies who lived among the country people, and were one in feeling with them. And that line of songstresses which began at the dawn of last century with Lady Wardlaw, author of the ballad of "Hardyknute," and Lady Grisell Baillie, if it did indeed begin with them, has never since been interrupted. It was carried on through the middle of last century by Miss Elliot and Miss Rutherford, taken up by Lady Anne Lindsay, authoress of "Auld Robin Gray," and, to pass over others, was brought down to our own day by Lady Nairne, the greatest of them all. Indeed, if asked to name the singer of the half-dozen best Scottish songs after Burns, I know not to whom I should turn before this last-named lady. Lord Cockburn has portrayed a generation of vigorous strong-featured Scottish dames, such as has made our more proper fair ones stand aghast. Those I have named, who belonged some to the same, others to an earlier age, would prove, if it had needed proof, that there were other things in our grandmothers' and great-grandmothers' hearts besides masculine vigour and trenchant humour—other tones on their tongues than the unseemly words which his Lordship has recorded. The fact is, these old dames were brimful of character, which swelled over in some into strong-mindedness, or humour, or sarcasm, in others into tender-hearted and deep pathos, as in those songs they have left behind.

Enough has now, I hope, been said to prove that Burns was not, as some think, the creator of Scottish song; that it was in vigorous existence, and that many a lovely strain had been sung up and down Scotland, long ere he was born; that he had a great background of song to draw upon, that he was born into an age and country with "an atmosphere of legendary melody" floating all about, and that his great merit was to have drunk it into his heart of hearts, and re-uttered it in deeper, clearer, more varied compass than it had ever before attained. And—a thing that should never be forgotten—he purified it. It could hardly be that the popular heart of any country could pour itself so freely forth in all its moods without uttering some things base. And the earlier collections—Herd's, for instance—contain evidence enough that, when unrestrained,

"Auld Scotland has a raucle tongue."

And though among Burns's own songs there are some which we could wish he had not written, yet we, who have inherited his labours, can hardly know how much he did to purify and elevate their prevailing tone; how many songs he purged of their baser leaven; how many tunes which he found attached to most unworthy words he married to healthy and beautiful words of his own.

This naturally suggests one thought which must not be passed by. I said, at the outset, that there is no mood of soul unexpressed in these songs. To this, however, I must make one marked exception. Considering what the Scottish people have been— a devout people they have been, notwithstanding all that modern statistics urge against them—and considering how they loved their songs, it is strange how seldom these contain any direct expression of Christian feeling or aspiration. From this we might be apt to infer that song belonged to one class of men, religion to another. But any one who has known our older Scottish peasantry, knows that this is untrue, that the devoutness and the songs did not dwell in separate, but in the same hearts, so that the modern line is hardly an exaggeration which speaks of them as a people—

"Who sang by turns
The psalms of David and the songs of Burns."

To give one instance. Margaret Laidlaw, mother of the Ettrick Shepherd, was known for her remarkable piety all over the Ettrick Forest—a piety which had come down to her from ancestors who, at the beginning of the last century, had been intimate with the good Thomas Boston, minister of Ettrick. Yet her mind was a very storehouse of legendary lore and popular melody, from which two poets gathered materials for their early inspiration. Scott, when traversing the Border hills on his ballad-raids, took down many of the finest in his *Border Minstrelsy* from old Margaret's lips. From her, too, her son imbibed that rich wealth of legend, and that deep feeling of the old superstitions, which he employed his manhood in setting to prose and rhyme, and from which he has woven that delicate fairy poetry which has borne its consummate flower in the "Bonny Kilmeny."

How, then, are we to account for this marked absence of religious feeling from the songs, if it existed in the hearts, of the people? Partly from the undoubted fact that, two hundred years ago and less, many of the popular songs were so coarse as to justify the ministers in setting their faces against them. Partly also from another and more permanent cause—the divorce that Scottish religion has too much made between things secular and things profane. Song and all things pertaining to it were, it is to be feared, branded as unchristian by the religious teachers. Yet the love of it was too strong to be thus put down. It lived on in men's minds a separate life, railed off by a partition wall from their conscious religion. And yet there is no warrant in the nature of things for such a divorce. Even if there were no other such song, Lady Nairne's "Land o' the Leal" alone would for ever remove the barrier, and prove how easily Scottish melody can rise into the purest air of religion.

These songs naturally divide themselves into three eras:—Songs before Burns; songs of Burns and his few song-making contemporaries; songs since Burns. Some authors belonging to the third era were among us as but yesterday. Many still in middle life remember Hogg, and it is but a few years since Lady Nairne passed away. And now the question rises somewhat sadly, Is the roll of Scottish song-makers for ever closed? Can the old inspiration live and breathe new melodies in so changed a world? Have not high farming, with its bothy system in the east, coal mines and manufactories in the west, money-getting everywhere, put out the old life of which song was the effluence? Is not the shriek of the railway whistle scaring it from all our hills, or is it tough enough to over-live steam, and normal schools, and mechanics' institutes, and all that they imply? A question I do not care to enter on. Only that beautiful saying of Allan Cunningham's comes painfully to mind,—" The fire that burns up the whins on the braeside to make way for the ploughshare, destroys also the nests of a thousand song-birds." It may be so. For artificial cultivation of minds, as of fields, we must pay many penalties, and the loss of the power of song may be of them. And yet, not without a sigh can we let it go, if go it must. General information may be good, popular science good; and yet to me the heart that can carol forth one lilt, with the true old melody in it, is more precious than tons of useful information, and whole libraries of popular science.[1]

[1] [In the foregoing essay there are some sentences and even short paragraphs, which are to be found also in a later production of the author, viz., "Scottish Song and Burns" in *Aspects of Poetry*, p. 200; but these could not be taken from the text without injury to the present paper, which contains much that is of great interest, not to be found elsewhere.]

## IX.—THE ETTRICK SHEPHERD.[1]

LAST summer, after some years' absence, I looked once more on the Vale of Yarrow, and as we descended upon it from the west, I saw the last gleam of sunset just touch the face of "still St. Mary's lake," and then pass upward to linger long upon the round green backs of the hills that surround it, Bowerhope, Herman Law, and the rest. Next morning, long before sunrise, I watched the first dawn fall upon the still lake, and the mountains that embosom it, and in that awful stillness it seemed as though the love that so many hearts have lavished on them was still lingering there to spiritualise their natural loveliness. Soon, while on the top of a hill to the northward, I saw the sun come up from behind the highest hill between Yarrow and Ettrick, opening out and illumining the long Vale of Yarrow eastward. There in the fresh light lay on the hill-side the old forsaken kirkyard of St. Mary's, that sanctuary of the middle age, from which the chapel has long vanished, though the burial-ground remains, giving its name to the lake which lies beneath it, and gathering to

[1] [Last lecture delivered by Prinçipal Shairp at Oxford, as Professor of Poetry, November 1884.]

itself from time to time the dust of one or another old shepherd of the forest. Farther down stood out prominent in the sunlight the roofless but still stalwart tower of Dryhope, to which, nearly four centuries ago, rode the foremost sons of Border chivalry to woo the fair Mary Scott, the flower of Yarrow, most beautiful lady of her age. Farther down still, just where the Vale winds out of sight, the sunrise touched the mouth of the Douglas Burn, where it joins the Yarrow—that dark glen, the scene in old time of the Douglas Tragedy, and in later days the meeting-place where Walter Scott first found his friend William Laidlaw. "All around me was, what Mr. Ruskin calls pre-eminently the singing country, that which has most naturally expressed its noble thoughts and passions in song." "The singing country" Mr. Ruskin calls all the Border district of Scotland. But if the whole of the Border be so, it is the Vales of Yarrow and Ettrick which are the heart and centre of the singing. The Forest of Ettrick, which is nearly identical with the county of Selkirk, now suggests, mainly, the two sister Vales of Yarrow and Ettrick, which, after running parallel to each other for nearly twenty miles, at length unite and flow in one stream into Tweed. This district, in the time of the Stuart kings covered with natural wood, and full of deer, was a great royal hunting ground, as one of the oldest of the ballads sings.

> "Ettrick Forest is a fair Forest,
> In it growes mony a seemlie tree,
> There's hart and hind, and dae and rae,
> And of a' wild bestes great plentie."

But the trees and the deer have long since vanished, and left only green softly outlined sheep-covered hills, that overlap and flow gently into each other, "great, round-backed, friendly, solemn hills, too plain to be grand, too simple and pure to be commonplace," and at the feet and round the folds of these hills, the clear streams " glide the green hills under," and, with the burns that join them from every *hope* and *cleuch*, make a soothing, some say, a melancholy music.

Every one knows how Walter Scott and Wordsworth have shed consecration on these vales. Few know so well the great back-ground of song coming down from an immemorial past that has made that region dear to the Scottish people. And still fewer, in England at least, know the more recent poet, native to the Forest, whose whole life and poetry are identified with Ettrick and Yarrow, and whose reputation, though high in Scotland, has scarcely reached to the south of the Border. The poet I mean is James Hogg, better known as the Ettrick Shepherd. Perhaps by way of contrast to the tone and the studies of this place, I may be allowed to dwell for once on this most unacademic of men and of poets—this inspired child of nature, this voice of the Border Hills.

Whatever may be the shortcomings of the Ettrick Shepherd's poetry, there are those who love it more than much modern poetry that is more highly prized. For it takes them to the natural and primitive sources of all poetry—the high fresh well-heads of song as they burst from the very heart of the mountains and of their inhabitants. To say the truth, they find bracing and refreshment in turning from the trim parterres and artificial terraces of most modern poetry, loaded as they are with scent of musk, and hot-house perfumes, to the open hillsides up which Hogg leads them, where the music is the sighing of the mountain burns, and the cry of the curlew and the plover, and the only fragrance is that of the wild thyme and purple heather.

It was while Sir Walter Scott was still engaged in making his raids into the Border dales, in search of those Ballads which make up his immortal *Minstrelsy*, that the first light falls on James Hogg, the Ettrick Shepherd. As early as 1792, Scott had begun to ransack Liddesdale, and had carried out of it spoil which appeared in the first volumes of the *Minstrelsy*. When in 1800 he was appointed Sheriff of Selkirkshire, the Ettrick Forest lay within his jurisdiction, and he was not long ere he plunged into that chosen sanctuary of legend and song. In one of the earlier of his excursions to the Yarrow, he passed up the secluded Douglas Burn, and there, in the solitary farm of Blackhouse, found

William Laidlaw, of whom he at once made a friend, and who continued to be his amanuensis and companion till his life closed.

William himself, something of a poet, and author of one of the finest modern songs, "Lucy's Flittin'," supplied Scott with some ballads he was in search of, but told him that he had a young friend, who had lived for ten years as a herd under his father's roof, and who possessed a still larger store of ballads than he himself did. This friend was now over the hills in Ettrick, and thither Scott at once made Laidlaw accompany him. The rest must be told in Hogg's own words in his racy autobiography:—

"One fine day in the summer of 1801, as I was busily engaged working in the fields at Ettrick House, Wat Shiel came over to me, and said that 'I boud gang away down to the Ramseycleuch, as fast as my feet could carry me, for there war some gentlemen there wha wantit to speak to me.' 'Wha can be at the Ramseycleuch that want me, Wat?' 'I couldna say, for it wasna me that they spak' to i' the by-ganging. But I'm thinking it's the Shirra an' some o' his gang.'"

"The Shirra" was the name by which the young Sheriff was known among the Selkirkshire people.

That night was spent by Scott with Laidlaw and Hogg, singing and reciting ballads, under the roof of Mr. Brydone, the master whom Hogg then served. Hogg speaks of it as the day on which Scott "found him in the wilderness." Thenceforth till the end of his life Scott treated the Shepherd as a friend. For in Hogg he had found not only a memory retentive of all the ballads and legendary lore of the Forest, but an imagination smitten with love of his country's songs, and capable himself of adding to their number. But Hogg's mother, Margaret Laidlaw, had a memory more stored with the ballads which Scott was in quest of than even her son's.

When he visited her cottage, old Margaret chanted to him the ballad of "Auld Maitlan'," with which Scott was greatly delighted. He asked her if it had ever been printed. "Oo, na, na, sir; it was never prented i' the world. Except George Warton and James Steward, there was never ane o' my sangs prented, till ye prented them yoursel', and ye hae spoilt them a'thegither. They war made for singing, an' no for reading; and they 're nouther right spelled, nor right setten doun."

But much as Scott valued this great friend of ballads, "the personal history of Hogg," as Lockhart says, "interested Scott even more than any ballad he got from him." For in him Scott had met with "perhaps the most remarkable man that ever wore the shepherd's plaid."

At the time Scott first found him, Hogg was about thirty. And this is the description Laidlaw gives of his appearance then. He was rather above the middle height, of faultless symmetry of form, of almost unequalled agility and swiftness. His face was round and full, and of a ruddy complexion, with light blue eyes that beamed with gaiety, glee, and good humour, the effect of the most exuberant animal spirits. "His head was covered with redundant light brown hair, which he was obliged to wear coiled up under his hat. On entering church on a Sunday, where he was all his life a regular attender, he used, on lifting his hat, to raise his right hand to assist a graceful shake of his head, in laying back his long hair, which rolled down his shoulders."

James Hogg was sprung from a long race of shepherds, who had for ages been dwellers in the Forest. His uneuphonious surname has not the meaning which it at first suggests, but was a corruption—so Professor Veitch tells us—of the old Scandinavian name of Haig of Bemerside. His father was originally a shepherd, then tried a farm—failed in the venture, and in his old age was forced to take again to his original calling.

James was one of four sons, and so poor were their parents that, at the age of six, James was taken from school, and sent to herd cows, for one lamb and a pair of shoes as his half-year's wage. His whole school time was less than six months. When he left school he could with difficulty read the Bible and the Psalms in metre. Thus Hogg started in life's race far less well equipped than Burns, who was for his time a well-educated man—indeed, with more mental training than most sons of Scottish lairds at that day received. Six months at school, a little reading—hardly any writing, and no ciphering—seem but a poor outfit for a literary career. But Hogg had teachers who did more for him than many schoolmasters could have done. Within doors he had his mother, out of doors a lonely and lovely country, to which every fibre of his being responded. Margaret Laidlaw had, as I have already said, a wonderful memory, stored with all that was oldest and best in songs and ballads of the Forest—with tales of frays and forays, and all that was wild and weird in the legends of the Border. Round the winter hearth she would gather her children, sing those ancient songs, tell those old-world tales, till they sank into their hearts deeper than the six Standards—the modern code of these days—are ever likely to do. This was the well-head from which her son drew his inspiration in after years.

His mother, however, was more than a repository of old-world lore; she was a devout and religious woman—one of many dwellers in the Forest in whom was still vital the influence of a once famous minister of Ettrick—Boston, author of *The Fourfold State;* and it is remarkable how, in her mind, and that of others of her kind, a whole world of superstition lived on, side by side with genuine Christian faith, apparently in perfect harmony. Years ago I used to hear much about Margaret Laidlaw from one who as a girl had been her servant. She told me how in the morning as she went about her work, old Margaret would ask her if she had that morning worshipped God. If the answer was that she had not, Margaret would reply, "Gie me nane o' your work, till ye have first gi'en your Maker His praise." It is noteworthy that Scotland's three greatest poets were all the children of religious households. What Burns's father was all know from the portrait his son drew of him—I believe, a faithful portrait—in *The Cottar's Saturday Night*. Of Walter Scott's father, his son tells, that "his religion was devoutly sincere—Calvinism of the strictest kind; while his mother's religion, though equally sincere, was of a less austere cast," and therefore, we may believe, more congenial to her son's taste. Is it too much to believe that, in each of these three poets, not only their characters were heightened, but their imaginations were deepened by the religious atmosphere that filled their first homes?

From his sixth year onward each summer found the boy, James Hogg, with a new master, advanced from cow-herding to shepherding and tending of horses; at length, as he reached manhood, he found a permanent and genial home as shepherd on the farm of Blackhouse, up the Douglas Burn, under a kindly master, the father of his friend, William Laidlaw. In that lone and legend-haunted glen, and on the heights around it, Hogg passed ten years, and these years were the budding time of his genius. It would be hard to find another spot so fitted to feed a young and vivid imagination, as that Douglas Burn.

And add to the influence of earth and sky the warm home he had in that farm-house, where the farmer, old Mr. Laidlaw, treated him more as a son than a servant, and made him free of a well-stocked library, from which the shepherd lad was allowed to take Milton, and Pope, and Thomson, and read them for the first time on the hillside; while for bosom friend he had his master's son William, a youth of the same tastes as himself—he, too, a latent poet. With this kindly home to shelter him, and the influence around him during those ten years, Hogg lived in a perfect school of song. All day long, up the hills, he was crooning his songs in rough spontaneous measure. The difficulty was to get them written down when they were once composed. The art of writing, which he had not acquired at school, he had now to teach himself on the hillside, in order to preserve the songs he had made.

But is it possible to conceive a finer singing-school for a poet? Let us hear how one who knows it better than any now living—Professor Veitch—in his volume, *History and Poetry of the Border*, has described it:—

"I like to picture Hogg during those years as he herded on the Hawkshaw Rig up the Douglas Burn. There on a summer day, during those ten years, you would find on the hill a ruddy-faced youth, of middle height, of fine and agile form, with beaming, bright blue eyes and a profusion of light brown hair that fell over his shoulders, long, fair, and lissom as a woman's. The time is between the middle of July and the middle of September, when his duty was 'to summer the lambs.' While these are quietly pasturing, he sets to work, produces a sheet or two of paper folded and stitched, has an inkhorn stuck in a hole in his waistcoat, and a stump of a pen. There he thinks out his verses, writes them, in fact, all through on the tablet of his memory, and then as best he may (with infinite difficulty) gets them put down on paper.

"It is a lone, wild scene this Hawkshaw Rig. The heights shut him in on the north and west, while on the east the moorland opens and widens to the head of the watershed of the Quair. Awe and solitude, legendary tale, and the shadows of old memories are all round about the shepherd singer. But there is also a sweet, strange beauty, for the heather is in bloom, and there are numberless gentle birks down in the cleuch, and green spots of rare grassy beauty by the burnside ; and the many-branched feeders of the burn themselves make a soft, pulsing, intermittent sough and hum that charms the ear, and inclines the soul to tenderness and all gentle thoughts and feelings. It is as if soft beauty of sight and sound lay quiet at the heart of solitude and fear."

To these words of Professor Veitch let us add Hogg's own description of what those years and scenes had done for him :—

> " O list the mystic lore sublime
> Of fairy tales of ancient time ;
> I learned them in the lonely glen,
> The last abodes of living men,
> Where never stranger came our way,
> By summer night or winter day ;
> Where neighbouring hind or cot was none,
> Our converse was with heaven alone,
> With voices through the clouds that sung
> And brooding storms that round us hung.
> .   .   .   .   .   .
> Of themes like these, when darkness fell,
> Grey-headed sires the tales would tell ;
> When doors were barred and eldern dame
> Plied at her task beside the flame,

> That through the smoke and gloom alone
> On dim and umbered faces shone;
> The bleat of mountain goat on high
> That from the cliff came quavering by;
> The echoing rock, the rushing flood,
> The cataract's swell, the moaning wood;
> The undefined and mingled hum,
> Voice of the desert never dumb!
> All these have left within this heart
> A feeling, tongue can ne'er impart;
> A wildered and unearthly flame,
> A something that's without a name."

During those years at Blackhouse Hogg was composing his first songs. Rude they were, for he was yet unskilled in metre, but fresh and spontaneous, for they came straight from the heart. Many of these never reached print, but they fled from lip to lip like wild-fire through the Forest, and delighted the maidens and shepherds, who sang them at all their merry-makings, and called their author "Jamie the Poeter." Their admiration was all the reward he then asked for. The first of his songs that reached a wider public was one called "Donald Macdonald," written in the year 1800, when Bonaparte was threatening invasion to our shores. That song, full of patriotic feeling, and breathing defiances to the Frenchmen, took the heart of the people—spread far and wide, and was sung at every public gathering, but no one cared to ask the author's name.

Hogg was seven-and-twenty before he ever heard the name of Burns. In the year after Burns died, a wandering, half-witted lad came to him on the hill-side, repeated to him "Tam O'Shanter," and told him something about Burns and his early death. Hogg listened till his soul fired with the thought—Might not I become his successor in Scottish song? Nothing can more show how secluded Hogg's early life must have been than the fact that he should have lived six-and-twenty years while Burns was alive, and never have heard his name! The ten years' service with the Laidlaws was just over, and Hogg was working with his father in Ettrick, when Scott, as Hogg expresses it, "found him in the wilderness." That first meeting with Scott was the great turning-point in his life. The intercourse with Scott then begun, and his approval of the young shepherd's attempt at song fanned the flame of his poetic aspiration. But Hogg did not at once throw down the crook and take the pen. He still clung to sheep-farming, and, with two hundred pounds he had saved from his earnings at Blackhouse, leased, along with another, a sheep-farm in the Hebrides, sang his "Farewell to Ettrick," and went westward; but before he had set foot on the farm his lease was questioned, he had to sell his lambs at a dead loss, and return to Ettrick nearly penniless. Nothing daunted, he went back again to shepherding in Nithsdale, and there, as he tended his sheep on Queensberry Hill, Allan Cunningham, attracted by the fame of his songs, sought and found him. During his shepherding on Queensberry he was busy composing new songs.

About this time Scott's third volume of the *Border Minstrelsy* appeared, containing the Editor's "Imitations of the Ancient Ballads." With these Hogg was by no means pleased; and immediately, he tells us, "I chose a number of traditional facts, and set about imitating the manner of the Ancients myself." When he had satisfied himself, he went to Edinburgh, dined with Scott at his house in Castle Street—that first famous dinner which Lockhart has immortalised in the *Life*—submitted his ballads to Scott, who highly approved, and got Constable to publish them.

*The Mountain Bard*, for that was the name of the book, did much to extend Hogg's reputation; something, too, to replenish his purse. For these ballads and a prose treatise on sheep Hogg received three hundred pounds. This sum was too much for his buoyant spirit. On the strength of it he immediately took two sheep-farms. But his ewes and lambs all died, and once more he was left penniless. It was bad enough to lose his all; it was worse to find that by his failure he had forfeited the good opinion of all his neighbours in the Forest. Thrifty Scotland at that time held the losing of money in a foolish venture to be more than a misfortune—it was a sin. Hogg found he had lost caste. Cold and averted looks met him where he had expected sympathy and aid. His old employer even would not again take into service a man who had dabbled in poetry and failed in farming. So in February 1810 he threw his plaid around him, turned his back on the Forest, and set his face to Edinburgh. Only three things he could do—be a shepherd, or a farmer, or an author. The two former were closed against him; he resolved to try the third. But this too was uphill work. He soon found that literary poems were not more highly rated by Edinburgh publishers than his shepherding by Ettrick sheep-farmers.

The next three years spent in Edinburgh were the most precarious and perilous of Hogg's existence. A rustic, though a man of genius, inexperienced, credulous, impulsive, thrown upon town life with nothing but his pen to live by, who could have wondered had he come to shipwreck? These dreary years were spent in continual writing—songs, poems, prose tales, editing a weekly periodical called *The Spy*, attempts at the drama, interminable wrangle with publishers, the more substantial ones looking askance at Hogg's wares, the inferior ones promising him high prices, and going bankrupt before they paid him a penny—these make up the tale of his town life.

Then, if ever, Hogg might have gone the same way as Burns did. But from this, spite of all his follies, imprudence, and absurdities, he was preserved by the warmth and geniality of his heart, which always drew to him staunch friends who kept him from drifting upon the rocks. Chief among these was Mr. John Grieve—a well-to-do Edinburgh tradesman —a native of the Forest, who loved Hogg, believed in his genius, made his house his home, saw that he wanted for nothing. Hogg says he had been starved out of it, but for Mr. Grieve [1] and one or two other like men. Then, though moving in another social sphere, there was Sir Walter Scott, who, while pouring forth his own creations, and rising daily in the world's fame, never forgot his humbler brother poet, but gave him counsel and tried in all directions to find posts for Hogg—Militia ensignship, excise officer, bailiff—and when these failed, arranged with publishers for him, bore with Hogg's absurd vanity, assisted him in every way, gave him all his influence, only refused to write prefaces or poems for him, or to review his books. In all literary history there is no nobler example of a strong man's holding out a hand to struggling genius than the bearing of Sir Walter Scott to Hogg from the first day he saw him till the last,—such sound-headed, true-hearted magnanimity, which no insult could alienate, no failure discourage.

At length, mainly owing to the advice and encouragement of his friend Grieve, Hogg girt himself to one more poetic effort. The result was

[1] [Mr. Grieve, of an old Border stock, was a man of great worth. He died in 1836, and is buried in the old Churchyard of St. Mary's Kirk.]

"The Queen's Wake," in 1813. This was the supreme stroke of his genius. It took the world by storm, silenced all detraction, passed rapidly through several editions, won for the shepherd everywhere the reputation of a true poet, and man of original genius, secured for him the acquaintance of Wilson, Lockhart, Southey, Wordsworth, even Byron,—made him, in fact, free of that great poetic brotherhood which then illumined England. "The Queen's Wake" indeed made his reputation, but not his fortune. He ought to have received for it, Scott says, from £100 to £200. But his publishers failed as usual, and Hogg got never a farthing. Poetry has very seldom fed its sons, and it would not have fed Hogg. He would still have had to struggle on in Edinburgh as a literary hack, or at least a journeyman.

At length, in a little more than a year after the appearance of this poem, relief came from another quarter. He had already received some patronage from the Buccleuch family, on whose lands he and his parents had lived—especially from the good Duchess Harriet. To her Hogg, on first going to Edinburgh, had dedicated a collection of songs called *The Forest Minstrel*, and had received from her in return £100. This good lady died in 1814, and on her deathbed said to her husband that she hoped he would remember the poor poet when she was no more. The Duke regarded this as "a legacy from his departed wife," and soon after gave Hogg a small farm called Altrive Lake, on the banks of Yarrow, about the middle of its course. For this small farm it was understood the rent should be merely nominal, and none was ever asked.

In this way Hogg at last, in the four-and-fortieth year after his long and stormy voyage, found a haven —"a cosie beild," as Scott calls it, "a habitation once more," as Hogg himself says, "among my native moors and streams, where every face was that of a friend, and each house was a home"—"an independent lairdship," which was a residence for himself, as well as a shelter for his aged father, then of more than eighty years.

Much has been said by Carlyle and other literary men of the neglect with which the Scottish nobility treated Burns, though, to say the truth, if another Burns, with his proud temper, were to appear to-day, it would be hard to say what could be done for him. Little has been said of the really thoughtful kindness which the House of Buccleuch extended to James Hogg—a kindness which saved him from we know not what disaster. Hogg was really forty-five when he entered this "cosie beild" with the green hills all about him—the Yarrow water sounding in his ears—his own burn running by his door affording him excellent trout-fishing, with leave to shoot grouse and black game on the neighbouring hills. When he was fifty he married a damsel from Dumfriesshire, much younger, and of somewhat higher station than himself. Some have said that the wives of most poets have been miserable. It was not so with the wife of Altrive Lake.

It would have been well if Hogg could have confined himself to his one small domain. But he must needs be a sheep farmer on a great scale. So he became tenant at a high rent of the farm of Mount Benger, on the north side of Yarrow, just opposite Altrive Lake, and after struggling for seven years in debt and difficulty, at the close of his lease was once again left penniless, having lost £2000 on this luckless enterprise. During all these years the losses he had by sheep he tried to make up by continual literary labour — novels, tales, poems; one epic at least, called "Queen Hynde," the best Epic ever produced in Scotland, he himself allowed; it flowed from his pen and brought him in considerable subsidies. But this was toil for livelihood, not inspiration. It was, as has been well said, with the heathery hillock for a seat, his knee for a writing-desk, his collie and sheep for his companions, that he had composed the greater part of "The Queen's Wake," and the best of his songs.

In his Autobiography he says : " One may think on reading these memoirs that I must have worn out a life of misery—quite the reverse. I never knew either man or woman so uniformly happy as I have been. This is partly owing to a good constitution, partly to the conviction that a heavenly gift, conferring powers of immortal song, was inherent in my soul. Indeed so smooth and happy has my married life been that on a retrospect I cannot distinguish one part from another, save by some remarkably good days of fishing, shooting, and curling on the ice." The world has been hearing a good deal of late of a Scottish man of genius who like Hogg was originally a peasant, but one of the most dyspeptic of men. Hogg was of altogether a different type— eminently eupeptic, genial, sunny-hearted—irascible only when he thought his genius was under-rated. There was a saying common in Oxford in our undergraduate time that all the Scots in the University belonged to one of two classes, the controversial Scot, or the convivial Scot. Carlyle was a specimen of the former, the Ettrick Shepherd of the latter type, and yet his conviviality was kept in bounds as that of Burns was not.

There are many more incidents in the life of Hogg which I might have touched on had time allowed: his converse with other poets—pre-eminently his meeting Wordsworth at Traquair Manse and leading him upwards through the New Hall Glen and by Glenlude down into Yarrow—a day which the Lake Poet immortalised in his "Yarrow Visited;"—his having been in a great part the originator of *Blackwood's Magazine*, and his writing for one of its earliest numbers the Chaldee MS. once famous, now forgotten;—his introduction by his friend Christopher North as the leading figure in his " Noctes," where the Shepherd appears a strange mixture—half inspired genius and half buffoon—Scott's disapproval of this, and the pain it gave his wife and family, while he himself took it almost too good-humouredly —his last pathetic interview with Walter Scott in 1830, when they walked down the Yarrow together from the Gordon Arms past Mount Benger; Scott then disabled and saddened, leaning heavily on the stalwart Shepherd's arm;—his visit to London for the first and last time, in the spring of 1832, when London made of him its literary Lion for the hour, and feasted, fêted, and bedinnered him more than enough. Soon after this visit his health began to fail. His robust frame was at last giving way under the prolonged strain which mind and body had from youth undergone.

He died in November 1835, and the shepherds carried him over the hills that divided Yarrow from Ettrick, and laid him in his own Ettrick kirkyard, only a few steps from the cottage in which he was born—that cottage which I grieve to say has disappeared. The green turf that wraps his grave is covered with daisies (gowans he called them), as the poet had wished it to be.

It was over him that Wordsworth sang his last really inspired strain. When both were in their prime Wordsworth had once hinted a doubt whether Hogg belonged of right to the brotherhood of Poets;

a hint which Hogg deeply resented. But Wordsworth did his best to repair the wrong, by chanting this over the Shepherd's grave :—

"When first, descending from the moorlands,
    I saw the stream of Yarrow glide
Along a bare and open valley,
    The Ettrick Shepherd was my guide.

When last along its banks I wandered,
    Through groves that had begun to shed
Their golden leaves upon the pathways,
    My steps the Border Minstrel led.

The Mighty Minstrel breathes no longer,
    'Mid mouldering ruins low he lies,
And death upon the braes of Yarrow
    Has closed the Shepherd-Poet's eyes."

The poverty which is the proverbial lot of poets fell to Hogg in the fullest measure. His whole life was a struggle against it. But notwithstanding his incessant ups and downs and his not infrequent crashes, he overcame, and reached the end in safety. What might have been his fate but for the timely intervention of his ducal benefactor, who shall say? Genial and society-loving to the extreme, yet he was not wrecked by this disposition, or by those fiercer passions which have run other poets upon the rocks.

His character, as he bore himself towards his fellow-men, had two very different sides. Towards publishers, poets, and the whole literary order, he was touchy, testy, irritable. This arose not only from his vanity about his own powers, though that was excessive, but still more because he felt that any depreciation of his genius was cutting away the whole standing-ground from beneath him. If he was not a man of original genius, he was nothing but a common and very unsuccessful shepherd. No one experienced more of his vanity and irascibility than Scott did, but in his delineation of this, Lockhart has been too unsparing—somewhat too bitterly indignant. It was quite another side he turned towards the Yarrow people. To his brother shepherds he was all kindness and geniality. One whom I used to meet, and who knew Hogg well, said that he prided himself on belonging to the humble but intelligent shepherd-race, that he claimed the headship of their clan, and that when he was quite at ease he cared more to talk of sheep than of poetry. In my youth I used to hear Yarrow people who remembered him speak of him, and it always was with kindness. "He was a kind-hearted chield was James Hogg, and gied himself nae airs, but spak' to the poorest as he did to the highest." Or as an old Border woman, well known on Yarrow, used to say, "James Hogg was a gey sensible man, for a' the nonsense he wrait."

I have heard how in the season when salmon came up Yarrow to spawn, he would gather a great company of shepherds at Blackhouse, and, after feasting them well, would set them loose when it grew dark down the Douglas stream, every one with his lighted torch or leister, to burn the water, and hunt the salmon, and how he would stand on the bank watching, with the shepherd lads, as they floundered down the stream, cheering them on with his jovial laugh. You may believe that these men both loved and were proud of their poet.

The mould in which all the Shepherd's poetry was cast was that of the ballad and the song—the ballad of the Borders, and the song which is native to Scotland. These were the forms his ear had drunk in at his mother's knee, long before he could either read or write. And though he did attempt other and more ambitious forms, he never succeeded in any but the two kinds I have named.

As to the substance which Hogg wrought into his poems it may be given in his own words. "Dear me, Sir Walter," James once said, "ye can never suppose that I belong to your school o' chivalry? Ye are the king o' that school, but I'm king o' the mountain and fairy school, which is a far higher ane nor yours."

We may laugh at Hogg's vanity, and may decline to esteem his school of poetry as highly as he did, but these words show that Hogg knew where his real strength lay. The realm of the supernatural was his own domain. No other poet in our language has ever described fairy-land so well, or embodied the whole underwork of ghosts, spectres, wraiths, brownies, water-kelpies, dead-lights, with such an eerie thrilling sense of their reality; and the reason was this, that to him they were real existences. He had reached full manhood before he felt the atmosphere of the nineteenth century, and began to disbelieve these things. Therefore, when he came to describe that wild, weird world and its denizens, he did it, not as one standing outside of it, and drawing upon it for literary purposes, but as one who still stood within it, or under its shadow. In this region he has no equal; not even Walter Scott can match him. It is his hold in this region that gives its charm to his best poem, "The Queen's Wake," and to his best prose fiction, "The Brownie of Bodsbeck."

The genius of Hogg was essentially lyrical, yet he was ambitious to compose a long poem, and he made several attempts to do so. But "The Queen's Wake" was the only one in which he really succeeded. And the reason of his success, perhaps, was this, that in "The Queen's Wake" he hit upon a happy conception which enabled him, while still working in his own lyrical vein, to combine all the products of it into a complete and harmonious whole. The conception is this. Mary Stuart, on her return from France to assume the throne of her barbarous country, is supposed to have overheard among the crowd which welcomed her first landing, the song of an aged minstrel, and to have asked, "Was ever song so sweet before?" Argyll assures her that this was but a sorry strain compared with those of the great Highland bards. Mary, desiring to know more of the native minstrelsy, orders a festival or wake to be forthwith proclaimed, to be held at Holyrood at the ensuing Christmas-tide, when every minstrel, Highland and Lowland, from far and near, is commanded to attend, and join in a contest for the supremacy in song. Each is bidden come in native garb, and sing a song or ballad, truly Scottish in character; the prize was to be a harp. The contest takes place in Holyrood, in the presence of the queen and her ladies, and the lords and barons of her court. John Knox, you may believe, was not there. Thirteen bards appear; each is described, and the country he came from. The Shepherd's wanderings all Scotland over, and especially his frequent excursions into the Highlands, enabled him to describe the scenery and the legends of the most widely sundered regions, and to contrast well the several bards and their song. This variety forms one of the chief charms of the poem. Many of the bards' songs are of high mark—hardly one of them but has a touch of the weird and supernatural. The two best, to my taste, though neither won the prize harp, are "Kilmeny" and "The Fate of Macgregor." "Kilmeny" is a tale of fairyland, sung by a Highland bard from Loch Earn side. The Land of Fairy was, as I have said, Hogg's peculiar domain; and "Kilmeny" is his finest picture of it. The poem is founded on a local tradition of a child carried away from the wood of Plora, on Tweedside, near Traquair. "Kilmeny" is a girl of seven years, who disappears mysteriously from earth, and, though sought long and far, is never found. At length—

> "When many lang day had come and fled,
> When grief grew calm, and hope was dead,
> . . . . .
> Late, late, in a gloamin', when all was still,
> When the fringe was red on the westlin hill,
> The wood was sere, the moon i' the wane,
> The reek o' the cot hung o'er the plain,
> Like a little wee cloud in the world its lane ;
> When the ingle lowed wi' an eerie leme,
> Late, late in the gloamin' Kilmeny came hame.
>
> 'Kilmeny, Kilmeny, where have ye been?
> Lang hae we sought both holt and dean ;
> By linn, by ford, by greenwood tree,
> Yet you are halesome and fair to see.
> Where gat ye that joup o' the lily sheen?
> That bonnie snood o' the birk sae green?
> And these roses, the fairest that ever were seen?
> Kilmeny, Kilmeny, where have ye been?'
>
> Kilmeny looked up with a lovely grace,
> But nae smile was seen on Kilmeny's face;
> As still was her look, and as still was her e'e,
> As the stillness that lay on the emerant lea,
> Or the mist that sleeps on a waveless sea.
> For Kilmeny had been, she kenn'd not where,
> Kilmeny had seen what she could not declare ;
> Kilmeny had been where the cock never crew,
> Where the rain never fell, and the wind never blew.
> But it seemed as the harp of the sky had rung,
> And the airs of heaven played round her tongue,
> When she spake of the lovely forms she had seen,
> And a land where sin had never been;
> . . . . . .
> The land of vision, it would seem,
> A still, an everlasting dream."

Covered with flowers she had fallen asleep in an earthly wood, and

> "She kenn'd nae mair, nor opened her e'e,
> Till waked by the hymns of a far countrie."

In that region she had been carried from world to world, all of them beautiful, and they are all described. One is like this earth, only glorified.

> "She saw a sun on a summer sky,
> And clouds of amber sailing by;
> A lovely land beneath her lay,
> And that land had lakes and mountains gray;
> And that land had valleys and hoary piles,
> And marled seas and a thousand isles."

After seven years in the land of thought, Kilmeny besought the spirits who tended her to carry her back to earth, that she may tell her friends and the maidens of her native country how well it is in that land with those who have been pure and spotless here.

After she had seen her friends and delivered her message,

> "When a month and a day had come and gane,
> Kilmeny sought the greenwood wene;
> There laid her down on the leaves sae green,
> And Kilmeny on earth was never mair seen.
> But O! the words that fell from her mouth
> Were words of wonder, and words of truth!
> But all the land were in fear and dread,
> For they kendna whether she was living or dead.
> It was na her hame, and she couldna remain;
> She left this world of sorrow and pain,
> And returned to the land of thought again."

In quite another mood is the eleventh bard's song.

He belongs to the clan Alpine race, and like his clan has an imagination filled with wild deeds and stories of the nether world. The tale is of the fate of one of the chiefs of Macgregor, and opens with his brother's rousing call to come forth and lead his clan to battle. For this thrilling and descriptive poem we refer our readers to the poet's works. "The Queen's Wake" is Hogg's highest effort in the shape of a long and regularly constructed poem, and will continue to be the most lasting monument of his genius. In itself, apart from the circumstances of the author, it has intrinsic value; but when we regard it as the work of a man, who at the age of twenty could read but indifferently, and had yet to teach himself to write, it is one of the greatest marvels of natural genius that I know.

But perhaps his genius comes out nowhere more naturally and spontaneously than in his songs. Here he was most truly himself. He tossed off these songs as the mood came upon him with an ease and a rapidity which made him perhaps too careless of correction or after thought. If Burns stands as alone and supreme in song-writing as Shakespeare does in the drama, the second place among Scottish songsters belongs of right to the Shepherd, or perhaps to the Shepherd along with Lady Nairne. One great advantage he had in that he was a musician by nature, playing well on the violin, and with voice good enough to delight every social gathering with the singing of his own songs. His songs struck many chords, but every note in them, whether of joy or sorrow, is healthy, such as could be sung without discord in the open air and face of nature. Of these songs, some are pathetic, some love-songs, some humorous—others national songs. He passes from one to the other with the greatest ease and naturalness.

The morning he welcomes with the skylark :—

> "Bird of the wilderness,
> Blithesome and cumberless,
> Sweet be thy matin o'er moorland and lea !
> Emblem of happiness,
> Blest is thy dwelling-place,
> Oh, to abide in the desert with thee !"

And he closes the day with that sweetest of strains of rustic love-making,

> "When the kye comes hame."

When he turns his back on his native Ettrick and goes forth not knowing whither, he breathes a touching farewell to his old home :—

> "Thy roof will fa,' thy rafters start,
> How damp an' cauld thy hearth will be !
> Ah, sae will soon ilk honest heart,
> That erst was blithe an' bauld in thee !
> . . . . .
> Fareweel, my house an' burnie clear !
> My bourtree bush an' bowzy[1] tree ;
> The wee while I maun sojourn here,
> I 'll never find a hame like thee !"[2]

But it was as the collector of the Jacobite

[1] [Branching out, bushy.]
[2] From *The Auld Man's Fareweel to his Wee House.*]

minstrelsy and the composer of many beautiful additions to it that Hogg has done most for Scottish song. The three great risings in favour of the House of Stuart from Inverlochy and Killiecrankie to Culloden had called forth a great flood of song, partly Gaelic, partly Scottish, in which Scotland had poured forth her love for her ancient race of kings. This was lying scattered all about the Lowlands, and especially the Highlands, and Hogg, in his frequent excursions into the latter, was touched by its pathetic beauty. Burns no doubt had sung one or two Jacobite songs, but he was by nature more of a Jacobin than a Jacobite. But Hogg, being by nature a true and loyal Tory, his political as well as his natural feelings went warmly with the cause.

When however he tried to gather the Gaelic Jacobite songs from those who could sing them in the Highland glens, he found great difficulty, for the people suspected that this sassenach stranger might possibly mean to inform against them to the Government, and was collecting these things with some hostile intent. The fear of the English was then still so strong among the Gael, that it was only through the intervention of some Highland ladies that Hogg obtained from the natives those mournful "laments" for Culloden such as the "Farewell to Glen Shalloch," "The Stuarts of Appin," and "Flora Macdonald's Farewell." After guiding the wandering prince in safety through the outer isles and to the verge of Skye next the mainland, Flora is imagined to have said "farewell," and to sit watching the boat that bore him as it passed out of sight.

> "Far over yon hills of the heather sae green,
>    An' down by the corrie that sings to the sea,
> The bonnie young Flora sat sighing her lane,
>    The dew on her plaid, and the tear in her e'e.
> She look'd at a boat wi' the breezes that swung
>    Away, on the wave, like a bird of the main,
> An' aye as it lessen'd, she sigh'd and she sung,
>    Fareweel to the lad I shall ne'er see again.
> Fareweel to my hero, the gallant an' young,
>    Fareweel to the lad I shall ne'er see again."

These are the songs one loved in boyhood, and mature judgment does not disown them.

It is hardly possible not to compare, by way of conclusion, the genius and poetry of Burns with the genius and poetry of Hogg. Burns's best songs may have more force and weight, but they are not more original or more straight from the heart. Except that these men were both born in a humble place, both full of fire, there is no other resemblance. Burns was a ploughman, Hogg a shepherd, and this counts for much. Burns lived among the plough-fields of an agricultural country, and depicted it: Hogg in a secluded, beautiful pastoral region, and from this he drew his pictures. Burns dealt with the real and actual features of Scottish life: Hogg's imagination fled from the real, and delighted in romance and legend and fairy visions. Their views and their tempers differed widely. Burns, with all his genial fellowship, has a large leaven of social discontent, and bitterness against the classes above him: Hogg, while his mind was as independent as that of Burns, had no quarrel with the gradation of ranks and the social order, though he found himself at the bottom of the ladder. Ayrshire with its sturdy ploughman and the political weavers of its "westlan'" villages, is not more different from pastoral Yarrow and its stalwart simple-minded shepherds, than Burns is from Hogg. Each in his poetry reflected fully the country and the society in which they were born and the influences amid which they were nurtured. But all things have changed since they two lived. Can Scotland ever rear another Burns or another Ettrick Shepherd?

## X.—HENRY VAUGHAN, SILURIST.[1]

"THE entire forgetfulness into which poetry, which, though not of the very highest order of all, is yet of a very high one, may fall, is strikingly exemplified in the fact that, as nearly as possible, two centuries intervened between the first and the second editions of Vaughan's poems. The first edition of the first part of *Silex Scintillans* appeared in 1650, the second edition of the book in 1847."[2] So writes Archbishop Trench in the notes to his delightful volume of selections called *Household Poetry*. It is to Henry Lyte, author of the well-known hymn "Abide with me! fast falls the eventide," that the credit is due of having disinterred the long-forgotten poetry of Henry Vaughan. In 1847 Lyte published a volume containing all, or nearly all, Vaughan's religious poems, prefacing the work by an interesting account of the life of the poet. More recently, the indefatigable Mr. Grosart has devoted four closely packed volumes of "The Fuller Worthies' Library" to the complete works, in verse

---

[1] [Delivered as a Lecture from the Chair of Poetry, Oxford, 9th May 1883, and afterwards contributed to the *North American Review*.]

2. Second (enlarged) ed. 1655.

and prose, of Henry Vaughan. This work contains everything that came from Vaughan's pen, with all things known about him, both those we care, and some things we do not care, to remember. When Lyte's edition appeared, the late Dr. John Brown found in the newly discovered Vaughan a kindred spirit, and in one of his beautiful essays has shed around the Silurist the light of his appreciative and sympathetic genius.

Henry Vaughan belongs to that small band of Royalist poets of the Caroline era who stand discriminated from the host of dashing, rollicking, cavalier lyrists, by being essentially religious poets. What attracted them to the Royal Cause was not its worldly splendour; but they identified it with that refinement of feeling and that deep and sober piety which seem to have descended to us from Catholic ages. The others of the group to which Vaughan belongs are Crashaw, Sandys, and George Herbert, not to mention Quarles, with his homely *Emblems*, or Herrick, whose genius seems more secular than religious. But Henry Vaughan, interesting as he is from his character and his peculiar environment, has this special note to arrest our attention, that in him we hear, for the first time, some ethereal tones, some finer cadences, which, after his death, went silent in English poetry for more than a hundred years, only to revive in some of the higher strains of Wordsworth and Coleridge and Keble. Admirers of Shelley will catch a cadence here and there in Vaughan which reminds them of their favourite.

Henry Vaughan and his brother Thomas came of a fine old Cymric race belonging to South Wales. It is as a native of South Wales, and dearly loving it, that he styled himself Henry Vaughan, Silurist, from the name Silures, which Tacitus, about the close of the first Christian century, applied to the inhabitants of South Wales. The Vaughans traced their lineage back to Sir Roger Vaughan of Bredwardine, who went with Henry V. to his wars in France, and died on the field of Agincourt. This Sir Roger is said to have been knighted by the king, along with a comrade, Sir David Gam,—reckoned also among Vaughan's ancestors,—as he lay dying on the field. Welsh heralds traced the race of Sir Roger back to mythic times even to one Carodoc Fraich-Fas, a knight of Arthur's Round Table. From Sir Roger in the ninth degree came Henry Vaughan of Tretower and Newton in Brecknockshire, the father of the poet. It has been doubted whether there are any descendants of the poet still extant; but Mr. Grosart, the latest editor of Vaughan's works, has, in a minute and laborious biography, made it probable that Dr. Charles J. Vaughan, of the Temple Church, the present Dean of Llandaff, is a lineal descendant and representative of the poet, as is also Mr. H. Halford Vaughan, sometime Professor of Modern History in Oxford. It is also noted that the poet's family were by intermarriage akin to George Herbert, whom he calls his master. The old family seat of the Vaughans, Tretower Castle, is now a mouldering ruin. Thomas Vaughan, grandfather of the poet, left it for the humbler mansion of Scethrog, or Newton, a little distant from Tretower, in the beautiful valley of the Usk. Here Henry, the poet, and his twin brother were born in 1621. Of their mother, strange to say, nothing, not even the name, is known.

Scethrog by the Usk is said to be a fitting birthplace for a poet. His eyes in childhood must have looked on distant mountains, "the Brecknockshire Beacons," and all about him were wooded knolls, and side glens with their waters running down to the Usk. Shakespeare is said once to have visited the Vale of Usk, and to have taken the name Puck, according to Malone, from Cwn-Pooky, "the Goblin Vale," one of those side glens belonging to the Vaughans. The Usk, with its sights and sounds, murmurs often through Vaughan's verse. Here is one of his many notices of it :—

> "Garlands, and songs, and roundelays,
> Mild, dewie nights and sunshine days,
> The Turtle's voice, joy without fear,
> Dwell on thy bosom all the year.
>
> To thee the wind from far shall bring
> The odours of the scattered spring,
> And loaden with the rich arreare
> Spend it in spicie whispers here."

When the two lads were eleven years old, 1632,

they were sent to a parsonage a short distance from their home, where the Rev. Matthew Herbert undertook their education. This good man his two pupils ever afterward regarded with reverence and affection. In 1638 the twin brothers passed from their retired vale to Jesus College, Oxford, then, as now, the favourite resort of young Welshmen. Little or nothing is known as to how they fared at Oxford. Like all the young patricians of Wales at that time, they were devoted cavaliers, and all they saw and heard at Oxford would increase their loyalty. Oxford had not yet forgotten that famous reception it had given to Charles I. two years before, which has since become one of its most cherished historic memories. 1638, the year of the Vaughans entering Jesus, was the year when the Covenant first broke out in Scotland, and with it all the troubles of the king. That same year, too, Charles was at Woodstock, whither all the magnates of Oxford resorted to pay him homage. Perhaps even then the two brothers may have caught sight of the king. Or if they remained in Oxford till the close of 1642, they may have been present when he retired to Oxford, after the battle of Edgehill, and may have gazed on that beautiful sad face which Vandyck has immortalised, and which has impressed itself indelibly on all generations since. However this may be, it seems certain that in the year 1641 Vaughan addressed some verses to the king, which appeared in a volume called *Eucharistica Oxoniensis*. This steadfast loyalty breathes through all his poetry, and did not abate when Charles I. had been succeeded by his less attractive son. Mr. Grosart, the diligent and devoted editor of Vaughan's works, himself a nonconformist and a descendant of the Puritans, pulls a ludicrously long face over Vaughan's "Royalism," as he calls it. This is the one blot which he sees in his favourite poet. Even his decided High Churchmanship he lets pass with comparatively little comment. Vaughan came to Oxford when this way of thinking had there set strongly in. It had not always been so. At the beginning of the seventeenth century Puritanism had it all its own way within the University. Humphrey, a disciple of Zwingli, who was Professor of Theology, with the two Abbots, one Master of University and Vice-Chancellor, the other Master of Baliol, all of the Genevan school, commanded the situation. But Laud, who was ordained in 1600, within thirty years reversed all that. From the first he had set Humphrey, the Abbots, and Reynolds at defiance; and by 1630 he had gathered around himself a body of theologians of his own views, who have since been known as the Caroline Divines. Laud, as he had himself been befriended by the saintly Bishop Andrewes, in his turn helped forward and encouraged Jeremy Taylor, Sanderson, Bramhall, Bethel, Hammond, and Nicholas Farrar with his devoted family. Oxford, then, as now, the home of violent reactions, was, when the

Vaughans entered it, in strong recoil from Puritanism, and the tide of High Church theology was in full flow. "Laud," says Mozley, "was the first High Churchman;" and in this sense he was, that "a theological school which was a mere handful when he commenced life at Oxford had, mainly through his influence, spread over the country in all directions. Oxford itself, from being a focus of Calvinism, had come round, and scarcely knew its reflection in the theology of Jeremy Taylor and Hammond."

It is not likely that this theology much affected the two lads during their Oxford residence, but, in after years, when they came to think for themselves, these were the views which they firmly adopted. There is no record that either of the brothers graduated. When they left Oxford, Thomas took up arms on the king's side, and as to Henry, while it is uncertain whether he joined the royal army, it is certain that he suffered imprisonment for the royal cause. He would seem to have sojourned for some time in London, as is proved by a rhapsody of his, commemorating convivial evenings at the Globe Tavern. The great wits who once haunted it were all gone,—Shakespeare, Ben Jonson, and the rest,—but to Vaughan's imagination their memories were still there. There is a sort of bacchanalian swagger about this piece which sounds strange to those who know Vaughan's maturer style.

In 1646 Vaughan gave to the world his earliest

poetic venture, in a small collection of love verses, addressed, many of them, to Amoret and Etesia. Who these fair ones were, whether one damsel or two, or one under different names, does not appear. These verses are full of ardours and wistful sighs, expressed in the conceits usual to the love-poetry of that time. Vaughan afterwards abjured them with what seems superfluous contrition; for there is nothing in them to call for repentance, unless all love-poetry be sinful.

When the two brothers had to choose professions, Thomas was ordained, soon afterward evicted from his charge by the Scrutinisers of the Parliament, retired to Oxford, wrote works on alchemy and magic, and died in 1665. Henry became a country doctor, though whence he got his diploma does not appear, and settled before 1647 in Brecon, then called Brecknock, the country town of his native region. From a poem of his, written about this time, his new quarters do not seem to have been much to his mind. All things in the town and neighbourhood he found set to the new Puritan and Republican régime. This is the way he describes it:—

"Here's brotherly Ruffs and Beards, and a strange sight
Of high monumental Hats, ta'en at the fight
Of eighty-eight; while every Burgesse foots
The mortal Pavement in eternall boots."

In a more serious strain, speaking of the abolition

of the Christmas Festival by the Puritans, he exclaims—

> "Alas! my God, thy birth now here
> Must not be numbered in the year."

This uncongenial neighbourhood he soon quitted, to settle in his native Scethrog, or Newton, a home which he never afterward left. There he became the Gideon Gray of his native district, and between his duties as a country doctor and his occupation as a poet, found his time amply filled. This is what the late Dr. John Brown, well entitled to speak on such a subject, says of his daily rounds :—

> "Though what Sir Walter says of the country surgeon is too true, that he is worse fed and harder wrought than any one else in the parish, except his horse, still, to a man like Vaughan, to whom the love of nature and its scrutiny was a constant passion, few occupations could have furnished ampler and more exquisite manifestations of her magnificence and beauty. Many of his finest descriptions give us quite the notion of their having been composed while going his rounds on his Welsh pony among the glens and hills, and their unspeakable solitudes."

Soon after settling in Wales, Vaughan married, but the name of his wife is not known. Her married life was brief, but the impression left on Vaughan by her character was lasting. His pathetic poem, entitled "Mourning for the Young Dead," surely alludes to her:—

> "Sleep, happy ashes! blessed sleep!
> While hapless I still weep;
> Weep that I have outlived
> My life, and unrelieved
> Must—soul-less shadow—so live on,
> Though life be dead, and my joy gone."

Lyte says that in time Vaughan married again, but Mr. Grosart, though he sought for evidence of this, found none. He is willing, however, to accept it on Lyte's authority. Before 1650 Vaughan was visited by a serious and prolonged illness, which brought him to the verge of the grave. The death of his first wife, so young and good, followed by this long illness, wrought a great change in him, and he came out of this double affliction another man. The religious bent which his mind then took it never afterward lost. Just about that time he became acquainted with the poems of George Herbert, whom he not only greatly admired as a poet, but welcomed as a spiritual guide and comforter. Taking Herbert as his model in form, he composed during his illness "sacred poems and private ejaculations," which are a faithful transcript of the experience through which he had recently passed. These he gave to the world, in 1650, in a volume styled *Silex Scintillans*, suggesting by this title that the poems were sparks struck from a flinty heart. About the same time his twin-brother Thomas was publishing another collection of Henry's poems, under the title *Olor Iscanus*, or the Swan of Usk. This latter volume contained his more outward thoughts and observations; and though Henry, in his now altered mind, would gladly have burnt these, as well as his love-poems, there does not seem to be anything in either of which he needed to be ashamed. In 1655 came the second part of *Silex Scintillans*, and, in 1675, a small volume entitled *Thalia Rediviva*, in the same style and spirit as the two parts of *Silex Scintillans*. The twin-brother, Thomas, died early in 1665. Henry lived till he was seventy-three, and died in his native place on April 23, 1695, and was laid in the neighbouring churchyard of Llansaintfread. On his tombstone were inscribed these contrite words, prepared by himself:—

"H. V. M.D. Siluris
Servus Inutilis
Peccator Maximus
Hic jaceo
Gloria . . . . . . Miserere."

"Henry Vaughan, M.D., Silurist;
An Unprofitable Servant;
Chief of Sinners,
Here I lie.
Glory to God . . . Have mercy upon me!"

Vaughan has sometimes been spoken of as a mere imitator of Herbert; and such was his reverence for the Poet of *The Temple* that he would have held it an honour to be so styled. In the preface to *Silex Scintillans*, after speaking of the licentiousness that tainted most of the poetry of that day, Vaughan says:—"The first that with an effectual success attempted a diversion of this foul and overflowing stream was the blessed man Mr. George Herbert, whose holy life and verse gained many converts, of whom I am the least." Herbert was, no doubt,

Vaughan's instructor in religious truth and the kindler of his piety. *The Temple* Vaughan probably knew by heart; and, naturally enough, when he began himself to versify, he adopted its metres, and here and there reproduced its cadences, just as we find Keble, two centuries later, sometimes recalling Herbert's tones. But after making full allowance for the influence of Herbert upon Vaughan, and the consequent likeness of their thoughts, it remains true that, as a poet, Vaughan contains in himself a fountain of inspiration, an intensity of feeling, and a subtle music, which Herbert never attained to. Archbishop Trench, a good judge of such matters, has well said:—"As a theologian, Vaughan may be inferior, but as a poet he is certainly superior to Herbert, who never wrote anything so purely poetical as 'The Retreate.'"

Yet Vaughan never has been, and never will be, a popular poet. His subjects and his style alike forbid this—his subjects, because they all lie in a region of spiritual meditation which will probably never attract the many; his style, because it has no high colouring, and nothing of that sustained finish and perfect workmanship to which most of our great modern poets have accustomed us. From Vaughan, an ordinary reader will be repelled by his utterance, often broken and imperfect; by thoughts good in themselves but condensed to obscurity; by halting rhythms and broken music. Often you are pleased, shall I say? or provoked, to find one or two verses of fine thought, beautifully expressed, yet imbedded in a surrounding mass of inferior workmanship. Only in a few poems, when his best mood is on him, does he kindle into expression, bright, vivid, intense, from end to end.

One of the most noticeable qualities of Vaughan is his inwardness. A meditative spirit by nature, this tendency was doubtless deepened by the religious change which he passed through. The phases of that experience are recorded in many poems in the first part of *Silex*, such as "The Emblem," "The Call," "The Relapse," "Affliction," "The Tempest," "The Pilgrimage." The last of these contains an aspiration which Vaughan often expresses—some may call it unhealthy, others will feel it to be spiritual. It certainly has a warrant in the Psalms:—

> "As birds robb'd of their native wood,
> Although their diet may be fine,
> Yet neither sing, nor like their food,
> But with the thought of home do pine;
>
> So do I mourn, and hang my head;
> And, thou, Thou dost me fulness give,
> Yet look I for far better bread,
> Because by this man cannot live.
>
> O feed me then! and since I may
> Have yet more days, more nights to count,
> So strengthen me, Lord, all the way,
> That I may travel to Thy Mount."

The personal experience which these poems reveal

is for depth and spirituality unsurpassed by Baxter, or Bunyan, or any of the best of the Puritans. And in Vaughan, as in Herbert, it has this further advantage—the intensity of their personal religion, is saved from individualism by the continual sense of an external and catholic standard of devotion. They found it a support and confirmation of their faith to feel that they were not resting on their own isolated experiences, but were only following the footsteps of "those who had gone before them—those multitudes in the primitive time who had believed and taught and worshipped as they did."

There is, however, another and rarer way in which Vaughan's inwardness shows itself. In common with all idealists, he feels strongly that the spirit in man is the only reality, that visible things are but shadows, a mere screen hiding from men the eternal world. This is the way he expresses it in his poem called "Cock-crowing:"—

> "Only this Veyle which Thou hast broke,
> And must be broken yet in me,
> This Veyle, I say, is all the cloke
> And cloud which shadows me from Thee.
>   This Veyle Thy full-eyed love denies,
>   And only gleams and fractions spies.
>
> O take it off! make no delay,
> But brush me with Thy light, that I
> May shine unto a perfect day;
> And warme me at Thy glorious Eye!
>   O take it off! or till it flee,
>   Though with no Lilie, stay with me."

The feeling to which I have alluded, and which these lines express, is part of Vaughan's Platonic mysticism—a spiritual imaginativeness, vouchsafed only to the finer order of mind. To many, mysticism is a word of evil import, suggesting only something vague, shadowy, and unreal. But there is a true as well as a false mysticism. If one may say it with reverence, the writings of St. John are pervaded with that true mystic insight that enabled him to apprehend sayings and intimations of his Master which escaped the other Apostles. There are touches of mysticism interlining here and there the robust thought of Shakespeare. Spenser, too, has it; indeed, none of the higher poets are without it. The mystic element is finely interfused through the thoughts of Vaughan; indeed, it is the element in which his mind naturally expands itself and seems most at home. Take this opening of a poem called "The World:"—

> "I saw Eternity the other night;
> Like a great Ring of pure and endless light;
> All calm as it was bright;
> And round beneath it, Time in hours, days, years,
>     Driv'n by the spheres
> In a vast shadow moved, in which the world
>     And all her train were hurl'd."

This is the solemn background against which Vaughan sees all the transitory ongoings of man. The mystery of the universe by which he is encompassed haunts him; he longs to penetrate to the heart of it. This feeling often breaks out, and he finds in the nature of his own soul the key which opens furthest into the secret. Thus in his poem "Vanity of Spirit," he says :—

"I summoned Nature ; pierced through all her store ;
Broke up some seales, which none had touched before ;
. . . . . . And having past
Through all her creatures, came at last
To search myself, where I did find
Traces and sounds of a strange kind.
Here of this mighty stream I found some rills
With echoes beaten from the eternal hills.
Weake beames and fires flashed to my sight,
Like a young East, or moone-shine night,
Which showed me in a nook cast by
A piece of much antiquity,
With hieroglyphicks quite dismembered,
And broken letters scarce remembered.
I took them up, and, much-joyed, went about
T' unite those pieces, hoping to find out
The mystery ; but this ne'er done,
The little light I had was gone.
It grieved me much. At last said I,
Since in those veyls my eclipsed eye
May not approach Thee,—for at night
Who can have commerce with the light?—
I'le disapparell, and to buy
But one half-glance, most gladly dye."

This ideal faculty in Vaughan, this mystic longing to see the spiritual side of things, was combined with another power which seems quite opposed to it —a faithful eye to see and seize the exact form and features of natural things. Vaughan has been compared, for his mysticism, to William Blake. But there is this striking difference in their mysticism :

in Blake it quite absorbs his powers of observation, as well as all his other faculties. "I assert for myself," says Blake, "that I do not behold the outward creation; to me it is hindrance." This was not at all the way with Vaughan. He rejoiced in rural sights and sounds for their own sake, and could reproduce them accurately and faithfully, without any subjective intrusion. The sound of waters, clouds with their shadows and gleams, and birds are special favourites with him. Here is his morning address to a bird :—

> "Hither thou com'st, the busie wind all night
> Blew through thy lodging: where thy own warm wing
> Thy pillow was: and many a sullen storm,
> For which coarse man seems much the fitter born,
>    Rained on thy bed,
>    And harmless head;
> And now, as fresh and cheerful as the light,
> Thy little heart in early hymns doth sing."

But such dwelling on outward objects for their own sake is with Vaughan comparatively rare. Usually, he portrays them in their relation to the human spirit—the action of things on thought, and of thought on things. What Mrs. Barrett Browning finely said of Wordsworth is as true of Vaughan: "His eye is his soul." In the words of Coleridge: "To read the great book of Nature in a figurative sense, and to find therein correspondencies and symbols of the spiritual world," this which has been "the music of gentle and pious minds in all ages," was Vaughan's peculiar delight. But for this characteristic of all high poetry, which is so strong in Vaughan, we have, after his time, to wait till it reappeared in the poetry of the nineteenth century.

It would have been pleasant to have lingered over his many allusions to his native Usk, over the "Waterfall," over his frequent images taken from birds and their ways, and over the beautiful surprises with which he startles and delights us, often in the midst of the plainest ground.

There is one poem to which I have not adverted, though it is one of the finest and most sustained of all Vaughan's poems. I mean that entitled "Communion with the Holy Dead," beginning thus:—

> "They are all gone into the world of light!
> And I alone sit lingering here!
> Their very memory is fair and bright,
> And my sad thoughts doth clear."

But as it has found its way into almost every collection of poetry, and is known where nothing else about Vaughan is known, I may presume that it is familiar to all.

But I cannot conclude without referring to Vaughan's peculiar feeling about childhood, for of all his characteristics this is the most original and the most delightful. In his poem called "The Retreate" it is that he has expressed most fully the ideal light in which he looked back upon childhood :—

> "Happy those early dayes, when I
> Shined in my angell infancy !
> Before I understood this place
> Appointed for my second race,
> Or taught my soul to fancy aught
> But a white Celestial thought ;
> When yet I had not walkt above
> A mile or two from my first love,
> And looking back, at that short space,
> Could see a glimpse of his bright face :
> When on some gilded cloud or flowre
> My gazing soul would dwell an hour,
> And in those weaker glories spy
> Some shadows of eternity ;
> Before I taught my tongue to wound
> My conscience with a sinfull sound,
> Or had the black art to dispence
> A severall sinne to every sence,
> But felt through all this fleshly dresse
> Bright shootes of everlastingnesse.
>
> O, how I long to travell back,
> And tread again that ancient track !
> That I might once more reach that plaine
> Where first I left my glorious traine ;
> From whence the Inlightened spirit sees
> That shady City of Palm trees.
> But ah ! my soul with too much stay
> Is drunk, and staggers in the way !
> Some men a forward motion love,
> But I by backward steps would move,
> And, when this dust falls to the urn,
> In that state I came, return."

Here is a wonderful anticipation of the main conception of Wordsworth's great ode. The first to point this out was, as far as I know, Archbishop

Trench, who, in the first edition of his *Household Book of English Poetry*, wrote thus :—

"This poem, apart from its proper beauty, has a deeper interest, as containing in the germ Wordsworth's still higher strain, namely, his 'Ode on Intimations of Immortality from Recollections of Early Childhood.' I do not mean that Wordsworth had ever seen this poem when he wrote his. But the coincidences are so remarkable that it is certainly difficult to esteem them accidental; but Wordsworth was so little a reader of anything out of the way—and, at the time when his ode was composed, the *Silex Scintillans* was altogether out of the way, a book of such excessive rarity, that an explanation of the points of contact must be sought elsewhere."

That this was spoken rashly, the Archbishop learnt before the second edition of his Household Poetry Book appeared, for a correspondent informed him that he (the correspondent) had a copy of the first edition of the Silex, incomplete and very much damp-stained, which he had bought at a sale of Wordsworth's books. So Wordsworth, we may be sure, had read "The Retreate," and if he read it could not have failed to be arrested by it. No doubt, the whole conception is expanded by Wordsworth into a fulness of thought and a splendour of imagery which Vaughan has nowhere equalled. But the points of resemblance between the two poets are numerous and remarkable. The Platonic idea of ἀνάμνησις is at the root of both—the belief that this is not our first state of existence, that we are haunted by broken memories of an ante-natal life. Indeed, this belief was held by Vaughan, and expressed in several of his other poems much more explicitly than it is by Wordsworth.

Mr. George MacDonald has closely compared "The Retreate" and Wordsworth's great ode, and has shown that if Wordsworth says,

> "There was a time
> When earth, and every common sight,
> To me did seem
> Apparelled in celestial light,"

Vaughan has

> "Happy those early days, when I
> Shined in my angell infancy."

If Wordsworth speaks of a time when he was haunted by

> "Blank misgivings of a creature
> Moving about in worlds not realised,"

Vaughan recalls a time,

> "Before I understood this place
> Appointed for my second race."

> "Heaven lies about us in our infancy,"

says Wordsworth; Vaughan speaks of being filled by

> "A white celestial thought."

If Wordsworth says that

> "Trailing clouds of glory do we come
> From God, who is our home,"

Vaughan speaks of his childhood as a time

> "When yet I had not walkt above
> A mile or two from my first love,
> And looking back at that short space
> Could see a glimpse of his bright face."

Wordsworth calls childhood

> "the hour
> Of splendour in the grass, of glory in the flower."

Vaughan speaks of it as a time

> "When on some gilded cloud or flowre
> My gazing soul could dwell an hour."

But if there are these marked resemblances, there are differences hardly less marked. The fading of the early vision Wordsworth attributes to custom, lying upon the soul

> "with a weight
> Heavy as frost, and deep almost as life."

Vaughan, on the other hand, traces it to a moral cause: to wit, his teaching

> "his tongue to wound
> His conscience with a sinfull sound,"

and learning

> "the black art to dispence
> A severall sinne to every sence."

And Wordsworth has not brought home the sense of immortality present in the vivid feelings of childhood so penetratingly as Vaughan has done in these two consummate lines :—

> "And felt through all this fleshly dresse
> Bright shootes of everlastingnesse."

There is another poet who has touched very beautifully the subject of childhood,—I mean William Blake, in his "Songs of Innocence." But between Blake's treatment of it and that of the other two poets, there is this great difference: they, from their mature manhood, recall the bright instincts they had in childhood, and reflect, and even philosophise, upon them; Blake, on the other hand, throws himself entirely out of his present manhood, and prattles the very feelings he had as a child,—about the green fields, the lambs, the angels, and God. Some of these poems of Blake's are, perhaps, the very best expression ever given to baby-life, its innocence, its simplicity, its happiness, its religiousness.

But some one may here interpose and say, Why all this fine talk about childhood; is it not a mere piece of sentimentalism, without any ground in reality? They who speak thus would seem to have a great authority upon their side. Mr. Matthew Arnold, in the preface to his "Selections from Wordsworth," has said—

"The idea of the high instincts and affections coming out in childhood . . . this idea, of undeniable beauty as a play of fancy, has in itself not the character of poetic truth of the best kind; it has no real solidity. The instinct of delight in Nature and her beauty had, no doubt, extraordinary strength in Wordsworth as a child; but to say that universally this instinct is mighty in childhood, and tends to die away afterwards, is to say what is extremely doubtful. In many people, especially in the majority of educated persons, the love of nature is nearly imperceptible at ten years old, but strong and operative at thirty. In general, we may say of those high instincts of early childhood what Thucydides says of the early achievements of the Greeks, that probably they were no very great things."

Alas! for poetry, if the perceptions of the so-called éducated man are to be made its norm and canon. The ordinary educated man is apt to be a very artificial product, and unless he has to begin with some original spring of nature that lies deeper than his education, his sentiments and his judgments of poetry, as of other things, are, for the most part, strictly limited by the standards that pass current for the time in the circle to which he belongs. Judged even by so solid and respectable a faculty as ordinary common sense, poetry would fare but badly, —would be put down as something extravagant and fantastic,—"a convenient way of talking nonsense." It is probably true enough that to few has been granted a childhood so bright and imaginative as Vaughan, Blake, and Wordsworth could look back to; that few persons in any generation could say that the poems above alluded to reproduce exactly their childhood's experience. Of course, the remembrance that each one has of his or her childhood must depend on the conditions which surrounded their home,—whether their childhood was passed in town or in the country, and whether in a beautiful or an unattractive neighbourhood. But most persons of any sensibility who have spent some part of their childhood in a pleasant country must, I should think, in looking back, be aware that, next to the warmth of home affection and companionship, the things that most made their happiness were the sunshine, the green fields, the beasts and birds, the mountains, the clear streams, and the sea-shore. In the rural sights and sounds around them they rejoiced, though they knew not at the time what it was they rejoiced in. There are few, I suppose, who cannot recall from their childhood one or two at least of "those heavenly days which cannot die," when the innocent brightness of the morning was about them, as yet undimmed by any shadow of mortality, and there were loving voices in the garden that have long been still. Such moments may have been few, as they were fleeting; but they must have thrilled us when they were here, else how could we recall them now? The remembrance of them may have waxed so faint that it seldom now revisits us, save perhaps for a moment, when reawakened by some long-forgotten tone or some scent that breathes of that early time. But no doubt they lie far down in most of us, those remembrances, buried fathoms deep, under layer on layer of custom, conventionality, commonplace, it may be, of worldliness. Is it not, then, one of the finest gifts of the true poet that he can pierce through those coatings with which later experience has incrusted our better nature, and re-awaken the child's heart that still slumbers within us? As Miss Annie Keary, one of the best of modern depictors of childhood, has expressed it: "There is a mental atmosphere common to all children, which changes so gradually that only a few observers, or, rather, a few imaginative people who have lived vividly the childlife, and so kept a good deal of its atmosphere imbedded in their memory, ever succeed in bringing it back."

To have succeeded in bringing it back, this is the good office which Vaughan and Blake and Wordsworth have performed. Those fine and ethereal, yet evanescent instincts, which most men and women in childhood have in some measure shared, these poets have preserved in their hearts so tenaciously, and expressed in their poems so vividly, that they awaken, even in ordinary minds, some recollection of them. Can any poet render to his fellow-men a truer, more delicate, service?

There is, however, it must be noted, one thought about childhood in Vaughan which Wordsworth has not. It is this,—that hereafter in the perfected Christian manhood the child's heart will reappear. "Of such is the kingdom of heaven."

Vaughan's poem of "The Retreate" closes with the wish that

"When this dust falls to the urn,
In that state I came, return."

Again, in another poem he calls childhood

"An age of mysteries, which he
Must live twice who would God's face see,
Which angels guard, and with it play,
Angels! whom foul men drive away."

It is a beautiful and, I trust, a true faith, that a day is coming when the soul shall put off all the incrustations it has gathered here, when we shall regain all that we have lost, and combine the matured wisdom of the man with all that is lovely in the child. And so our life is rounded both ways by a childhood—the imperfect childhood we pass through here—the perfect childhood which shall be hereafter.

FINIS.

---

Printed by T. and A. CONSTABLE, Printers to Her Majesty,<br>at the Edinburgh University Press.

BY THE SAME AUTHOR.

## I.
## STUDIES IN POETRY AND PHILOSOPHY.

Fourth Edition, with Portraits of the Author and Thomas Erskine by W. HOLE, A.R.S.A.

Crown 8vo, 7s. 6d.

CONTENTS.—Wordsworth, Coleridge, Keble, The Moral Motive Power, Thomas Erskine, and John Brown.

## II.
## CULTURE AND RELIGION
## IN SOME OF THEIR RELATIONS.

Seventh Edition. Extra fcap. 8vo, 3s. 6d.

"A wise book, and unlike a great many other wise books, has that carefully shaded thought and expression which fits Professor Shairp to speak for Culture no less than for Religion."—*Spectator*.

## III.
## KILMAHOE.
## A HIGHLAND PASTORAL.

WITH OTHER POEMS.

Ex. fcap. 8vo, 6s.

EDINBURGH : DAVID DOUGLAS.

15A Castle Street,
Edinburgh, *January* 1887.

# LIST OF BOOKS PUBLISHED BY
# DAVID DOUGLAS.

**The Political State of Scotland.**
By Sir Charles Adam, Bart. Crown 8vo. [*In the Press.*

**On the Philosophy of Kant.**
By Robert Adamson, M.A., Professor of Logic and Mental Philosophy, Owens College; formerly Examiner in Philosophy in the University of Edinburgh. Ex. fcap. 8vo, 6s.

**The Age of Lead: A Twenty Years' Retrospect.**
In three Fyttes. "Vae Victis." Second Edition. Sm. crown 8vo, 2s. 6d.

**The Correspondence of Sir Patrick Waus of Barnbarroch**, during the latter half of the Sixteenth Century, from originals in the Family Charter-Chest. Edited by R. Vans Agnew. Demy 8vo, 21s.

**The New Amphion; Being the Book of the Edinburgh** University Union Fancy Fair, in which are contained sundry Artistick, Instructive, and Diverting Matters, *all now made publick for the first time.* 12mo, Illustrated, 5s.

"An especially dainty little morsel for the lovers of choice books."—*Academy.*
"There is no need to say that the book is valuable. It will be eagerly and widely sought for. . . . The external appointments are such as would charm the most fastidious bibliomaniac."—*Scotsman.*

**Stories by Thomas Bailey Aldrich.**
The Queen of Sheba. 1s., or in cloth, gilt top, 2s.
Marjorie Daw, and other Stories. 1s., or in cloth, gilt top, 2s.
Prudence Palfrey. 1s., or in cloth, gilt top, 2s.
The Stillwater Tragedy. 2 vols. 2s., or in cloth, gilt top, 4s.
From Ponkapog to Pesth. [*In the Press.*
"Mr. Aldrich is, perhaps, entitled to stand at the head of American humourists."—*Athenæum.*
"*Marjorie Daw* is a clever piece of literary work."—*Saturday Review.*

**Johnny Gibb of Gushetneuk in the Parish of Pyketillim,** with Glimpses of Parish Politics about A.D. 1843. By William Alexander. Eighth Edition, with Glossary, Ex. fcap. 8vo, 2s.

Seventh Edition, with Twenty Lithographic Illustrations—Portraits and Landscapes—by George Reid, R.S.A. Demy 8vo, 10s. 6d. Net.

"A most vigorous and truthful delineation of local character, drawn from a portion of the country where that character is peculiarly worthy of careful study and record."—*The Right Hon. W. E. Gladstone.*

**Life among my Ain Folk.**
By William Alexander, Author of "Johnny Gibb of Gushetneuk."
Ex. fcap. 8vo. Second Edition. Cloth, 2s. 6d. Paper, 2s.

**Notes and Sketches of Northern Rural Life in the** Eighteenth Century, by William Alexander, the Author of "Johnny Gibb of Gushetneuk." Ex. fcap. 8vo, 2s. Cloth, 2s. 6d.

## American Authors.

Latest Editions. Revised by the Authors. In 1s. volumes. By Post, 1s. 2d.
Printed by Constable, and published with the sanction of the Authors.

By W. D. HOWELLS.
A FOREGONE CONCLUSION.
A CHANCE ACQUAINTANCE.
THEIR WEDDING JOURNEY.
A COUNTERFEIT PRESENTMENT.
THE LADY OF THE AROOSTOOK. 2 vols.
OUT OF THE QUESTION.
THE UNDISCOVERED COUNTRY. 2 vols.
A FEARFUL RESPONSIBILITY.
VENETIAN LIFE. 2 vols.
ITALIAN JOURNEYS. 2 vols.
THE RISE OF SILAS LAPHAM. 2 vols.

By FRANK R. STOCKTON.
RUDDER GRANGE.
THE LADY OR THE TIGER?

By GEO. W. CURTIS.
PRUE AND I.

By J. C. HARRIS.
(*Uncle Remus.*)
MINGO, AND OTHER SKETCHES.

By GEO. W. CABLE.
OLD CREOLE DAYS.

By B. W. HOWARD.
ONE SUMMER.

By JOHN BURROUGHS.
WINTER SUNSHINE.
PEPACTON.
LOCUSTS AND WILD HONEY.
WAKE-ROBIN.
BIRDS AND POETS.
FRESH FIELDS.

By OLIVER WENDELL HOLMES.
THE AUTOCRAT OF THE BREAKFAST TABLE. 2 vols.
THE POET. 2 vols.
THE PROFESSOR. 2 vols.

By G. P. LATHROP.
AN ECHO OF PASSION.

By R. G. WHITE.
MR. WASHINGTON ADAMS.

By T. B. ALDRICH.
THE QUEEN OF SHEBA.
MARJORIE DAW.
PRUDENCE PALFREY.
THE STILLWATER TRAGEDY. 2 vols.

By B. MATTHEWS and H. C. BUNNER.
IN PARTNERSHIP.

By WILLIAM WINTER.
SHAKESPEARE'S ENGLAND.

\*\*\* *Other Volumes of this attractive Series in preparation.*

Any of the above may be had bound in Cloth extra, at 2s. each vol.

"A set of charming little books."—*Blackwood's Magazine.*
"A remarkably pretty series."—*Saturday Review.*
"These neat and minute volumes are creditable alike to printer and publisher."—*Pall Mall Gazette.*
"The most graceful and delicious little volumes with which we are acquainted."—*Freeman.*
"Soundly and tastefully bound . . . a little model of typography, . . . and the contents are worthy of the dress."—*St. James's Gazette.*
"The delightful shilling series of 'American Authors' introduced by Mr. David Douglas has afforded pleasure to thousands of persons."—*Figaro.*
"The type is delightfully legible, and the page is pleasant for the eye to rest upon; even in these days of cheap editions we have seen nothing that has pleased us so well."—*Literary World.*

## American Statesmen.

A Series of Biographies of men conspicuous in the Political History of the United States. Edited by JOHN T. MORSE, Jun.

Small crown 8vo, price 6s. each vol.

1. THOMAS JEFFERSON. By JOHN T. MORSE, Jun.
"Mr. Morse tells the story of his career with terseness and perspicuity, yet with sufficient fulness, and in a charming literary style."—*Aberdeen Free Press.*

2. SAMUEL ADAMS By JAMES K. HOSMER.
"A man who, in the history of the American Revolution, is second only to Washington."
"Remarkable for its firmness of spirit and its moderation of tone. His book furnishes the best account with which we are acquainted, in readable compass, of the controversies between the colonists and the representatives of the Imperial Government in Massachusetts that led the way to the Declaration of Independence."—*Scotsman.*

3. ALEXANDER HAMILTON. By HENRY CABOT LODGE.
With a Preface containing the "Declaration of Independence," "Articles of Confederation," and the Constitution of the United States.

## Modern Horsemanship. A New Method of Teaching
Riding and Training by means of pictures from the life. By E. L. ANDERSON. New and Revised Edition containing some observations upon the mode of changing lead in the Gallop. Illustrated by 28 Instantaneous Photographs. Demy 8vo. 21s.

## Vice in the Horse and other Papers on Horses and
Riding. By E. L. ANDERSON, Author of "Modern Horsemanship." Illustrated. Demy 8vo, 5s.

## The Gallop.
By E. L. ANDERSON. Illustrated by Instantaneous Photography. Fcap. 4to, 2s. 6d.

## Scotland in Early Christian Times.
By JOSEPH ANDERSON, LL.D., Keeper of the National Museum of the Antiquaries of Scotland. (Being the Rhind Lectures in Archæology for 1879 and 1880.) 2 vols. Demy 8vo, profusely Illustrated. 12s. each volume.
*Contents of Vol. I.*—Celtic Churches—Monasteries—Hermitages—Round Towers—Illuminated Manuscripts—Bells—Crosiers—Reliquaries, etc.
*Contents of Vol. II.*—Celtic Medal-Work and Sculptured Monuments, their Art and Symbolism—Inscribed Monuments in Runics and Oghams—Bilingual inscriptions, etc.

## Scotland in Pagan Times.
By JOSEPH ANDERSON, LL.D. (Being the Rhind Lectures in Archæology for 1881 and 1882.) In 2 vols. Demy 8vo, profusely Illustrated. 12s. each volume.
*Contents of Vol. I.*—THE IRON AGE.—Viking Burials and Hoards of Silver and Ornaments—Arms, Dress, etc., of the Viking Time—Celtic Art of the Pagan Period—Decorated Mirrors—Enamelled Armlets—Architecture and Contents of the Brochs—Lake-Dwellings—Earth Houses, etc.
*Contents of Vol. II.*—THE BRONZE AND STONE AGES.—Cairn Burial of the Bronze Age and Cremation Cemeteries—Urns of Bronze-Age Types—Stone Circles—Stone Settings—Gold Ornaments—Implements and Weapons of Bronze—Cairn Burial of the Stone Age—Chambered Cairns—Urns of Stone-Age Types—Impliments and Weapons of Stone.

## Scotland as it was and as it is.
By the DUKE OF ARGYLL. 2 vols. Demy 8vo, Illustrated. [*In the Press.*

## Crofts and Farms in the Hebrides:
Being an account of the Management of an Island Estate for 130 Years. By the DUKE OF ARGYLL. Demy 8vo, 83 pages, 1s.

## Continuity and Catastrophes in Geology.
An Address to the Edinburgh Geological Society on its Fiftieth Anniversary, 1st November 1883. By the DUKE OF ARGYLL. Demy 8vo, 1s.

## The History of Liddesdale, Eskdale, Ewesdale, Wauchopedale, and the Debateable Land.
Part I. from the Twelfth Century to 1530. By ROBERT BRUCE ARMSTRONG. The edition is limited to 275 copies demy quarto, and 105 copies on large paper (10 inches by 13). 42s. and 84s.

## Morning Clouds:
Being divers Poems by H. B. BAILDON, B.A. Cantab., Author of "Rosamund," etc. Ex. fcap. 8vo, 5s.

*By the same Author.*

## First Fruits. 5s.     Rosamund. 5s.

## On Both Sides. By FRANCES C. BAYLOR. 1 vol. 6s.

## Dr. Heidenhoff's Process.
By EDWARD BELLAMY. Crown 8vo, 6s.

## Miss Ludington's Sister: a Romance of Immortality.
By EDWARD BELLAMY, Author of "Dr. Heidenhoff's Process." Crown 8vo, 6s.

## LIST OF BOOKS

**Bible Readings.**
Extra fcap. 8vo, 2s.

**The Voyage of the Paper Canoe.**
A Geographical Journey of 2500 miles, from Quebec to the Gulf of Mexico, during the year 1874-75. By N. H. BISHOP. With Maps and Plates. Demy 8vo, 10s. 6d.

**On Self-Culture:**
Intellectual, Physical, and Moral. A *Vade-Mecum* for Young Men and Students. By JOHN STUART BLACKIE, Emeritus Professor of Greek in the University of Edinburgh. Sixteenth Edition. Fcap. 8vo, 2s. 6d.
"Every parent should put it into the hands of his son."—*Scotsman.*
"Students in all countries would do well to take as their *vade-mecum* a little book on self-culture by the eminent Professor of Greek in the University of Edinburgh."—*Medical Press and Circular.*
"An invaluable manual to be put into the hands of students and young men."—*Era.*
"Written in that lucid and nervous prose of which he is a master."—*Spectator.*
"An adequate guide to a generous, eager, and sensible life."—*Academy.*
"The volume is a little thing, but it is a *multum in parvo*, ... a little locket gemmed within and without with real stones fitly set."—*Courant.*

*By the same Author.*

**On Greek Pronunciation.** Demy 8vo, 3s. 6d.

**On Beauty.**
Crown 8vo, cloth, 8s. 6d.

**Lyrical Poems.**
Crown 8vo, cloth, 7s. 6d.

**The Language and Literature of the Scottish Highlands.** Crown 8vo, 6s.

**Four Phases of Morals:**
Socrates, Aristotle, Christianity, and Utilitarianism. Lectures delivered before the Royal Institution, London. Ex. fcap. 8vo, Second Edition, 5s.

**Songs of Religion and Life.** Fcap. 8vo, 6s.

**Musa Burschicosa.**
A book of Songs for Students and University Men. Fcap. 8vo, 2s. 6d.

**War Songs of the Germans.** Fcap. 8vo, 2s. 6d. cloth; 2s. paper.

**Political Tracts.** No. 1. GOVERNMENT. No. 2. EDUCATION. 1s. each.

**Gaelic Societies. Highland Depopulation and Land** Law Reform. Demy 8vo, 6d.

**Homer and the Iliad.**
In three Parts. 4 vols. Demy 8vo, 42s.

**Love Revealed: Meditations on the Parting Words of** Jesus with His Disciples, in John xiii.-xvii. By the Rev. GEORGE BOWEN, Missionary at Bombay. New Edition. Small 4to, 5s.
"No true Christian could put the book down without finding in himself some traces of the blessed unction which drops from every page."—*Record.*
"Here is a feast of fat things, of fat things full of marrow."—*Sword and Trowel.*
"A more stimulating work of its class has not appeared for many a long day."—*Scotsman.*
"The present work is eminently qualified to help the devotional life."—*Literary World.*
"He writes plainly and earnestly, and with a true appreciation of the tender beauties of what are really among the finest passages in the New Testament."—*Glasgow Herald.*

**"Verily, Verily," The Amens of Christ.**
By the Rev. GEORGE BOWEN, Missionary at Bombay. Small 4to, cloth, 5s.
"For private and devotional reading this book will be found very helpful and stimulative."—*Literary World.*

**Daily Meditations by Rev. George Bowen, Missionary**
at Bombay. With Introductory Notice by Rev. W. HANNA, D.D., Author of "The Last Day of our Lord's Passion." New Edition. Small 4to, cloth, 5s.

"These meditations are the production of a missionary whose mental history is very remarkable. . . . His conversion to a religious life is undoubtedly one of the most remarkable on record. They are all distinguished by a tone of true piety, and are wholly free from a sectarian or controversial bias."—*Morning Post.*

**Works by John Brown, M.D., F.R.S.E.**
HORÆ SUBSECIVÆ. 3 Vols. 22s. 6d.
    Vol. I. Locke and Sydenham. Fifth Edition, with Portrait by James Faed. Crown 8vo, 7s. 6d.
    Vol. II. Rab and his Friends Thirteenth Edition. Crown 8vo, 7s. 6d.
    Vol. III. John Leech. Fifth Edition, with Portrait by George Reid, R.S.A. Crown 8vo, 7s. 6d.

*Separate Papers, extracted from "Horæ Subsecivæ."*

RAB AND HIS FRIENDS. With India-proof Portrait of the Author after Faed, and seven India-proof Illustrations after Sir G. Harvey, Sir Noel Paton, Mrs. Blackburn, and G. Reid, R.S.A. Demy 4to, cloth, 9s.
MARJORIE FLEMING: A Sketch. Being a Paper entitled "Pet Majorie; A Story of a Child's Life fifty years ago." New Edition, with Illustrations. Demy 4to, 7s. 6d. and 6s.
RAB AND HIS FRIENDS. Cheap Illustrated Edition. Square 12mo, ornamental wrapper, 1s.
LETTER TO THE REV. JOHN CAIRNS, D.D. Second Edition, crown 8vo, sewed, 2s.
ARTHUR H. HALLAM. Fcap., sewed, 2s.; cloth, 2s. 6d.
RAB AND HIS FRIENDS. Sixty-sixth thousand. Fcap., sewed, 6d.
MARJORIE FLEMING: A Sketch. Sixteenth Thousand. Fcap., sewed, 6d.
OUR DOGS. Twentieth thousand. Fcap., sewed, 6d.
"WITH BRAINS, SIR." Seventh thousand. Fcap., sewed, 6d.
MINCHMOOR. Tenth Thousand. Fcap., sewed, 6d.
JEEMS THE DOOR-KEEPER: A Lay Sermon. Twelfth thousand. Price 6d.
THE ENTERKIN. Seventh Thousand. Price 6d.
PLAIN WORDS ON HEALTH. Twenty-seventh thousand. Price 6d.
SOMETHING ABOUT A WELL: WITH MORE OF OUR DOGS. Price 6d.

**From Schola to Cathedral. A Study of Early Christian**
Architecture in its relation to the life of the Church. By G. BALDWIN-BROWN, Professor of Fine Art in the University of Edinburgh. Demy 8vo, Illustrated, 7s. 6d.

The book treats of the beginnings of Christian Architecture, from the point of view of recent discoveries and theories, with a special reference to the outward resemblance of early Christian communities to other religious associations of the time.

**The Capercaillie in Scotland.**
By J. A. HARVIE-BROWN. Etchings on Copper, and Map illustrating the extension of its range since its Restoration at Taymouth in 1837 and 1838. Demy 8vo, 8s. 6d.

**A Vertebrate Fauna of Sutherland, Caithness, and**
West Cromarty, by J. A. HARVIE-BROWN, F.R.S.E., F.Z.S., Vice-President Royal Physical Society, Edinburgh; Member of the British Ornithologists' Union, etc., and T. E. BUCKLEY, B.A., F.Z.S., Member of the British Ornithologists' Union, etc. Small 4to, cloth, with Map and Plates, price 21s. to Subscribers. [*In the Press.*

**The History of Selkirkshire; Chronicles of Ettrick Forest.**
By T. CRAIG-BROWN. Two vols. Demy 4to, Illustrated. £4, 10s. to Subscribers.

**Pugin Studentship Drawings. Being a selection from**
Sketches, Measured Drawings, and details of Domestic and Ecclesiastic Buildings in England and Scotland. By G. WASHINGTON-BROWNE, F.S.A. Scot., Architect. 1 vol. Folio, Illustrated. [*In the Press.*

**Select Hymns for Church and Home.**
By R. BROWN-BORTHWICK. Second Edition. 16mo, 1s. 6d.

## LIST OF BOOKS

**"The Red Book of Menteith" Reviewed.**
By GEORGE BURNETT, Advocate, Lyon King of Arms. Small 4to, 5s.

**Next Door. A Novel.** By CLARE LOUISE BURNHAM. Crown 8vo, 7s. 6d.
"A strangely interesting story."—*St. James's Gazette.*

**John Burroughs's Essays.**
Six Books of Nature, Animal Life, and Literature. Choice Edition. Revised by the Author. 6 vols., cloth, 12s.; or in smooth ornamental wrappers, 6s.; or separately at 1s. each vol., or 2s. in cloth.

WINTER SUNSHINE. | FRESH FIELDS.
LOCUSTS AND WILD HONEY. | BIRDS AND POETS.
WAKE-ROBIN. | PEPACTON.

"Whichever essay I read, I am glad I read it, for pleasanter reading, to those who love the country, with all its enchanting sights and sounds, cannot be imagined."—*Spectator.*
"Mr. Burroughs is one of the most delightful of American Essayists, steeped in culture to the finger ends."—*Pall Mall Gazette.*

FRESH FIELDS. By JOHN BURROUGHS. Library Edition. Crown 8vo, 6s.
SIGNS AND SEASONS. Library Edition. Crown 8vo, 6s.

**Dr. Sevier: A Novel.**
By GEO. W. CABLE, Author of "Old Creole Days," etc. In 2 vols., crown 8vo, price 12s.

**Old Creole Days.**
By GEO. W. CABLE. 1s.; and in Cloth, 2s.
"We cannot recall any contemporary American writer of fiction who possesses some of the best gifts of the novelist in a higher degree."—*St. James's Gazette.*

**Memoir of John Brown, D.D.**
By JOHN CAIRNS, D.D., Berwick-on-Tweed. Crown 8vo, 7s. 6d.

**My Indian Journal.**
Containing Descriptions of the principal Field Sports of India, with Notes on the Natural History and Habits of the Wild Animals of the Country. By Colonel WALTER CAMPBELL, Author of "The Old Forest Ranger." Small demy 8vo, with Illustrations by Wolf, 16s.

**Life and Works of Rev. Thomas Chalmers, D.D., LL.D.**
MEMOIRS OF THE REV. THOMAS CHALMERS. By Rev. W. HANNA, D.D., LL.D. New Edition. 2 vols. crown 8vo, cloth, 12s.
DAILY SCRIPTURE READINGS. Cheap Edition. 2 vols. crown 8vo, 10s.
ASTRONOMICAL DISCOURSES, 1s.
COMMERCIAL DISCOURSES, 1s.
SELECT WORKS, in 12 vols., crown 8vo, cloth, per vol. 6s.
  Lectures on the Romans. 2 vols.
  Sermons. 2 vols.
  Natural Theology, Lectures on Butler's Analogy, etc. 1 vol.
  Christian Evidences, Lectures on Paley's Evidences, etc. 1 vol.
  Institutes of Theology. 2 vols.
  Political Economy, with Cognate Essays. 1 vol.
  Polity of a Nation. 1 vol.
  Church and College Establishments. 1 vol.
  Moral Philosophy, Introductory Essays, Index, etc. 1 vol.

**Lectures on Surgical Anatomy.**
By JOHN CHIENE, M.D., Professor of Surgery in the University of Edinburgh. In demy 8vo. With numerous Illustrations drawn on Stone by BERJEAU. 12s. 6d.
"The book will be a great help to both teachers and taught, and students can depend upon the teaching as being sound."—*Medical Times and Gazette.*

**Lectures on the Elements or First Principles of Surgery.**
By JOHN CHIENE, M.D., Professor of Surgery in the University of Edinburgh. Demy 8vo, 2s. 6d.

## Traditional Ballad Airs.
Arranged and Harmonised for the Pianoforte and Harmonium. By W. CHRISTIE, M.A., and the late WILLIAM CHRISTIE, Monquhitter. Demy 4to, Vols. I. and II. 42s. each.

## The Odes of Horace.
Translated by T. RUTHERFORD CLARK, Advocate. 16mo, 6s.

## Archibald Constable and his Literary Correspondents:
a Memorial. By his Son, THOMAS CONSTABLE. 3 vols. demy 8vo, 36s., with Portrait.

"He (Mr. Constable) was a genius in the publishing world. . . . The creator of the Scottish publishing trade."—*Times.*

## The Dandie Dinmont Terrier: Its History and Characteristics.
Compiled from the most Authentic Sources. By CHARLES COOK. Illustrated by Portraits of Authentic Specimens of the Pure Breed. Drawn and Etched by W. HOLE, A.R.S.A. Royal 8vo, 21s.

"His history of various celebrated Dandies, his pedigrees, and his anecdotes of Dandies' doings, are so well compiled and so interesting, that every one who owns a pet Dandie, let alone all who take an interest in dogs in general, will read the book with great interest."—*Pall Mall Gazette.*

"Mr. Cook's work teems with interest, and, quite unique of its kind, it will no doubt be found on the drawing-room table of all who take an interest in this particular strain of Scottish terriers."—*Field.*

## The Earldom of Mar, in Sunshine and in Shade, during
Five Hundred Years. With incidental Notices of the leading Cases of Scottish Dignities of King Charles I. till now. By ALEXANDER, EARL OF CRAWFORD AND BALCARRES, LORD LINDSAY, etc. etc. 2 vols. demy 8vo, 32s.

## The Crime of Henry Vane: a Study with a Moral.
By J. S. of Dale, Author of "Guerndale." Crown 8vo, 6s.

## A Clinical and Experimental Study of the Bladder
during Parturition. By J. H. CROOM, M.B., F.R.C.P.E. Small 4to, with Illustrations, 6s.

## Wild Men and Wild Beasts.
Adventures in Camp and Jungle. By Lieut.-Colonel GORDON CUMMING. With Illustrations by Lieut.-Colonel BAIORIE and others. Small 4to, 24s.

Also a cheaper edition, with *Lithographic* Illustrations. 8vo, 12s.

## Prue and I.
By GEORGE WILLIAM CURTIS. 1s. paper; or 2s. cloth extra.

*Contents.*—Dinner Time—My Chateaux—Sea from Shore—Titbottom's Spectacles —A Cruise in the Flying Dutchman—Family Portraits—Our Cousin the Curate.

"This is a dainty piece of work, and well deserved reprinting."—*Athenæum.*

"These charming sketches will be enjoyed by all cultured readers."—*Daily Chronicle.*

## Burnt Njal.
From the Icelandic of the Njal's Saga. By Sir GEORGE WEBBE DASENT, D.C.L. 2 vols. demy 8vo, with Maps and Plans, 28s.

## Gisli the Outlaw.
From the Icelandic. By Sir GEORGE WEBBE DASENT, D.C.L. Small 4to, with Illustrations, 7s. 6d.

## A Daughter of the Philistines: A Novel.
Crown 8vo, 6s. Also a cheaper edition in paper binding, 2s.

"The story is very powerfully told, possesses a piquantly satirical flavour, and possesses the very real attraction of freshness."—*Scotsman.*

"It is cleverly and brightly written."—*Academy.*

## A Manual of Chemical Analysis.
By Professor WILLIAM DITTMAR. Ex. fcap. 8vo, 5s.

TABLES FORMING AN APPENDIX TO DITTO. Demy 8vo, 3s. 6d.

**A Chat in the Saddle; or Patroclus and Penelope.**
By THEO. A. DODGE, Lieut.-Colonel, United States Army. Illustrated by 14 Instantaneous Photographs. Demy 8vo, half-leather binding, 21s.

**The Fireside Tragedy, etc.**
By Sir GEORGE DOUGLAS, Bart. Fcap. 8vo, 5s.

**Veterinary Medicines; their Actions and Uses.**
By FINLAY DUN. Sixth Edition, revised and enlarged. Demy 8vo, 15s.

**Social Life in Former Days;**
Chiefly in the Province of Moray. Illustrated by Letters and Family Papers. By E. DUNBAR DUNBAR, late Captain 21st Fusiliers. 2 vols. Demy 8vo, 19s. 6d.

**Letters of Thomas Erskine of Linlathen.**
Edited by WILLIAM HANNA, D.D., Author of the "Memoirs of Dr. Chalmers," etc. Fourth Edition. Crown 8vo, 7s. 6d.

**The Unconditional Freeness of the Gospel.**
By THOMAS ERSKINE of Linlathen. New Edition, revised. Crown 8vo, 3s. 6d.

*By the same Author.*

**The Brazen Serpent:**
Or, Life coming through Death. Third Edition. Crown 8vo, 5s.

**The Internal Evidence of Revealed Religion.**
Crown 8vo, 5s.

**The Spiritual Order,**
And other Papers selected from the MSS. of the late THOMAS ERSKINE of Linlathen. Third Edition. Crown 8vo, 5s.

**The Doctrine of Election,**
And its Connection with the General Tenor of Christianity, illustrated especially from the Epistle to the Romans. Second Edition. Crown 8vo, 6s.

**Three Visits to America.**
By EMILY FAITHFULL. Demy 8vo, 9s.

**Ogham Inscriptions in Ireland, Wales, and Scotland.**
By the late SIR SAMUEL FERGUSON, President of the Royal Irish Academy, Deputy Keeper of the Public Records of Ireland, LL.D., Queen's Counsel, etc. (Being the Rhind Lectures in Archæology for 1884.) 1 vol. demy 8vo.
[*In the Press.*]

**Twelve Sketches of Scenery and Antiquities on the**
Line of the Great North of Scotland Railway. By GEORGE REID, R.S.A. With Illustrative Letterpress by W. FERGUSON of Kinmundy. 4to, 15s.

**Guide to the Great North of Scotland Railway.**
By W. FERGUSON of Kinmundy. Crown 8vo; in paper cover, 1s.; cloth cover, 1s. 6d.

**Letters and Journals of Mrs. Calderwood of Polton,**
from England, Holland, and the Low Countries, in 1756. Edited by ALEX. FERGUSSON, Lieut.-Colonel, Author of "Henry Erskine and his Kinsfolk." Demy 8vo, Illustrated, 18s.

**The Laird of Lag; A Life-Sketch of Sir Robert Grierson.**
By ALEX. FERGUSSON, Lieut.-Colonel, Author of "Mrs. Calderwood's Journey." Demy 8vo, with Illustrations, 12s.

**Autobiography of Mrs. Fletcher**
(of Edinburgh), with Letters and other Family Memorials. Edited by her Daughter. Third Edition. Crown 8vo, 7s. 6d.

**L'Histoire de France.**
Par M. LAME FLEURY. New Edition, corrected to 1883. 18mo, cloth, 2s. 6d.

PUBLISHED BY DAVID DOUGLAS.  9

### The Deepening of the Spiritual Life.
By A. P. FORBES, D.C.L., Bishop of Brechin. Seventh Edition. Paper, 1s.; cloth, 1s. 6d. Calf, red edges, 3s. 6d.

### Kalendars of Scottish Saints,
With Personal Notices of those of Alba, etc. By ALEXANDER PENROSE FORBES, D.C.L., Bishop of Brechin. 4to, price £3, 3s. A few copies for sale on large paper, £5, 15s. 6d.

"A truly valuable contribution to the archæology of Scotland."—*Guardian.*

"We must not forget to thank the author for the great amount of information he has put together, and for the labour he has bestowed on a work which can never be remunerative."—*Saturday Review.*

### Missale Drummondiense. The Ancient Irish Missal in
the possession of the Baroness Willoughby d'Eresby. Edited by the Rev. G. H. FORBES. Half-Morocco, Demy 8vo, 12s.

### Forestry and Forest Products.
Prize Essays of the Edinburgh International Forestry Exhibition 1884. Edited by JOHN RATTRAY M.A., B.Sc., and HUGH ROBERT MILL, D.Sc. Demy 8vo, Illustrated, 9s.

### Fragments of Truth:
Being the Exposition of several Passages of Scripture. Third Edition. Ex. fcap. 8vo, 5s.

### Studies in English History.
By JAMES GAIRDNER and JAMES SPEDDING. Demy 8vo, 12s.

*Contents.*—The Lollards—Sir John Falstaff—Katherine of Arragon's First and Second Marriages—Case of Sir Thomas Overbury—Divine Right of Kings—Sunday, Ancient and Modern.

### Gifts for Men.
By X. H. Crown 8vo, 6s.

"There is hardly a living theologian who might not be proud to claim many of her thoughts as his own."—*Glasgow Herald.*

### Sketches, Literary and Theological:
Being Selections from the unpublished MSS. of the Rev. GEORGE GILFILLAN. Edited by FRANK HENDERSON, Esq., M.P. Demy 8vo, 7s. 6d.

### The Roof of the World:
Being the Narrative of a Journey over the High Plateau of Tibet to the Russian Frontier, and the Oxus Sources on Pamir. By Brigadier-General T. E. GORDON, C.S.I. With numerous Illustrations. Royal 8vo, 31s. 6d.

### Works by Margaret Maria Gordon (née Brewster).
THE HOME LIFE OF SIR DAVID BREWSTER. By his Daughter. Second Edition. Crown 8vo, 6s. Also a cheaper Edition. Crown 8vo, 2s. 6d.

WORK; Or, Plenty to do and How to do it. Thirty-Sixth Thousand. Fcap. 8vo, cloth, 2s. 6d.

WORKERS. Fourth Thousand. Fcap. 8vo, limp cloth, 1s.

LITTLE MILLIE AND HER FOUR PLACES. Cheap Edition. Fifty-eighth Thousand. Limp cloth, 1s.

SUNBEAMS IN THE COTTAGE; Or, What Women may Do. A Narrative chiefly addressed to the Working Classes. Cheap Edition. Forty-fifth Thousand. Limp cloth, 1s.

PREVENTION; Or, An Appeal to Economy and Common Sense. 8vo, 6d.

THE WORD AND THE WORLD. Twelfth Edition. 2d.

LEAVES OF HEALING FOR THE SICK AND SORROWFUL. Cheap Edition, limp cloth, 2s.

THE MOTHERLESS BOY. With an Illustration by Sir NOEL PATON, R.S.A. Cheap Edition, limp cloth, 1s.

OUR DAUGHTERS; An Account of the Young Women's Christian Association and Institute Union. 2d.

HAY MACDOWALL GRANT OF ARNDILLY; His Life, Labours, and Teaching. New and Cheaper Edition. 1 vol. crown 8vo, limp cloth, 2s. 6d.

## LIST OF BOOKS

**Ladies' Old-Fashioned Shoes.**
By T. WATSON GREIG, of Glencarse. Folio, illustrated by 11 Chromolithographs. 31s. 6d.

**The Life of our Lord.**
By the Rev. WILLIAM HANNA, D.D., LL.D. 6 vols., handsomely bound in cloth extra, gilt edges, 30s.

Separate vols., cloth extra, gilt edges, 5s. each.

1. THE EARLIER YEARS OF OUR LORD. Fifth Edition.
2. THE MINISTRY IN GALILEE. Fourth Edition.
3. THE CLOSE OF THE MINISTRY. Sixth Thousand.
4. THE PASSION WEEK. Sixth Thousand.
5. THE LAST DAY OF OUR LORD'S PASSION. Twenty-third Edition.
6. THE FORTY DAYS AFTER THE RESURRECTION. Eighth Edition.

**The Resurrection of the Dead.**
By WILLIAM HANNA, D.D., LL.D. Second Edition. Fcap. 8vo, 5s.

**Mingo, and other Sketches in Black and White.**
By JOEL CHANDLER HARRIS (*Uncle Remus*). 1s.; and in cloth, 2s.

**Notes of Caithness Family History.**
By the late JOHN HENDERSON, W.S. 4to, 31s. 6d.

**Errors in the Use of English.**
Illustrated from the Writings of English Authors, from the Fourteenth Century to our own Time. By the late W. B. HODGSON, LL.D., Professor of Political Economy in the University of Edinburgh. Fifth Edition. Crown 8vo, 3s. 6d.

"Those who most need such a book as Dr. Hodgson's will probably be the last to look into it. It will certainly amuse its readers, and will probably teach them a good deal which they did not know, or at least never thought about, before."—*Saturday Review.*

"His conversation, as every one who had the pleasure of his acquaintance knows, sparkled with anecdote and epigram, and not a little of the lustre and charm of his talk shines out of those pages."—*The Scotsman.*

**Life and Letters of W. B. Hodgson, LL.D.**, late Professor of Political Economy in the University of Edinburgh. Edited by Professor J. M. D. MEIKLEJOHN, M.A. Crown 8vo, 7s. 6d.

**Sketches: Personal and Pensive.**
By WILLIAM HODGSON. Fcap. 8vo, 2s. 6d.

**"Quasi Cursores." Portraits of the High Officers and** Professors of the University of Edinburgh. Drawn and Etched by WILLIAM HOLE, A.R.S.A. The book is printed on beautiful hand-made paper by Messrs. T. & A. Constable. It contains 45 Plates (64 Portraits), with Biographical Notices of all the present Incumbents. The impression is strictly limited. Quarto Edition (750 Copies only for sale), £2, 10s. Folio Edition, Japan Proofs (100 Copies only for sale), £5, 10s.

"A work of great value and of high artistic merit, not merely in respect of the portraits, but also in respect of the typography, the paper, the binding, and the general get-up of the volume. . . . It does great credit to the resources of Edinburgh, both as a seat of learning, and as a centre of literary production on its mechanical side."—*Times.*

### The Breakfast Table Series.
In 6 vols. By OLIVER WENDELL HOLMES. New and Revised Editions, containing Prefaces and additional Bibliographical Notes by the Author.
Every man his own Boswell.
THE AUTOCRAT OF THE BREAKFAST TABLE. 2 vols., 2s.
THE POET AT THE BREAKFAST TABLE. 2 vols., 2s.
THE PROFESSOR AT THE BREAKFAST TABLE. 2 vols., 2s.
Also bound in dark blue cloth, at 2s. a vol., or in a neat cloth box, 15s.

"Small enough to be carried in any sensibly constructed pocket, clear enough in type to accommodate any fastidious eyesight, pleasant and instructive enough for its perusal to be undertaken with the certainty of present enjoyment and the prospect of future profit."—*Whitehall Review.*

Also a LIBRARY EDITION, in 3 vols. crown 8vo, printed at the Riverside Press, Cambridge, with a Steel Portrait of the Author, 10s. 6d. each volume.

A COMPLETE EDITION of the Poems of OLIVER WENDELL HOLMES, revised by the Author, in 3 vols. [*In the Press.*

### Traces in Scotland of Ancient Water Lines, Marine,
Lacustrine, and Fluviatile. By DAVID MILNE-HOME, LL.D., F.R.S.E. Demy 8vo, 3s. 6d.

### A Sketch of the Life of George Hope of Fenton Barns.
Compiled by his DAUGHTER. Crown 8vo, 6s.

### One Summer.
By BLANCHE WILLIS HOWARD. Paper, 1s.; cloth, 1s. 6d. and 2s.

### W. D. Howells's Writings:—
*In "American Author" Series.*
THE RISE OF SILAS LAPHAM. 2 vols., 2s.
A FOREGONE CONCLUSION. 1 vol., 1s.
A CHANCE ACQUAINTANCE. 1 vol., 1s.
THEIR WEDDING JOURNEY. 1 vol., 1s.
A COUNTERFEIT PRESENTMENT, and THE PARLOUR CAR. 1 vol., 1s.
THE LADY OF THE AROOSTOOK. 2 vols., 2s.
OUT OF THE QUESTION, and AT THE SIGN OF THE SAVAGE. 1 vol. 1s.
THE UNDISCOVERED COUNTRY. 2 vols., 2s.
A FEARFUL RESPONSIBILITY, and TONELLI'S MARRIAGE. 1 vol., 1s.
VENETIAN LIFE. 2 vols., 2s.
ITALIAN JOURNEYS. 2 vols., 2s.
All the above may be had in cloth at 2s. each vol.

*Copyright Library Edition.*
A MODERN INSTANCE. 2 vols., 12s.
A WOMAN'S REASON. 2 vols., 12s.
DR. BREEN'S PRACTICE. 1 vol., 3s. 6d.
INDIAN SUMMER. 1 vol., 6s.
THE MINISTER'S CHARGE; OR, THE APPRENTICESHIP OF LEMUEL BARKER. 1 vol., 6s.
TUSCAN CITIES: WITH ILLUSTRATIONS FROM DRAWINGS AND ETCHINGS OF JOSEPH PENNELL and others. 4to, 16s.

### A Memorial Sketch, and a Selection from the Letters
of the late Lieut. JOHN IRVING, R.N., of H.M.S. "Terror," in Sir John Franklin's Expedition to the Arctic Regions. Edited by BENJAMIN BELL, F.R.C.S.E. With Facsimiles of the Record and Irving's Medal and Map. Post 8vo, 5s.

### Jack and Mrs. Brown, and other Stories.
By the Author of "Blindpits." Crown 8vo, paper, 2s. 6d.; cloth, 3s. 6d.

### Zeph: A Posthumous Story.
By HELEN JACKSON ("H.H."). Author of "Ramona," etc. Crown 8vo, 6s.

### Epitaphs and Inscriptions from Burial-Grounds and
Old Buildings in the North-East of Scotland. By the late ANDREW JERVISE, F.S.A. Scot. With a Memoir of the Author. Vol. II. Cloth, small 4to, 32s.
Do.        do.              Roxburghe Edition, 42s.

## LIST OF BOOKS

**The History and Traditions of the Land of the Lindsays**
in Angus and Mearns. New Edition, Edited and Revised by the Rev. JAMES GAMMACK, M.A. Demy 8vo, 14s.
Do. do. Large Paper Edition (of which only 50 are printed), Demy 4to, Roxburghe binding, 42s.

**Memorials of Angus and the Mearns: an Account,**
Historical, Antiquarian, and Traditionary, of the Castles and Towns visited by Edward I, and of the Barons, Clergy, and others who swore Fealty to England in 1291-6. By the late ANDREW JERVISE, F.S.A. Scot. Rewritten and corrected by the Rev. JAMES GAMMACK, M.A. Illustrated with Etchings by W. HOLE, A.R.S.A. 2 vols. Demy 8vo, 28s.; Large Paper, 2 vols. Demy 4to, 63s.

**Pilate's Question, "Whence art Thou?"**
An Essay on the Personal Claims asserted by Jesus Christ, and how to account for them. By JOHN KENNEDY, M.A., D.D., London. Crown 8vo, 3s. 6d.

**Sermons by the Rev. John Ker, D.D., Glasgow.**
Thirteenth Edition. Crown 8vo, 6s.

**Sermons: Second Series: by the Rev. John Ker, D.D.**
Crown 8vo, 6s.

**The English Lake District as interpreted in the Poems**
of Wordsworth. By WILLIAM KNIGHT, Professor of Moral Philosophy in the University of St. Andrews. Ex. fcap. 8vo, 5s.

**Colloquia Peripatetica (Deep Sea Soundings):**
Being Notes of Conversations with the late John Duncan, LL.D., Professor of Hebrew in the New College, Edinburgh. By WILLIAM KNIGHT, Professor of Moral Philosophy in the University of St. Andrews. Fifth Edition, enlarged, 5s.

**Lindores Abbey, and the Burgh of Newburgh;**
Their History and Annals. By ALEXANDER LAING, LL.D., F.S.A. Scot. Small 4to. With Index, and thirteen Full-page and ten Woodcut Illustrations, 21s.
"This is a charming volume in every respect."—*Notes and Queries.*
"The prominent characteristics of the work are its exhaustiveness and the thoroughly philosophic spirit in which it is written."—*Scotsman.*

**Recollections of Curious Characters and Pleasant**
Places. By CHARLES LANMAN, Washington; Author of "Adventures in the Wilds of America," "A Canoe Voyage up the Mississippi," "A Tour to the River Saguenay," etc. etc. Small Demy 8vo, 12s.

**Essays and Reviews.**
By the late HENRY H. LANCASTER, Advocate; with a Prefatory Notice by the Rev. B. JOWETT, Master of Balliol College, Oxford. Demy 8vo, with Portrait, 14s.

**An Echo of Passion.**
By GEO. PARSONS LATHROP. 1s.; and in cloth, 2s.

**On the Philosophy of Ethics. An Analytical Essay.**
By S. S. LAURIE, A.M., F.R.S.E., Professor of the Theory, History, and Practice of Education in the University of Edinburgh. Demy 8vo, 6s.

**Notes on British Theories of Morals.**
By Prof. S. S. LAURIE. Demy 8vo, 6s.

**Leaves from the Buik of the West Kirke.**
By GEO. LORIMER. With a Preface by the Rev. JAS. MACGREGOR, D.D. 4to.

**Bible Studies in Life and Truth.**
By the Rev. ROBERT LORIMER, M.A., Free Church, Mains and Strathmartine. Crown 8vo, 5s.

**Sermons by the Rev. Adam Lind, M.A., Elgin.**
Ex. fcap. 8vo, 5s.

**Only an Incident.**
A Novel. By Miss G. D. LITCHFIELD. Crown 8vo, 6s.

PUBLISHED BY DAVID DOUGLAS. 13

**A Lost Battle.** A Novel. 2 vols. Crown 8vo, 17s.
"This in every way remarkable novel."—*Morning Post*.
"We are all the more ready to do justice to the excellence of the author's drawing of characters."—*Athenæum*.

**John Calvin, a Fragment by the Late Thomas M'Crie,** Author of "The Life of John Knox." Demy 8vo, 6s.

**The Parish of Taxwood, and some of its Older Memories.** By Rev. J. R. MACDUFF, D.D. Extra fcap. 8vo, illustrated, 3s. 6d.

**Principles of the Algebra of Logic, with Examples.** By ALEX. MACFARLANE, M.A., D.Sc. (Edin.), F.R.S.E. 5s.

**The Castellated and Domestic Architecture of Scot**land, from the Twelfth to the Eighteenth Century. By DAVID M'GIBBON and THOMAS ROSS, Architects. Vol. I. Containing about 500 Illustrations of Ground Plans, Sections, Views, Elevations, and Details. Royal 8vo. 42s.
Vol. II., completing the work. [*In the Press*.

**Memoir of Sir James Dalrymple, First Viscount Stair.** A Study in the History of Scotland and Scotch Law during the Seventeenth Century. By Æ. J. G. MACKAY, Advocate. 8vo, 12s.

**Storms and Sunshine of a Soldier's Life.** Lt.-General COLIN MACKENZIE, C.B., 1825-1881. With a Portrait. 2 vols. Crown 8vo, 15s.
"A very readable biography ... of one of the bravest and ablest officers of the East India Company's army."—*Saturday Review*.

**Nugæ Canoræ Medicæ.** Lays of the Poet Laureate of the New Town Dispensary. Edited by Professor DOUGLAS MACLAGAN. 4to, with Illustrations, 7s. 6d.

**The Hill Forts, Stone Circles, and other Structural Re**mains of Ancient Scotland. By C. MACLAGAN, Lady Associate of the Society of Antiquaries of Scotland. With Plans and Illustrations. Folio, 31s. 6d.
"We need not enlarge on the few inconsequential speculations which rigid archæologists may find in the present volume. We desire rather to commend it to their careful study, fully assured that not only they, but also the general reader, will be edified by its perusal."—*Scotsman*.

**The Light of the World.** By DAVID M'LAREN, Minister of Humbie. Crown 8vo, 6s.

**The Book of Psalms in Metre.** According to the version approved of by the Church of Scotland. Revised by Rev. DAVID M'LAREN. Crown 8vo, 7s. 6d.

**Omnipotence belongs only to the Beloved.** By Mrs. BREWSTER MACPHERSON. Extra fcap., 3s. 6d.

**Humorous Masterpieces from American Literature,** from 1810 to 1886. Edited by EDWARD T. MASON. Selections are made from the Works of: ALCOTT, ALDEN, ALDRICH, BALDWIN, BEECHER, BELLAMY, BROWNE, BUNNER, BUTLER, CABLE, CAVAZZA, CLEMENS, CONE, COZZENS, CRANE, CURTIS, DODGE, DUNNING, HALE, HARTE, HARRIS, HAWTHORNE, HOLMES, HOWE, HOWELLS, IRVING, JOHNSON, LANIGAN, LELAND, LOWELL, LUDLOW, M'DOWELL, MATTHEWS, OGDEN, PHELPS, QUINCEY, ROCHE, SAXE, SEBA, SMITH, STOFFORD, STOCKTON, STOWE, THORPE, THROWBRIDGE, WARNER, Etc. 3 vols. square 16mo, 3s. 6d. each vol.

**In Partnership. Studies in Story-Telling.** By BRANDER MATTHEWS and H. C. BUNNER. 1s. in paper, and 2s. in cloth.

**Antwerp Delivered in MDLXXVII. :** A Passage from the History of the Netherlands, illustrated with Facsimiles of a rare series of Designs by Martin de Vos, and of Prints by Hogenberg, the Lierixes, etc. By Sir WILLIAM STIRLING-MAXWELL, Bart., K.T. and M.P. In 1 vol. Folio, 5 guineas.
"A splendid folio in richly ornamented binding, protected by an almost equally ornamental slip-cover. ... Remarkable illustrations of the manner in which the artists of the time 'pursued their labours in a country ravaged by war, and in cities ever menaced by siege and sack.'"—*Scotsman*.

## LIST OF BOOKS

**Studies in the Topography of Galloway, with a List of** nearly 4000 Names of Places, and Remarks on their Origin and Meaning. By SIR HERBERT MAXWELL, Bart., M.P. 1 vol. demy 8vo. [*In the Press.*

**The History of Old Dundee, narrated out of the Town** Council Register, with Additions from Contemporary Annals. By ALEXANDER MAXWELL, F.S.A. Scot. 4to. Cloth, 21s.; Roxburgh, 24s.

**Researches and Excavations at Carnac (Morbihan),** The Bossenno, and Mont St. Michel. By JAMES MILN. Royal 8vo, with Maps, Plans, and numerous Illustrations in Wood-Engraving and Chromolithography.

**Excavations at Carnac (Brittany), a Record of Archæo-** logical Researches in the Alignments of Kermario. By JAMES MILN. Royal 8vo, with Maps, Plans, and numerous Illustrations in Wood-Engraving. 15s.

**The Past in the Present—What is Civilisation?** Being the Rhind Lectures in Archæology, delivered in 1876 and 1878. By ARTHUR MITCHELL, M.D., LL.D., Secretary to the Society of Antiquaries of Scotland. In 1 vol. demy 8vo, with 148 Woodcuts, 15s.

" Whatever differences of opinion, however, may be held on minor points, there can be no question that Dr. Mitchell's work is one of the ablest and most original pieces of archæological literature which has appeared of late years."—*St. James's Gazette.*

**In War Time. A Novel.** By S. WEIR MITCHELL, M.D. Crown 8vo, 6s.

**Roland Blake. A Novel.** By S. WEIR MITCHELL, M.D. Crown 8vo, 6s.

**Our Scotch Banks:** Their Position and their Policy. By WM. MITCHELL, S.S.C. Third Edition. 8vo, 5s.

**On Horse-Breaking.** By ROBERT MORETON. Second Edition. Fcap. 8vo, 1s.

**Ecclesiological Notes on some of the Islands of Scot-** land, with other Papers relating to Ecclesiological Remains on the Scottish Mainland and Islands. By THOMAS S. MUIR, Author of "Characteristics of Church Architecture," etc. Demy 8vo, with numerous Illustrations, 21s

**The Birds of Berwickshire.** By GEO. MUIRHEAD. 1 vol. demy 8vo, Illustrated. 10s. to Subscribers. [*In the Press.*

**Ancient Scottish Lake-Dwellings or Crannogs, with a** Supplementary Chapter on Remains of Lake-Dwellings in England. By ROBERT MUNRO, M.D., F.S.A. Scot. 1 vol. demy 8vo, profusely illustrated, 21s.

" A standard authority on the subject of which it treats."—*Times.*
" . . . Our readers may be assured that they will find very much to interest and instruct them in the perusal of the work."—*Athenæum.*

**"The Lanox of Auld:" An Epistolary Review of "The** Lennox, by William Fraser." By MARK NAPIER. With Woodcuts and Plates. 4to, 15s.

**Tenants' Gain not Landlords' Loss, and some other** Economic Aspects of the Land Question. By JOSEPH SHIELD NICHOLSON, M.A., Professor of Political Economy in the University of Edinburgh. Crown 8vo, 5s.

**Camps in the Caribbees: Adventures of a Naturalist** in the Lesser Antilles. By FREDERICK OBER. Illustrations, demy 8vo, 12s.

" Well-written and well-illustrated narrative of camping out among the Caribbees."—*Westminster Review.*
" Varied were his experiences, hairbreadth his escapes, and wonderful his gleanings in the way of securing rare birds."—*The Literary World.*

PUBLISHED BY DAVID DOUGLAS.     15

**Cookery for the Sick and a Guide for the Sick-Room.**
By C. H. Ogg, an Edinburgh Nurse. Fcap. 1s.

**The Lord Advocates of Scotland from the close of the**
Fifteenth Century to the passing of the Reform Bill. By G. W. T. OMOND,
Advocate. 2 vols. demy 8vo, 28s.

**Arniston Memoirs—From the 16th to the 19th Century.**
Edited from Family Papers by GEO. W. T. OMOND, Advocate. 1 vol. demy 8vo,
Illustrated. [In the Press.

**An Irish Garland.**
By Mrs. S. M. B. PIATT. Crown 8vo, 3s. 6d.

**The Children Out of Doors. A Book of Verses**
By TWO IN ONE HOUSE. Crown 8vo, 3s. 6d.

**Records of the Coinage of Scotland, from the earliest**
period to the Union. Collected by R. W. COCHRAN-PATRICK, M.P. Only two
hundred and fifty copies printed. Now ready, in 2 vols. 4to, with 16 Full-page
Illustrations, Six Guineas.
"The future Historians of Scotland will be very fortunate if many parts of their materials are so carefully worked up for them and set before them in so complete and taking a form."—*Athenaum.*
"When we say that these two volumes contain more than 770 records, of which more than 550 have never been printed before, and that they are illustrated by a series of Plates, by the autotype process, of the coins themselves, the reader may judge for himself of the learning, as well as the pains, bestowed on them both by the Author and the Publisher."—*Times.*
"The most handsome and complete work of the kind which has ever been published in this country."—*Numismatic Chronicle, Pt. IV.,* 1876.

**Early Records relating to Mining in Scotland:**
Collected by R. W. COCHRAN-PATRICK, M.P. Demy 4to, 31s. 6d.
"The documents . . . comprise a great deal that is very curious, and no less that will be important to the historian in treating of the origin of one of the most important branches of the national industry."—*Daily News.*
"Such a book . . . revealing as it does the first developments of an industry which has become the mainspring of the national prosperity, ought to be specially interesting to all patriotic Scotchmen."—*Saturday Review.*

**The Medals of Scotland: a Descriptive Catalogue of**
the Royal and other Medals relating to Scotland. By R. W. COCHRAN-PATRICK,
M.P. Dedicated by special permission to Her Majesty the Queen. Demy 4to,
with plates in facsimile of all the principal pieces, £3, 3s.

**Phœbe.**
By the Author of "Rutledge." Reprinted from the Fifth Thousand of the
American Edition. Crown 8vo, 6s.
"'Phœbe' is a woman's novel."—*Saturday Review.*

**Popular Genealogists;**
Or, The Art of Pedigree-making. Crown 8vo, 4s.

**The Gamekeeper's Manual: being Epitome of the Game**
Laws for the use of Gamekeepers and others interested in the Preservation of
Game. By ALEXANDER PORTER, Deputy Chief Constable of Roxburghshire.
Fcap. 8vo, 1s.

**Oils and Water Colours.**
By WILLIAM RENTON. Fcap., 5s.
"The book is obviously for the Artist and the Poet, and for every one who shares with them a true love and zeal for nature's beauties."—*Scotsman.*

**Kuram, Kabul, and Kandahar: being a Brief Record of**
the Impressions in Three Campaigns under General Roberts. By Lieutenant
ROBERTSON, 8th, "The King's," Regiment. Crown 8vo, with Maps, 6s.

## LIST OF BOOKS

### Scotland under her Early Kings.
A History of the Kingdom to the close of the 13th century. By E. WILLIAM ROBERTSON. In 2 vols. 8vo, cloth, 36s.

### Historical Essays,
In connection with the Land and the Church, etc. By E. WILLIAM ROBERTSON, Author of "Scotland under her Early Kings." 8vo, 10s. 6d.

### A Rectorial Address delivered before the Students of
Aberdeen University, in the Music Hall at Aberdeen, on Nov. 5, 1880. By THE EARL OF ROSEBERY. 6d.

### A Rectorial Address delivered before the Students of
the University of Edinburgh, Nov. 4, 1882. By THE EARL OF ROSEBERY. 6d.

### Rosetty Ends, or the Chronicles of a Country Cobbler.
By Job Bradawl (A. DEWAR WILLOCK), Author of "She Noddit to me." Fcap. 8vo, illustrated.

### Aberdour and Inchcolme. Being Historical Notices of
the Parish and Monastery, in Twelve Lectures. By the Rev. WILLIAM ROSS, LL.D., Author of "Burgh Life in Dunfermline in the Olden Time." Crown 8vo, 6s.

"If any one would know what Aberdour has been, or, indeed, what to some extent has been the history of many another parish in Scotland, he cannot do better than read these Lectures. He will find the task a pleasant one."—*Saturday Review.*

"We know no book which within so small a compass contains so varied, so accurate, and so vivid a description of the past life of the Scottish people, whether ecclesiastical or social, as Dr. Ross's 'Aberdour and Inchcolme.'"—*Scottish Review.*

"It seems a pity that so good a thing should have been so long withheld from a wider audience; but better late than never."—*Scotsman.*

### Notes and Sketches from the Wild Coasts of Nipon.
With Chapters on Cruising after Pirates in Chinese Waters. By HENRY C. ST. JOHN, Captain R.N. Small Demy 8vo, with Maps and Illustrations, 12s.

"One of the most charming books of travel that has been published for some time."—*Scotsman.*

"There is a great deal more in the book than Natural History.... His pictures of life and manners are quaint and effective, and the more so from the writing being natural and free from effort."—*Athenæum.*

"He writes with a simplicity and directness, and not seldom with a degree of graphic power, which, even apart from the freshness of the matter, renders his book delightful reading. Nothing could be better of its kind than the description of the Inland Sea."—*Daily News.*

### Notes on the Natural History of the Province of Moray.
By the late CHARLES ST. JOHN, Author of "Wild Sports in the Highlands." Second Edition. In 1 vol. royal 8vo, with 40 page Illustrations of Scenery and Animal Life, engraved by A. DURAND after sketches made by GEORGE REID, R.S.A., and J. WYCLIFFE TAYLOR; also, 30 Pen-and-Ink Drawings by the Author in facsimile. 50s.

"This is a new edition of the work brought out by the friends of the late Mr. St. John in 1863; but it is so handsomely and nobly printed, and enriched with such charming illustrations, that we may consider it a new book."—*St. James's Gazette.*

"Charles St. John was not an artist, but he had the habit of roughly sketching animals in positions which interested him, and the present reprint is adorned by a great number of these, facsimiled from the author's original pen and ink. Some of these, as for instance the studies of the golden eagle swooping on its prey, and that of the otter swimming with a salmon in its mouth, are very interesting, and full of that charm that comes from the exact transcription of unusual observation."—*Pall Mall Gazette.*

### A Tour in Sutherlandshire, with Extracts from the
Field-Books of a Sportsman and Naturalist. By the late CHARLES ST. JOHN, Author of "Wild Sports and Natural History in the Highlands." Second Edition, with an Appendix on the Fauna of Sutherland, by J. A. HARVIE-BROWN and T. E. BUCKLEY. Illustrated with the original Wood Engravings, and additional Vignettes from the Author's sketch-books. In 2 vols. small demy 8vo, 21s.

"Every page is full of interest."—*The Field.*

"There is not a wild creature in the Highlands, from the great stag to the tiny fire-crested wren, of which he has not something pleasant to say."—*Pall Mall Gazette.*

### Life of James Hepburn, Earl of Bothwell.
By Professor SCHIERN, Copenhagen. Translated from the Danish by the Rev. DAVID BERRY, F.S.A. Scot. Demy 8vo, 16s.

### Scotch Folk.
Illustrated. Fourth Edition enlarged. Ex. fcap. 8vo, 1s.

"They are stories of the best type, quite equal in the main to the average of Dean Ramsay's well-known collection."—*Aberdeen Free Press.*

### Studies in Poetry and Philosophy.
By the late J. C. SHAIRP, LL.D., Principal of the United College of St. Salvator and St. Leonard, St. Andrews. Fourth Edition, with Portraits of the Author and Thomas Erskine, by WILLIAM HOLE, A.R.S.A. Crown 8vo, 7s. 6d

"In the 'Moral Dynamic,' Mr. Shairp seeks for something which shall persuade us of the vital and close bearing on each other of moral thought and spiritual energy. It is this conviction which has animated Mr. Shairp in every page of the volume before us. It is because he appreciates so justly and forcibly the powers of philosophic doctrine over all the field of human life, that he leans with such strenuous trust upon those ideas which Wordsworth unsystematically, and Coleridge more systematically, made popular and fertile among us."—*Saturday Review.*

"The finest essay in the volume, partly because it is upon the greatest and most definite subject, is the first, on *Wordsworth.* . . . We have said so much upon this essay that we can only say of the other three that they are fully worthy to stand beside it."—*Spectator.*

### Culture and Religion.
By PRINCIPAL SHAIRP. Seventh Edition. Fcap. 8vo, 3s. 6d.

"A wise book, and unlike a great many other wise books, has that carefully shaded thought and expression which fits Professor Shairp to speak for Culture no less than for Religion."—*Spectator.*

"Those who remember a former work of Principal Shairp's, 'Studies in Poetry and Philosophy,' will feel secure that all which comes from his pen will bear the marks of thought, at once careful, liberal, and accurate. Nor will they be disappointed in the present work. . . . We can recommend this book to our readers."—*Athenæum.*

"We cannot close without earnestly recommending the book to thoughtful young men. It combines the loftiest intellectual power with a simple and childlike faith in Christ, and exerts an influence which must be stimulating and healthful."—*Freeman.*

### Kilmahoe, a Highland Pastoral,
And other Poems. By PRINCIPAL SHAIRP. Fcap. 8vo, 6s.

### Shakespeare on Golf. With special Reference to St. Andrews Links. 3d.

### The Divine Comedy of Dante Alighieri, The Inferno.
A Translation in Terza Rima, with Notes and Introductory Essay. By JAMES ROMANES SIBBALD. With an Engraving after Giotto's Portrait. Small Demy 8vo, 12s.

"Mr. Sibbald is certainly to be congratulated on having produced a translation which would probably give an English reader a better conception of the nature of the original poem, having regard both to its matter and its form in combination, than any other English translation yet published."—*Academy.*

## The Use of what is called Evil.
A Discourse by SIMPLICIUS. Extracted from his Commentary on the Enchiridion of Epictetus. Crown 8vo, 1s.

## The Near and the Far View,
And other Sermons. By Rev. A. L. SIMPSON, D.D., Derby. Ex. fcap. 8vo, 5s.

"Very fresh and thoughtful are these sermons."—*Literary World.*

"Dr. Simpson's sermons may fairly claim distinctive power. He looks at things with his own eyes, and often shows us what with ordinary vision we had failed to perceive. . . . The sermons are distinctively good."—*British Quarterly Review.*

## Archæological Essays.
By the late Sir JAMES SIMPSON, Bart. Edited by the late JOHN STUART, LL.D. 2 vols. 4to, 21s.

1. Archæology.
2. Inchcolm.
3. The Cat Stane.
4. Magical Charm-Stones.
5. Pyramid of Gizeh.
6. Leprosy and Leper Hospitals.
7. Greek Medical Vases.
8. Was the Roman Army provided with Medical Officers?
9. Roman Medicine Stamps, etc. etc.

## The Art of Golf.
By SIR WALTER SIMPSON, Bart., Captain of the Hon. Company of Edinburgh Golfers. Illustrated. Demy 8vo. [*In the Press.*

## The Four Ancient Books of Wales,
Containing the Cymric Poems attributed to the Bards of the sixth century. By WILLIAM F. SKENE, D.C.L., Historiographer-Royal for Scotland. With Maps and Facsimiles. 2 vols. 8vo, 36s.

## Celtic Scotland: A History of Ancient Alban.
By WILLIAM F. SKENE, D.C.L., Historiographer-Royal for Scotland. In 3 vols. Demy 8vo, 45s. Illustrated with Maps.

I.—HISTORY and ETHNOLOGY.  II.—CHURCH and CULTURE.
III.—LAND and PEOPLE.

"Forty years ago Mr. Skene published a small historical work on the Scottish Highlands which has ever since been appealed to as an authority, but which has long been out of print. The promise of this youthful effort is amply fulfilled in the three weighty volumes of his maturer years. As a work of historical research it ought in our opinion to take a very high rank."—*Times.*

## The Gospel History for the Young:
Being lessons on the Life of Christ, Adapted for use in Families and Sunday Schools. By WILLIAM F. SKENE, D.C.L., Historiographer-Royal for Scotland. Small Crown 8vo, 3 vols., with Maps, 5s. each vol., or in cloth box, 15s.

"In a spirit altogether unsectarian provides for the young a simple, interesting, and thoroughly charming history of our Lord."—*Literary World.*

"This 'Gospel History for the Young' is one of the most valuable books of the kind."—*The Churchman.*

## Scottish Woodwork of the Sixteenth and Seventeenth
Centuries. Measured, Drawn, and Lithographed by J. W. SMALL, Architect. In one folio volume, with 130 Plates, Four Guineas.

## Shelley: a Critical Biography.
By GEORGE BARNETT SMITH. Ex. fcap. 8vo, 6s.

## The Sermon on the Mount.
By the Rev. WALTER C. SMITH, D.D. Crown 8vo, 6s.

## Life and Work at the Great Pyramid.
With a Discussion of the Facts ascertained. By C. PIAZZI SMYTH, F.R.SS.L. and E., Astronomer-Royal for Scotland. 3 vols. Demy 8vo, 56s.

## Madeira Meteorologic:
Being a Paper on the above subject read before the Royal Society, Edinburgh, on the 1st of May 1882. By C. PIAZZI SMYTH, Astronomer-Royal for Scotland. Small 4to, 6s.

### Saskatchewan and the Rocky Mountains.
Diary and Narrative of Travel, Sport, and Adventure, during a Journey through part of the Hudson's Bay Company's Territories in 1859 and 1860. By the EARL OF SOUTHESK, K.T., F.R.G.S. 1 vol. demy 8vo, with Illustrations on Wood by WHYMPER, 18s.

*By the same Author.*

### Herminius:
A Romance. Fcap. 8vo, 6s.

### Jonas Fisher:
A Poem in Brown and White. Cheap Edition. 1s.

### The Burial of Isis and other Poems.
Fcap. 8vo, 6s.

### Darroll, and other Poems.
By WALTER COOK SPENS, Advocate. Crown 8vo, 5s.

### Rudder Grange.
By FRANK R. STOCKTON. 1s.; and cloth, 2s.

"'Rudder Grange' is a book that few could produce, and that most would be proud to sign."—*Saturday Review*.

"It may be safely recommended as a very amusing little book."—*Athenæum*.

"Altogether 'Rudder Grange' is as cheery, as humorous, and as wholesome a little story as we have read for many a day."—*St. James's Gazette*.

"The minutest incidents are narrated with such genuine humour and gaiety, that at the close of the volume the reader is sorry to take leave of the merry innocent party."—*Westminster Review*.

### The Lady or the Tiger? and other Stories.
By FRANK R. STOCKTON. Contents. THE LADY OR THE TIGER? THE TRANSFERRED GHOST. THE SPECTRAL MORTGAGE. THAT SAME OLD 'COON. HIS WIFE'S DECEASED SISTER. MR. TOLMAN. PLAIN FISHING. MY BULL CALF. EVERY MAN HIS OWN LETTER WRITER. THE REMARKABLE WRECK OF THE "THOMAS HYKE." 1s.; and cloth, 2s.

"Stands by itself both for originality of plot and freshness of humour."—*Century Magazine*.

### Christianity Confirmed by Jewish and Heathen Testimony, and the Deductions from Physical Science, etc.
By THOMAS STEVENSON, F.R.S.E., F.G.S., Member of the Institution of Civil Engineers. Second Edition. Fcap. 8vo, 3s. 6d.

### What is Play?
A Physiological Inquiry. Its bearing upon Education and Training. By JOHN STRACHAN, M.D. Fcap., 1s.

### Good Lives: Some Fruits of the Nineteenth Century.
By A. M. SYMINGTON, D.D. Small Crown 8vo, 3s. 6d.

### Sketch of Thermodynamics.
By P. G. TAIT, Professor of Natural Philosophy in the University of Edinburgh. Second Edition, revised and extended. Crown 8vo, 5s.

### Talks with our Farm-Servants.
By An Old Farm-Servant. Crown 8vo; paper 6d., cloth 1s.

### Walden; or, Life in the Woods.
By H. D. THOREAU. Crown 8vo, 6s.

### Tommie Brown and the Queen of the Fairies; a new
Child's Book, in fcap. 8vo. With Illustrations, 4s. 6d.

*Let pain be pleasure and pleasure be pain.*

"There is no wonder that children liked the story. It is told neatly and well, and is full of great cleverness, while it has that peculiar character the absence of which from many like stories deprives them of any real interest for children."—*Scotsman*.

20 LIST OF BOOKS PUBLISHED BY DAVID DOUGLAS.

**Our Mission to the Court of Marocco in 1880,** under Sir JOHN DRUMMOND HAY, K.C.B., Minister Plenipotentiary at Tangier, and Envoy Extraordinary to His Majesty the Sultan of Marocco. By Captain PHILIP DURHAM TROTTER, 93d Highlanders. Illustrated from Photographs by the Hon. D. LAWLESS, Rifle Brigade. Square Demy 8vo, 24s.

**The Upland Tarn: A Village Idyll.**
Small Crown, 5s.

**Mr. Washington Adams in England.**
By RICHARD GRANT WHITE. 1s.; or in cloth, 2s.
"An impudent book."—*Vanity Fair.*
"This short, tiresome book."—*Saturday Review.*
"Brimful of genuine humour."—*Montrose Standard.*
"Mr. White is a capital caricaturist, but in portraying the ludicrous eccentricities of the patrician Britisher he hardly succeeds so well as in delineating the peculiar charms of the representative Yankee."—*Whitehall Review.*

**Rosetty Ends, or the Chronicles of a Country Cobbler.**
By Job Bradawl (A. DEWAR WILLOCK), Author of "She Noddit to me." Fcap. 8vo, Illustrated.

**The Botany of Three Historical Records:**
Pharaoh's Dream, the Sower, and the King's Measure. By A. STEPHEN WILSON. Crown 8vo, with 5 plates, 3s. 6d.

**"A Bushel of Corn."**
By A. STEPHEN WILSON. An investigation by Experiments into all the more important questions which range themselves round a Bushel of Wheat, a Bushel of Barley, and a Bushel of Oats. Crown 8vo, with Illustrations, 9s.
"It is full of originality and force."—*Nature.*
"A monument of painstaking research."—*Liverpool Mercury.*
"Mr. Wilson's book is interesting not only for agriculturists and millers, but for all who desire information on the subject of corn, in which every one is so intimately concerned."—*Morning Post.*

**Songs and Poems.**
By A. STEPHEN WILSON. Crown 8vo, 6s.

**Reminiscences of Old Edinburgh.**
By DANIEL WILSON, LL.D., F.R.S.E., Professor of History and English Literature in University College, Toronto, Author of "Prehistoric Annals of Scotland," etc. etc. 2 vols. post 8vo, 15s.

**The India Civil Service as a Career for Scotsmen.**
By J. WILSON, M.A. 1s.

**Christianity and Reason:**
Their necessary connection. By R. S. WYLD, LL.D. Extra fcap. 8vo, 3s. 6d.

**Shakespeare's England.**
By WILLIAM WINTER. Contents. THE VOYAGE. THE BEAUTY OF ENGLAND. GREAT HISTORIC PLACES. RAMBLES IN LONDON. A VISIT TO WINDSOR. THE PALACE OF WESTMINSTER. WARWICK AND KENILWORTH. FIRST VIEW OF STRATFORD-ON-AVON. LONDON NOOKS AND CORNERS. RELICS OF LORD BYRON. WESTMINSTER ABBEY. THE HOME OF SHAKESPEARE. UP TO LONDON. OLD CHURCHES OF LONDON. LITERARY SHRINES OF LONDON. A HAUNT OF EDMUND KEAN. STOKE-POGIS AND THOMAS GRAY. AT THE GRAVE OF COLERIDGE. ON BARNET BATTLEFIELD. A GLIMPSE OF CANTERBURY. THE SHRINES OF WARWICKSHIRE. A BORROWER OF THE NIGHT. 1s., paper, or 2s., cloth extra.

EDINBURGH: DAVID DOUGLAS, CASTLE STREET.

www.ingramcontent.com/pod-product-compliance
Lightning Source LLC
Chambersburg PA
CBHW030424020526
44112CB00045B/786